High School Prom

Marketing, Morals and the American Teen

ANN ANDERSON

McFarland & Company, Inc., Publishers
Jefferson, North Carolina, and London

LIBRARY OF CONGRESS CATALOGUING-IN-PUBLICATION DATA

Anderson, Ann, 1951–
High school prom : marketing, morals and
the American teen / Ann Anderson.
p.   cm.
Includes bibliographical references and index.

ISBN 978-0-7864-6700-6
softcover : acid free paper ∞

1. Proms — United States.   2. Proms — Social
aspects — United States.   I. Title.
GV1746.A63 2012   793.3′808837318 — dc23   2012027893

BRITISH LIBRARY CATALOGUING DATA ARE AVAILABLE

Front cover images © 2012 Shutterstock

Manufactured in the United States of America

*McFarland & Company, Inc., Publishers
Box 611, Jefferson, North Carolina 28640
www.mcfarlandpub.com*

High School Prom

ALSO BY ANN ANDERSON

Snake Oil, Hustlers and Hambones:
The American Medicine Show
(McFarland, 2000; paperback 2005)

Table of Contents

Preface

Picture a lavishly costumed group in a beautiful setting teeming with movement, sound and emotion. It could be a scene from a Shakespeare play or a grand opera, but I'm actually talking about high school proms. They are the ultimate high school event, in some cases more eagerly anticipated than graduation. The senior prom has been a fixture of teenage life ever since the invention of high school. The dance encapsulates and magnifies all the drama of American adolescence, which is why prom is both a perennial theme in popular culture and a subject of academic inquiry.

Lest you think that proms are kids' stuff, consider the billions of dollars in annual revenue created by these events. Proms have evolved from modest tea dances into an industry that supports legions of apparel and cosmetic makers, limousine services, caterers, hotels, magazine publishers, tanning salons — the list goes on, and the income they generate increases yearly.

Prom (alternately *prom* and *the prom* in the popular press) is the subject of countless novels, magazine articles, etiquette guides, television episodes, movies and doctoral dissertations. Prom memories are indelible. Prom affects people who didn't even attend. Prom-goers never forget it, and nongoers wonder what they missed. (To be fair, there are people who didn't go and never gave it another thought, but I haven't encountered many.) I mentioned my prom project to several people while in the process of research. None were neutral about the topic, and I heard more unsolicited personal stories than a bartender at last call.

Answers to questions about proms tend to be inconclusive. Is it true that teens lose their virginity on prom night? Yes and no. Do they spend too much money on prom? That depends on how you define "too much." Is prom vitally important? To many, yes. To others, secretly yes. Some would rather have crawled through their local shopping mall naked than go to prom, and they still recall with high intensity why they refused to attend. The ambiguities, contradictions and sheer emotional charge of the topic struck me as I explored it.

Prom has changed a lot over the years, and it has also stayed the same.

1

I was prompted to investigate the topic when my local paper, *The Oregonian*, reported the cancellation of a prom owing to the prevalence of "grinding." Today's kids call it dancing. Their teachers call it standing sex. My elders responded similarly on viewing the Twist. *Plus ça change, plus c'est la même chose.*

I decided to write about prom because it was a big deal when I was a high school senior in 1969. Today, it's a massively big deal, and I wondered how that came to pass. The story of prom is complicated. It's gone in and out of fashion along with the changes in society at large. As of this writing, it's roaring along and shows no sign of fading in popularity. To understand the prom, it's necessary to look at both the American teenager and the American high school, two phenomena that developed together but have not been around for all that long, relatively speaking. This book looks at many aspects of U.S. history and popular culture: money, sex, fashion, youth, dance, music, television, transportation, communication and even war. Prom encompasses them all.

Part I describes the history and development of prom over several decades, with a look at social and economic trends. Part II is about the prom industry and how the event has grown from an inexpensive hand-made party into a professional, costly red-carpet extravaganza, complete with paparazzi. Part III looks at prom in popular culture and how it's portrayed in film, television and literature.

This book is not a sociological study. I include statistics where relevant, but numbers don't necessarily tell the story. Teenagers are individuals, and I have a problem with classifying people as, say, African American male or Caucasian female, upper or lower class. I like professors, and I used to be one, but the academic approach is not exactly what I use here. Nor is this book a collection of reminiscences. Personal anecdotes offer color, but they won't paint the full picture, either. What's true for one student is not the case for another. Proms vary from decade to decade, person to person, school to school, region to region. I've drawn as complete a portrait as I can, but apart from calculations of dollars and cents, demographic charts, old photographs and other data, prom is a fundamentally subjective experience. That's its fascination.

So here's a disclaimer: I've done my homework, but I'm not an entirely objective student of this topic. Proms are primarily for and about teenage girls, and I used to be one of those, too. If you're a former teenage girl, you know what a vivid experience that was. I also used to be a high school student. Both of those facts are as wedded to my self-identity and approach as a writer as anything else in my long, eventful life. My personal feelings, therefore, seep into this study. I'll let you know, to the extent of my self-awareness, when I'm asserting my own opinion. (For the record, teenage boys figure into the story of prom, too, but as supporting players.)

Every school administration I approached with a request to observe a prom was as well-defended and opaque as the Kremlin. "Prom is for the kids. Your presence would make them uncomfortable," was the usual response, as predictable as kabuki theater and just as artificial. Every teenager I spoke to was willing, even eager to have me attend. Teens love to be seen. They live to be seen! Survey after survey confirms that today's teens desire fame above all other goals. They record their proms and post clips on YouTube for the world to see. Their prom photos are plastered all over Facebook and other social media. It simply doesn't wash that they would object to being observed by an actual reporter.

One gate-keeper in the Beaverton, Oregon, school district told me she would have to consult their legal department and see if their attorneys (note the plural) would be willing to draw up appropriate releases and indemnifying documents. School bureaucrats recoil at any possibility of liability issues or danger to the students, although at sixty years old, gray-haired and five feet tall, I'm as physically threatening as a piece of vanilla taffy. Their real worry is negative press, which is why I was even refused admittance to a pre-prom assembly. I asked another administrator if she was concerned that I would misinterpret what went on. The answer was yes, simple as that. School officials do not want outsiders watching them, or as she put it, "The principals don't want any extra variables." As for the prom itself, given the usual teenage pro-clivities for sex and substances, it's a good bet that any observer would spot something that school principals wouldn't want revealed. If I were in their place, I wouldn't want me at the prom, either. Proms, fraught with potential for mishaps, are a perennial headache for administrators. As far as they're con-cerned, there's no up-side to scrutiny. That said, there's more than one way to hem a prom dress, and I got my story.

Teenagers have always had their lingo, but these days they don't employ it in phone conversations. They text. Thumb-typing is more conducive to tightly condensed messages than lengthy descriptions. I learned to ask simple, easy-to-answer questions and interpret the contemporary adolescent code. I have never felt more on the downhill slope of the generational divide. My inner teenager lives, but my outer self is a geezer (another disclaimer).

For me, high school was a bewildering exercise in insecurity and tedium. I attended high school because I was legally required to do so, but I was itching to graduate, turn eighteen, move to New York City and become an actress. (I did.) I attended prom because I received an invitation, and it never occurred to me to turn it down. The boy who asked me confirmed my mid-dle-caste designation in our school's hierarchy. There is no more definitive marker of high school status than the person who asks you to the prom. My date was by no means one of the outcasts. He was in the large mass of ordinary students. We both knew that he had not invited a girl out of his league. I was smack in the center of his league, which is to say that I was one of those ordinary kids, too. But who needed ordinary? I wanted what every girl in my school wanted: popularity, the sine qua non of high school achievement. Never mind that I ranked in the top 10 percent of my class academically. I knew that in the arena where the high school game was really played — boys and dating — I was a washout. I never got the hang of dating owing to a lack of practice. I was asked out maybe once or twice in high school, which for the most part was fine with me. I didn't understand boys. Frankly, they made me nervous. Nevertheless, if I were to go to prom, I wanted an ideal escort — a football player, and never mind that I had no interest in football or any particular team member. I would have dissolved into stammering idiocy if one had invited me. Ever the high achiever, however, I craved a more desirable trophy than the debate club statuettes I had dutifully supplied for my parents' living room mantle. I wanted to make my prom entrance on the muscular arm of one of the really cute, popular boys, thereby validating my own worthiness. That was shallow of me, I know. But I was seventeen, and ours was a very competitive school.

My date and I knew that I wasn't going to get a better offer. I despised him for mirroring my own perceived social failure, and I took my insecurities out on him, poor guy. The evening was as disastrous as I felt it would be from the moment of the invitation — a self-fulfilling prophecy, no doubt. (My dress, I have to say, was heavenly — a pale blue jacquard silk skirt with a white lace V-neck bodice. Nobody forgets their prom dress.) To this day, though, I regret accepting my date's invitation because I didn't really want to go with him. For one thing, we had barely spoken to each other in our three years at Denver's George Washington High, and prom is the worst possible time to make a new friend. Self-conscious in my beautiful but uncomfortable dress, I was cold and monosyllabic from the minute he showed up, stoop-shouldered and reeking of fear and Jade East cologne. I knew I had to put him at ease or the evening would be a nightmare, but I didn't know how, or maybe I didn't want to. Predictably, the evening dragged on through a series of awkward silences, and as soon as the dance was over, I asked him to take me home, forgoing whatever post-prom festivity he had in mind. I could barely look at him from that moment on; the pain in his eyes was unmistakable and all my fault. I feel as badly about that today as I did then.

If I could have a do-over, I would first reinvent the teenage me as a more sunny, confident and socially adept girl. I would appreciate my date, who, in hindsight, was a smart, nice kid, and probably would have been fun to know had I given him a chance. So J.M., wherever you are, I want you to know that I'm sorry.

Now for a few words of thanks. My research would be incomplete without the generous help from the staff at the Cedar Mill Community Library. I especially thank Michele Hjortung at the Interlibrary Loan desk for her invaluable assistance in gathering materials. To my friends who contributed photos and memorabilia: Linda Segall Anable, Liz Anderson, Jill Nicklas Andrews, Christina Saffran Ashford, Loretta Ayeroff, Veronica See Bryce, Howie Davidson, Mary Anne Erickson, Linda Kaye, Joe Malone, Pam Magnuson, Judith Sansom, Jillian Schmitz, Michael Sheck, and Thomas White; you're all prom kings and queens as far as I'm concerned. To my high school BFF, Cathy Loup, you're a good friend and an excellent editor. Thanks for all your help and feedback in the initial stages of the project. Thanks to John Cosgrove, owner of Decades Vintage Company; and to Paul Bassett, owner of Avalon in Portland, Oregon, for allowing me to photograph their authentic period clothes. Finally, a big high school cheer goes to my husband, Ken Anderson, photographer, digital image expert, sounding board and one-man pep squad. I could not have completed this project without your help. If I really could do it all over again, I'd go to the prom with you.

1. Promenade All

"Everybody is a teenage idol."
— Barry Gibb

Americans have always been fascinated by money and fame, which is how prom night came to be. At the turn of the twentieth century, newspaper society pages, *Harper's Bazaar*, *Ladies' Home Journal* and the like reported the doings of the wealthy and connected. Ordinary people couldn't get enough of it, and were especially interested in reports of debutante balls. The cosseted (and corseted) girls who made their formal debut into polite society were the tabloid fodder of their day. Demure in long, white dresses — the signifier of virginity was intentional — girls from the "best" families displayed themselves to the marriageable men of the upper crust (and to prospective mothers-in-law) so they too could become well-off matrons before the bloom was off the proverbial rose. Girls such as Emily Post and Alice Roosevelt exemplified good breeding and the good life. The debutante season was a gorgeous whirl that commenced with "coming out" (a phrase with a different connotation back then), and concluded with high-society weddings. Well-documented debutante parties provided daydreams for scores of ordinary women.

If a debutante's provenance was unimpressive, the size of her father's financial holdings could qualify her for entry into the social scene. Debutante balls signified wealth and class in a country that applauds the former and is decidedly uneasy about the latter. Money is money, but in the United States what is class? It may be a combination of family, wealth, achievement, charisma, fame, or something else, and no one has the definitive answer. In fact, the mere appearance of "class" (whatever it is) may be the thing itself. Would your daughter like to be a deb? Hire a hall, buy her a dress, invite some friends, *et voilà*! She's a debutante! Or maybe she's just a prom queen, but for one night, she captures the same magic. Prom is the democratic debutante ball. You don't even need to be a girl to enjoy the big night. Anyone who meets their school's requirements can attend, which is exactly the point.[1]

Prom is short for promenade, which is simply a slow walk, usually in pairs and as part of a formal ceremony. Some proms begin with a promenade, or "grand march." The first known reference to prom can be found in the biography of Amherst College student Dwight Morrow, who wrote in June 1884, "I have been invited over to the Smith Junior Prom." Morrow doesn't provide details about the dance, but his reference indicates that college proms were common by then.[2] Prom customs took odd form at times. The University of Texas required junior women to dress as men and escort senior women to the dance. The real men were supposed to sneak into the party, which usually meant disguising themselves as women. It was, apparently, good fun at the time. Student Jack Millard scored a coup at the 1923 prom by dressing as a coed and installing himself in a women's dorm room after the dance.[3]

Proms gradually filtered down to high schools and were probably modest tea dances at first, most likely in casual dress. By the 1920s, however, high schools that held proms were, as they said at the time, putting on the dog. Shrewsbury High in Massachusetts, for example, threw a prom in 1929 (shortly before the stock market crash) with decorations rumored to be "the most beautiful ever seen for any social function in town." The school newspaper reported that "Miss Virginia Mitchell wore a beautiful gown of changeable rose and violet taffeta; Miss Pauline Mulcahy attracted attention by her striking gown of brown and gold." The students danced to such tunes as "Tiger Rag" and "Mean to Me." Miss Loretta Giblin of Worcester performed "specialty numbers" — a fan dance and a "snappy tap dance." Ice cream was served at intermission. The evening was a big success.[4]

By the 1940s, high school proms were a tradition.[5] By the time the twenty-first century arrived, the prom had expanded into an event that would have beggared the most opulent debutante ball of 1900. But it's a long way from then to now, in more ways than one.

High school proms require three things: teenagers, high schools and dating, none of which existed in the early part of the twentieth century, at least not in the way we're used to thinking about them. In the early days of our country, the terms "teen" and "teenager" had not yet been coined. There was no special word for a person between the ages of thirteen and nineteen because no one regarded that cohort as a distinct group. Many people didn't even know their exact age. The number didn't matter. If you could do a job on your family farm or business, you worked. If not, your mother looked after you and gave you some schooling to the best of her ability. If you lived on a farm (and most people did in the early days of the republic), Mom taught summer classes to very young children and girls whose labor wasn't needed. Older children had their schooling in the winter when fields were dormant, and Dad may have undertaken their instruction. Students were not separated

A fashion model displays a summer debutante gown for the 1916 season (Library of Congress).

by age. A young man of eighteen would have studied alongside his eight-year-old sister.[6]

Parents depended on their children's labor. As writer Thomas Hine says of life before the twentieth century, "Everyone had to work long hours so that all could afford to live miserably."[7] The cohesive nuclear family wasn't the norm back then, either. Chances were good that one's father would have died in his forties from an accident, illness or just plain exhaustion. It was common for fatherless children to support their families.

Immigrant children typically worked from a very young age, and owing to a greater facility with English than their parents, they often became the family's primary breadwinners.[8] The rich, as always, did as they pleased, coming and going from their parents' home seasonally with a few months here and there of private or academy instruction.[9] What we think of as the formative years, by today's childrearing standards, were a fluid, dicey state of affairs. If adolescence is the time of life when young people are segregated from the working world and spend most of the day together, that wasn't the case a hundred years ago, even for those who attended school beyond age fourteen.[10]

At the turn of the prior century, there was no particular path laid out for young people. You worked at home or you worked where you could. If your folks paid more to feed and clothe you than your labor was worth, off you went to support yourself elsewhere. Girls often sought work in factories. Boys in coal country went into the mines. Others migrated to the cities and hustled on the streets or worked in department stores. Some served apprenticeships; others might have worked in a relative's workshop. The U.S. Census of 1900 showed that some 2 million children worked in "mills, mines, fields, factories, stores and on city streets."[11]

Adults worried about kids leaving home, especially the girls. How was a young lady to preserve her innocence in the workplace? Sexual activity at an early age was called "precocity," and was to be avoided at all costs.[12] An observer of the scene in 1858 wrote, "Early departure from the homestead is a moral crisis that many youth do not show themselves able to meet. It comes at a tender age, when judgment is weakest and passion and impulse strongest."[13] High school was viewed as a way of controlling rampant sexuality among the nation's youth. Public schools were charged with cultivating moral self-control as well as "the three R's," reading, (w)riting and (a)rithmetic. As the century wore on, births were spaced closer together, and families with a predominance of high school-aged children were common for the first time in the nation's history.[14]

Whenever possible, parents kept their children at home and sent them to the few high schools that existed, usually in bigger towns and cities, but attendance was low and often interrupted. Middle-class students, typically the children of shopkeepers and professional men, stayed for only a year or two. Most students were girls, and if they stayed until graduation, their diploma gave them entrée only to teaching.[15] Young men stayed in high school if they had the means to go on to college; otherwise they quit school and went to work. For most people prior to the twentieth century, this was the drill: brief childhood, early work with spotty schooling, early marriage, more work.

High schools caught on very gradually toward the latter part of the nineteenth century and into the early twentieth. The rise of industry and growth of cities expanded the economy, and more parents could afford to keep their children out of the work force for a few extra years. Mechanization reduced the need for farm hands, and young people were the most easily replaced moving part of any newly automated factory.[16] The economy was changing rapidly, and high schools prepared boys for new jobs in mechanical engineering, office and scientific work. Schools were also seen as important agents for civilizing young people, and educators supported clubs and school governments. Parents formed associations and involved themselves in the supervision of after-school activities, which they believed fostered obedience and cooperation.[17] Public schools introduced "age grading," grouping students by age instead of gender, family, reading level or some other criterion. Age grading led to social promotion because educators believed in moving students through the system with their age group.[18]

Between 1900 and 1920, the concept of adolescence as a transitional period between childhood and adulthood took hold, even if relatively few had the means to enjoy it.[19] Still, as Hine notes, "This widespread acceptance of the idea of high school was very, very slow in coming. The high school movement did not hit like a tidal wave, but rather, like a glacier, slowly insinuating itself into American life."[20] That said, three things fostered the establishment of adolescence.

The first was the enactment of child labor laws. The Keating-Owen Child Labor Act of 1916 banned the sale of products from any manufacturer that employed children under the age of fourteen, and also placed restrictions on mining and night work. The law was overturned in 1918 for overreaching its power to limit interstate commerce, but the trend was on, and other laws prohibiting child labor soon followed.[21] The second development was mandatory schooling, a state-by-state process that took over fifty years to complete. The District of Columbia was actually the first to require high school attendance in 1864, followed by Vermont in 1867. Mississippi was the last, passing such a law in 1918.[22] As high school attendance increased, it became the norm for American youngsters to spend most of the day with people their own age.[23] Eventually, high school attendance was taken for granted. Hine says that

High school is the threshold through which every young American must pass. Its classes impart knowledge we believe young people need to become good adults. Its athletics and extracurricular activities provide the principal stage for young people to explore their talents and find their strengths. It brings young people together, providing a fertile ground for the development of youth culture. By enrolling both young men and women, the high school gave teenagers control over their own social life, something that parents controlled before everyone went to high school. Without high school, there are no teenagers.[24]

(High school was also considered a way to curb precocity, although confining randy young men with nubile young women might seem counterproductive.) The third important change was the invention of the juvenile court system. The Chicago and Boston courts had begun trying juvenile cases in the late 1890s. Denver instituted a juvenile system in 1900. As separate courts for juvenile justice caught on, a person under the age of eighteen acquired a crucial, altogether new attribute: He or she was legally distinct from an adult.[25]

Dating is so much a part of our culture that it's hard to imagine the custom was completely unknown a scant century ago. Still, girls were girls and boys were boys and the twain did meet, even without the physical and social structure of a high school. Girls were generally around sixteen when they started keeping company with boys at church functions, community get-togethers and the like. Heavily supervised, these meetings were not dates — a better word is "courtship." As they grew older, young people managed to get together and enjoy more freedom.[26]

In the horse and buggy days, a young man did not "date" a young lady he fancied. He came "calling" at her home. First, he would ask permission from the girl or her mother, or he might leave his "calling card" with the maid and ask to see her. If he was denied, it meant he was not deemed suitable by the girl's family and should seek companionship elsewhere. If he was permitted entry, the young couple would sit and chat on the front porch or in the parlor under the watchful eyes of her family. Calling was a simple, rigid system that protected a girl from the pressures of a growing, restless population and any riff-raff that might drift her way. It also kept relationships securely under the stewardship of women. Calling was a private, middle- to upper-class affair that took place in the privacy of the home. Movie actress Loretta Young remarked, "I can't imagine dating a boy, meeting him only outside the home. What's a home and family for if it's not the center of one's life?"[27]

As the population shifted to cities in the early twentieth century, the old system broke down. Calling was impossible for lower-class folk and city dwellers whose family occupied one or two rooms. Front porches and parlors were in short supply for the surging immigrant population that lived in urban tenements. If a young man wanted to see a young lady, the encounter had to take place in public.

By the mid–1910s, "dating" had entered the common parlance, usually in connection with that most intriguing of characters, the college girl. The *Ladies' Home Journal* used the term in 1914, referring to a girl who allowed an especially popular boy "the monopoly of my 'dates.'" Writers O. Henry and Upton Sinclair, who were fascinated by the roiling expansion of city life, wrote about dating among the working class. Calling gradually disappeared and dating came to the middle class from both the upper and working classes. "Going out" was fashionable among the former and a necessity for the latter.

The car was another essential element in the development of dating. Henry Ford's Model T probably did more for dating than any other innovation. As writer Beth L. Bailey notes, "The rise of dating was usually explained, quite simply, by the invention of the automobile. Cars had given youth mobility and privacy, and so had brought about the system."[28] From the beginning, autos were symbols of masculine dominance and feminine allure, just as they are today. That advertising staple, a car draped with a beautiful woman, appeared in print ads in the 1920s. Apart from transporting one from point A to B, however, a car's added value was the private space it provided for sex. "If I had a car," one young New Yorker bragged, "there wouldn't be a virgin left in town."[29]

The impact of the shift from calling to dating was enormous. A date took place at the man's invitation and out in public. He, not she, was now in control. Furthermore, money became a central issue. There was no question that the man would do the asking and the paying. As Bailey writes, "In fact, the term date was associated with the direct economic exchange of prostitution at an early time.... Dating, like prostitution, made access to women directly dependent on money. Quite a few men did not hesitate to complain about the going rate of exchange." As one young man succinctly put it, "You don't win prom princesses. You buy them — like show horses."[30]

As dating took hold, men struggled to find a suitable rationale for what looked an awful lot like prostitution without the sex (or with it, depending on the individuals involved). Men supplied the money and women supplied their company. But the man supplied his company, too. Did that mean his company was worth less than hers? Was dating an investment that would lead to a future dividend? If the dividend was marriage, then wouldn't he be exchanging his salary for her household services, and if that was the case, then why not just hire a maid? If men were operating at a loss in the dating game, how could they recoup? The answer, according to many involved in the public discourse was *power*. Dating gave men control and made women dependent. What she had going for her was her feminine charm and the promise of ...

something. Dating was and is a process of bargaining. On it goes, and as we shall see, prom-goers still have to negotiate who pays for what and why.[31]

Parents who grew up before dating were appalled by its casualness. In their day, only engaged couples spent time alone. That a couple might go out (who knew where?) with no adult supervision was bad enough, but the lack of commitment was positively radical. Dating, especially if a couple went out only once or twice, was hardly a sign of marital intent. Adults were certain that nothing good could come of it.[32]

During the first decade of the twentieth century, young people went to dance halls, usually in groups of same-sex friends, where they would find dance partners once they got there. The music and dancing was ragtime, and it freaked out the old folks. Ragtime was unmistakably African American, which even in the abstract was bad enough for a lot of people. The real problem was the style itself, which required bodily contact. The old-fashioned European ballroom styles that adults enjoyed involved a certain amount of touching, but in a formal, courtly way, and strictly without swiveling torsos or swinging hips. Critics complained that ragtime dancing looked like simulated sex, and they weren't entirely wrong. New dances such as the Turkey Trot, the Bunny Hug and the Shimmy came along all the time. By the time a school principal had banned one dance, the kids were on to something else.[33]

Jazz was the rage in the 1920s, and partly because college students loved it, high school kids did too. Dancing to jazz was frenetic, not quite as overtly sexual as in ragtime days, but provocative enough to drive parents nuts. Jazz, like ragtime, is a black American invention, and once again its provenance was reason enough for some to declare it the work of the devil, raising its stock considerably among aficionados.[34] African Americans, by and large, did not attend high school, and those who did were relegated to substandard schools. But black Americans had a disproportionate influence in music and dance, creating styles and setting standards.

By the 1930s, dating and going to dances had become a competitive sport. A girl who attended a school dance did not expect or want to spend the entire evening with her date. She wanted other boys to "cut in" during a dance number, the more the better. Everyone knew the rules for cutting in. If you asked a girl to dance, you were responsible for her until someone cut in with a tap on the shoulder. Leaving her alone was not an option. It would have been unthinkably cruel to turn a girl into a wallflower. She might ask to leave the dance floor, but only if she spotted friends to whom she could escape. A girl who didn't attract multiple dance partners was "stuck." In the high school caste system that meant "untouchable." Getting stuck was such a grievous social failure that you couldn't even be stuck with the person who brought you. Many a male escort was known to throw pleading glances at his friends during the course of a "stuck" evening. If other boys didn't want to dance with your date, it reflected poorly on you. One apocryphal story in an advice book tells about a young man whose dance partner catches him waving a dollar bill at his friends behind her back. "Make it a five," she says, "and I'll go home." Conversely, bringing a girl with whom every boy wanted to whirl around the floor enhanced one's social standing. In a 1933 *Women's Home Companion* story, an elderly uncle explains the charm of cutting in to his niece:

> I took [Susan] to her first big dance and she almost backed out on me at the last minute, being frightened and all. Suppose no one cut in? I took care of that.... After three introductions, that girl hardly got her feet on the floor. They carried her around, passing her from one boy to another. A girl can't enjoy an experience like that today.... And a boy ought to know what it's like to see his girl competed for and appreciated. It makes a man in his teens feel important.

The old man's reminiscence is sweet, but fails to acknowledge that times had changed. In his day, men outnumbered women. Cutting in was a way to share scarce females in a noncombative fashion. The ratio of men to women narrowed as the country developed, but the custom was entrenched. During the Depression, when unemployment was high, the issue for women was the scarcity of acceptable (financially solvent) men with whom to dance. World War II created a shortage of male dance partners, yet cutting in persisted. At the war's end, there were statistically more women than men in the United States, and reality finally prevailed. At war's end, you danced "with the one who brung ya." By the 1950s young people were unaware that cutting in ever existed.[35]

In the 1920s and '30s, the idea of the perfect prom date was decades away. The system at the time was "dating and rating," and like other customs it filtered down from college to high school. One dated as widely as possible and the grapevine was the *Who's Who* of the social scene. Word spread quickly if a boy had access to a car, or if dating him meant riding the bus. Everyone knew which girls dressed stylishly or whose parents imposed an unreasonable curfew. The goal was popularity, which was weighed and measured as coldly as a cow at a stock show. The point of a date was to be seen, preferably with another popular person, as often as possible.[36] Dating and rating gave parents another reason to fret: Their influence on the system was nil. The high school gossip mill was the place for romantic guidance. "A girl's date would tell his friends what happened, the girl would tell hers, and pretty soon everybody knew," says Hine. "It wasn't advantageous in the long run for a girl to be known as 'fast,' because, while boys might rush to take her out, she might be excluded from the group. Girls looked for boys who were respectful, but not so 'bashful' they didn't try anything at all."

"Necking" and "petting" entered the vocabulary as adolescents tested the area between virginity and sexual experience. By the 1920s, petting meant anything short of intercourse. Petting parties became common, with couples surreptitiously eyeing each other to see how far to go. In other words, young people policed each other's sexual activity, and those who violated the unwritten rules invited vicious gossip. Boys could discreetly visit prostitutes for an education in sex, but girls were expected to remain chaste, even if that condition was something of a technicality. A girl who was known to be a virgin was "quality goods," and unwed pregnancy was strictly taboo.[37]

Jocks and cheerleaders have always topped the high school pecking order. For many years, the majority of high school teachers were women, spurring fears that too much female supervision would emasculate boys. The antidote for excessive feminine influence was sports. Football was deemed sufficiently brutal for the cultivation of manliness, and was therefore the first sport chosen for high school athletics. Legendary coach Vince Lombardi quipped, "A high school without football is in danger of deteriorating into a medieval study hall."[38] Girls were encouraged to attend games and root for their school's team, which led to cheerleading. As Hine writes, "That quintessential teen couple — the football player and his cheerleader girlfriend — was on hand to greet the twentieth century."[39] In the high school dating game, a dim handsome athlete beat a bright average-looking boy every time. Thus it ever was.

Just as dating replaced calling, going steady eventually replaced dating and rating. During the Depression, few people could afford a social round robin. In the war years, goods such as gasoline and clothing were rationed. A steady girl or boyfriend was the economical way to go, and provided emotional comfort in an insecure time. Going steady was less formal than an engagement, but served to place dibs on a future mate while awaiting a more prosperous future.[40]

In spite of all the dating and dancing, high school students in the late 1920s and early 1930s were eager to grow up and assume adult responsibilities. While taking their education seriously as preparation for imminent adulthood, they enjoyed the brief freedom of adolescence. In particular, they enjoyed the attention they received as the leading edge of a new consumer class. After all, the clothing, transportation, food and everything else that went with dating cost money. Young people knew they were having an unprecedented impact on the economy, and marketers knew they knew. By the late 1920s, a distinct youth culture was sprouting up. Then the Great Depression nearly nipped it in the bud.[41]

The stock market crash had an enormous impact on adolescents. By 1933, the most severe point of the Depression, one quarter of the 15 million unemployed Americans were between the ages of fifteen and twenty-four.[42]

(The numbers were worse for African and Mexican-Americans.) Young people whose parents could not support them hit the road. Hitchhiking and riding the rails, some 250,000 young vagabonds, girls included, traversed the country looking for a way to sustain themselves. This had two effects on high schools: On one hand, the dropout rate soared. On the other hand, those who weren't forced out of their homes went to school because there were no jobs. The net effect on enrollment was actually a sharp increase. There were fewer teachers, however, and school buildings deteriorated from lack of funding.[43]

The federal government eventually rescued young homeless males with New Deal programs such as the Civilian Conservation Corps (CCC), which maintained parks and wilderness areas. Three million young men were taken off the streets and paid $30 per month for a maximum nine-month stint in the CCC. The money was automatically sent home to their families. The National Youth Administration (NYA) provided vocational training for girls.[44] As the Depression worsened, the government did all it could to keep the nation's youth off the streets and out of the competition for very scarce jobs.

By 1939, 85 percent of children aged five to seventeen were in school. Away from their parents and under minimal supervision due to a dearth of teachers, high school students relied on each other for guidance, support, and approval. "For ever-growing numbers of young people," Hine writes, "the real life of going to work and starting a family was deferred, replaced by student life, played out almost entirely with people one's own age. The central role once performed by the family had been usurped by the aggressively modernizing institution of high school."[45] The formation of teen culture, endangered at the start of the Depression, picked up steam as high school attendance grew by default. Hine sums up the situation:

> This is the paradox: The austerity of the early 1930s could have killed youth culture, and for a time it appeared that it had. Yet, the enforced separation of young people from the economic mainstream and the emergence of high school as a the common experience of young Americans led directly to the emergence of teenagers as we know them today.[46]

New appellations such as *teeners*, *teensters* (used chiefly by marketers) and *teen-agers* appeared in print. The term *teenager* debuted in 1941, introduced into the lexicon by an anonymous writer.[47] "At first, the word, 'teen-ager' had a hyphen in the middle, a sign that the idea was new and might split apart at any time. By 1945, the word was almost always spelled 'teenager.' It was one word describing one new kind of person."[48] By 1944, the CCC and NYA had been disbanded. The U.S. economy was on a war footing, and those programs had outlived their usefulness. High school students assisted the war effort through a variety of civic activities, further solidifying their group spirit and identity. During the war, jobs for teens were plentiful because so many adult males were in the armed services. Teens whose activities were financially constrained during the Depression started spending again.[49]

The war expanded everyone's perspective as people from widely divergent backgrounds were forced to work together. As one Jewish enlistee said, "I got out of high school and three days later I was at boot camp in San Diego. Suddenly, I'm thrown in with people from Oklahoma, Texas, and the Southeast. Some of them had never used a toilet facility. I met guys who had never seen a Jew." The war gave many young men an education they never would have received in their home town high schools, and knitted disparate strands of a generation into a cohesive group.[50]

The cohort that went through high school during the Depression and World War II was not prone to brooding. They were an extroverted bunch who bucked up and made the best of things. Gender roles were sharply defined. Boys were expected to be manly; girls were girly. There was no such thing as sexually ambiguous clothing. A whiff of homosexuality could get you hurt. The emphasis was on team work and being "regular," a descriptor that confused no one.[51]

By 1944, dance clubs called "teen canteens" had sprung up everywhere. Although authorities were glad that minors had their own venues away from adults and alcohol, they were less sanguine about the actual dancing. The "hep" music was called *swing*, and a tune either swung or it didn't. Swing wasn't really about the notes, it was about how they were played. Musicians recognized it when they heard it. As for the dancers, if a song didn't make you move it wasn't swing.[52] Jitterbug (the name of the dance and the dancer), the Lindy Hop, and the Shim-Sham were some of the era's dances. Orchestras such as Benny Goodman's and Tommy Dorsey's had kids out of their seats and dancing up a cultural firestorm. "Trucking" and "shagging," leap-frogging and back-flipping, jitterbugging girls exposed their panties in public! Dance instructors considered the Lindy Hop and jitterbug too vulgar for the ballroom and refused to teach them. But teens didn't need formal instruction. They learned from each other and improvised new moves on the dance floor. Jitterbug champion Frankie Manning says about his invention of the "Over the Back" move, "We didn't know what to do because they didn't have any dance schools or anybody who knew how to do this step. She's back-to-back with me, and I flip her over my back, and she lands on her feet in front of me."[53]

Continuing a historical pattern, swing originated with African American musicians. Duke Ellington, Count Basie, Cab Calloway and other "cats" invented music for a subculture that the mainstream quickly co-opted. Within a short while, the Lindy Hop (and swing music) went from disrepute to "America's national dance." By the war years, African American influence on dance styles and popular music had made the old European dominance a relic of the prior century. In spite of the popularity of African American–inspired music, however, it was a long time until whites and blacks danced to it together.[54]

The prom was a different story from the teen canteen. You had to tone down your jitterbug moves in formal wear. (Prom dresses, like most women's clothes of the 30s and 40s were soft and swingy, often cut on the bias with an emphasis on shoulders.) Teens at the prom also danced as their parents did — a sedate foxtrot or a waltz. For many high school students during the war years, the prom (if their school had one at all) was a definitive end to childhood. Many young men enlisted in the service immediately after graduation. Girls went to work in factories or took care of young children so their mothers could work. Teen canteens and school dances were a last bit of youthful fun before embarking on very grownup business indeed.[55]

The Great Depression and World War II created the conditions for the advent of teen culture. The Depression made high school the only available path for many teenagers, which isolated them from the world of adults. The war provided the jobs and money for teens to become a new consumer class. "Bobby soxers," for instance, were high school girls who dressed in sweaters, plaid skirts, socks and saddle shoes, and were mad for jitterbugging and a skinny singer from New Jersey named Frank Sinatra. They spoke a lingo unknown to their parents, "wasted" their time with fan clubs, and spent their pocket money on lipstick, phonograph records and jukebox plays. Boys dressed in zoot suits — deliberately, provocatively outlandish outfits. Zoot suits, with their high-waisted baggy pants tapering at the ankle and mid-thigh–length jackets, were in Hine's words, "parodies of suits."[56] In the 1940s, the new group called *teenagers* had their own jargon, music, clothes and recreation. By the war's end, teens had money to spend, and spend it they did.[57] School was in session. The kids had to dance. It was time to plan the prom.

Saddle shoes, popular teen footwear in 1943 (Library of Congress).

2. Dancing to a New Beat

"This is the moment to slip into your dress.... Pat your hair in place again, fasten your necklace or bracelet, and step into your pumps.... And wheeee! Look now! There really is another you in the mirror. A you that is practically exuding a subtle new fascination, a wonderful femininity. Quickly, reach out for your flacon of perfume.... But, be careful—don't overdo it. The heat of your beating pulse will warm the scent and give it life—sending it out to greet all who come near you. You're off to a wonderful, wonderful time!"
— Glynne, *The American Girl Beauty Book*, 1954

The late 1940s and 1950s were the golden age of prom. Never before or since were teens so innocent, gender roles so crisp, and the event itself so normative. Girls wore wrist-length white gloves to set off dresses ballooned by layers of petticoats. Christian Dior's signature cinched waists and sweeping skirts permeated the fashion industry.[1] Like their mothers, girls loved anything with a hint of Parisian sophistication. Boys with crew-cuts wore white or black jackets with wide ties. They transported their dates in big American-made cars decked out with tailfins and dashboard buttons. At the prom, teens mamboed, waltzed and fox-trotted to "Cherry Pink and Apple Blossom White" and "The Tennessee Waltz." They swayed to records by singers such as Perry Como and Patti Page, the same entertainment their folks enjoyed. Boys paid for the evening — on average $15 worth — with money earned from part-time jobs.[2] They paid because splitting expenses ("going Dutch") would have been a withering loss of masculinity. Their dates dipped into babysitting money for dresses and grooming expenses. Girls waited for boys to open doors because exiting a car on their own was unfeminine.[3] As they were taught to do, boys took charge and girls were content to be passive and pretty. A nascent teen culture had not yet fully emerged. The postwar prom was an exercise in imitating the older generation.

Teens who were in high school immediately after the "big one" (as veterans like to call World War II) were in the middle of the "Silent Generation"

born between 1925 and 1942, so-
called for their disinclination to
challenge authority.[4] A sixteen-
year-old in 1946 had been born
into the Great Depression and
experienced rationing in the war
years. Between 1945 and 1960,
however, per capita income increased by 35 percent. Housing
starts exploded and stayed high
throughout the 1950s. At the war's
end, pent-up demand and dispos-
able cash ignited a national spending spree. The economy bloomed
with plentiful jobs, affordable cars
and newly constructed suburbs
such as Levittown that isolated its
mostly white, middle-class residents from the harsh realities of
the less fortunate.

The new medium of televi-
sion united the population with
bland, inoffensive images of what
a cheerful, prosperous society
should look like: Caucasian, gain-
fully employed, patriotic, church-
going, and ready to buy.[5] The
televised version of America was
not representative of reality: The
1950s saw a huge influx of Mexi-

Pink tulle and satin gown with wrap from
1950s.

can-American immigrants; by 1960, more Puerto Ricans lived in New York
City than San Juan, and African Americans populated large sections of North-
ern cities. Despite real-life demographics, TV shows were populated with the
white Andersons, Nelsons and Cleavers. The denial of diversity was so complete that even the Hispanic gardener on "Father Knows Best" was named
Frank Smith.[6]

The Silent Generation had an odd advantage — there weren't very many
of them because birth and immigration rates were low when they were born.
They were the first age cohort to receive an allowance instead of having to
earn every penny of their own spending cash. Parents lavished attention and
money on their kids, who happily accepted every bit of it. Teen girls caught

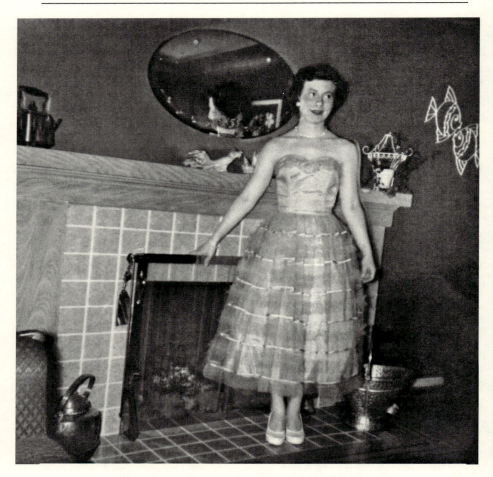

Judy Davies waits for her prom date, 1955 (Judith Sansom).

on to the new consumerism with a vengeance.[7] They loved to spend, but without a class of consumer goods to call their own, they bought the same items as their parents. Part-time jobs were easy to come by, but a teenager's primary job was being a teenager. A busy social life was seen as a necessary component of becoming a "well-rounded adult." As one writer counseled, "The Sunday school picnics, the cokes at the drugstore, the Friday night dances, teach the important lesson of getting along with people, especially those of the other sex. You have to be sure then, that your youngster's job doesn't slice deeply into his leisure."[8] Teens agreed. School and social activities were their world.

The era's teens were a modest, conservative group. As writer Frank Conroy said, "[We] became teenagers when to be a teenager was nothing, the lowest of the low." As in the early 1930s, circumstances retarded the formation of teen culture. All eyes were on high-schoolers' dads, the returning GIs who had saved the world from the Axis powers. Everyone, teenagers included, looked up to them. Eager to please their parents, postwar teens wanted to fit in. They disliked individualism and were suspicious of radical thinking. Just as writers of the period identified the gray-clad company man, the 1950s produced the "corporation teen."[9] All dressed up like Mom and Dad out for a special occasion, prom-goers embodied the fashionable enthusiasm for conformity.

Their parents, the "GI Generation," had produced a newly safe and prosperous world, and teenagers wanted nothing so much as to be an adult in that world. Marriage was glorified for a practical, if not altogether satisfying reason. Women who had enjoyed the freedom and personal income of wartime jobs had to say goodbye to all that for the men's sake. Returning GIs were eager to take the jobs previously held by women, and then marry and get on with their lives. They returned from the theaters of war worldly and sexually experienced. They were irresistible, and got married in droves. Large-scale domesticity ensued, fed by newly available consumer goods and a popular press that extolled the married state.[10] Teenagers thought their parents' scene looked pretty good. Fifteen-year-old girls assembled "hope chests" in anticipation of marriage, and indeed many girls in the late '40s and early '50s were engaged by the age of sixteen. One out of five was engaged by the age of nineteen. By 1956, the median age for a girl to marry was 20.1 years old — the youngest ever in twentieth century America.[11]

Like junior housewives, high percentages of teenage girls did the household cleaning and shopping. High schools taught home economics classes to prepare young ladies for marriage, motherhood and housework. Any school that didn't was deemed subpar.[12] Vocational training was standard for boys. Those in urban areas often took shop classes. They could find work right out of high school in the growing manufacturing sector, and make enough money to support a family. As one writer put it, "A small-town Iowa high school that neglects to teach farm management, crop planning or farm equipment repair is not doing its job." The purpose of "the modern 1950-style high school," he asserted, "is to prepare its students to do better the things they would do anyway,"[13] namely marriage, work and procreation. "High schools no longer are prep schools," he added. "They are finishing schools — not the fancy kind for wellborn young ladies — but literally the final dose of education for the majority of students, the ones who plunge directly from graduation into the world of jobs and everyday living."[14] Prom was like a junior wedding, a last chance to be free and fancy before a real wedding day, the prelude to a lifetime of domestic routine.

Ad for Keepsake diamond rings in October 1954 *Seventeen* targeting the era's marriage-minded girls.

Going steady — the adolescent version of marital monogamy — was the norm and the ideal. Peer pressure played a part. One magazine reported that 82 percent of boys and 76 percent of girls went steady because their friends did. Another stated reason for going steady was experience in getting along with the opposite sex, or put another way, rehearsal for marriage.[15] Going

This 1950 ad for New York Life Insurance Company uses prom as a metaphor for tradition and continuity. As her daughter looks on, a mom reminisces about the prom and her high school chum "Frank Wilson," now a trusted New York Life agent.

steady took all the pressure out of dating. Teens called it "social security." After an anxious September flurry of pairing off, you could relax, assuming you found someone. Going steady drove parents who had grown up in the dating and rating years crazy. The old style of dating many people was supposedly a developmental marker. Parents and social commentators thought going steady stunted your emotional growth. You were supposed to compete for the opposite sex's attention. As one writer warned, "To have your girl always assured at the end of a telephone line without having to work for her, to beat the other fellows to her, is bound to lessen your powers of personal achievement." Kids considered that argument and said *no sale*. Two generations looked at the dating game and assigned a completely different value to its competitiveness. In their parents' day, romantic set-backs were to be expected — one lived to date another day. Single '50s teens simply dropped out of the competition until the next school year. According to one girl, "At our school, if you don't find someone to go steady with by October, you just don't date that year." Another student said, "You either went steady or you never went." Steady couples didn't always stay together all academic year. In fact, many went steady on a serial basis, but if you didn't have someone's class ring or pin by prom time you didn't go to prom.[16]

In the dating and rating era, the game was having any date. In the 1950s, social competition revolved around the right prom date, and that meant money. Girls dressed to impress each other. They compared not only their gowns but their shoes, wraps, corsages (flowers were mandatory; orchids trumped gardenias), the means of transportation their dates provided and post-prom destinations. The rivalry around conspicuous consumption was so intense that some principals canceled proms to avoid "psychologically wounding" those who could not afford to attend.[17]

Contemporary girls think little of asking a boy to the prom, but in the 1950s, asking a boy for a date was an egregious faux pas. As one advice book admonished, "girls who [try] to usurp the right of boys to choose their own dates will ruin a good dating career. From the Stone Age, when men chased and captured their women, comes the yen of a boy to do the pursuing. You will control your impatience, therefore, and respect the time-honored custom of boys to take the first step."[18] How quickly "calling" faded from the collective memory! Framing dating in terms of "rights," "careers" and imaginary customs that connect Neanderthals to the 1950s is absurd in the twenty-first century. At the time, however, that point of view was common.

Postwar teens were avid to pair off yet remarkably naive about sex — many weren't exactly sure if French kissing or petting caused pregnancy. The notion of "going all the way" produced tremendous anxiety, whether or not one understood its precise anatomical meaning. It was absolutely understood and universally accepted, however, that "nice girl" meant "virgin."[19]

Teens looked to adults for guidance in matters intimate, but not necessarily to the adults at home. Professional advice-givers, such as syndicated columnists Ann Landers and her twin sister Dear Abby, dispensed the rules on how far a good girl could go. A typical bit of Landers' advice was, "When necking becomes the major interest and No. 1 indoor sport, you're playing with fire and you could get badly singed." It was a given that teenage boys would go as far as they could. "They'll take anything that's offered plus whatever they can talk a girl into giving," says Landers. "And to be blunt, a boy doesn't have much to lose." Girls had the burden of maintaining sexual limits because, Landers advises, "Girls get pregnant." Did prom-goers in the 1950s do the horizontal mambo? Only the couples know for sure, but if they did the deed it was probably in a car. Landers wrote, "The majority of teenagers who write to me about their sexual intimacies confess that the trouble started in a parked car." A

Ann Landers (Library of Congress).

prime spot for parking and all that ensued was the drive-in movie, or "passion pit." If a steamy movie was featured, that added to the "hazard." Landers goes on to say, "Add to this a full moon and a few cans of beer or a pint of bourbon which just happens to be in the glove compartment and you have a tailor-made setup for big trouble."[20] In the 1950s, unwed pregnancy was no joke. Writer Erica Jong recalls, "I remember the fear of pregnancy when I was in high school. I remember the terror — the girls who vanished, who went to the wilds of New Jersey and then were admitted to a New York hospital hemorrhaging. And some of them never returned. And some of them were sterilized for life. And some of them wanted to have babies later on and couldn't. So it was really scary."[21]

Advice columnists weren't the only writers focusing on teenagers by the early 1950s. Publications such as *Life*, *Look*, and *Time* often ran articles on teen life. Prom articles were a regular feature, probably because the accompanying photographs were fun to view. *Life* covered proms as early as 1937, captioning a photograph about an Antigo, Wisconsin dance, "Mrs. Fred Schmeisser humbly sits down on the floor as she applies the final stitches to her gallivanting daughter's homemade high school prom dress. The Schmeissers are typical of the plain self-respecting families who go to make up Antigo's 9,000 population."[22] Mrs. Schmeisser was a talented lady. Highly structured '50s patterns were not easy to sew. Pleats and gathers were hard enough, and darts were definitely not for the inexperienced seamstress. Every pattern had them, going up from the waist and in toward the armpit for bodice shaping. Ideally, they had to point directly to the center of a breast. A half-inch too high or low made the wearer look as if she had an extra pair of nipples.[23]

Fifties fashion, although beautiful to look at, was a trial to wear. The sexual anxiety of the period was reflected in the clothing. Structured, conical bras made teenage breasts (nowhere near prone to sagging) feel and look as forbidding as atomic-age rockets. Mandatory girdles cut off circulation and functioned like modern-day chastity belts.[24] Formal promwear, typically made of pastel-colored tulle, turned girls' bodies into exaggerations of the female shape. Fashion historian Ellen Melinkoff writes of the '50s, "The natural female figure was merely raw material that had to be poured, molded, whittled to perfection. How did it feel to be a living sculpture? Awful. But we endured in the name of womanhood."[25] A womanly look in the 1950s meant big breasts. Americans in the '50s were fixated on female chests. Men's magazines were full of photographs of Jayne Mansfield, Anita Ekberg and Mamie Van Doren

Panty girdles (at left), a compulsory 1960s undergarment. Modern girdles (at right), frequently worn under prom gowns, are called "body shapers."

look-alikes: leggy blondes with commodious bosoms. If nature hadn't endowed you with architecture like a battleship, "falsies" did the trick. We call them padded bras today, but in the '50s, one tucked foam pads into one's dress. (Tissues would do in a pinch. Today's falsies are often surgically implanted saline sacs.) Falsies had an awful tendency to pop out at inopportune moments, say at the prom. Melinkoff says, "There was no graceful way to handle it. You'd have to move to another state where nobody knew you."[26] Girls dressed for maximum sexual allure, while holding the line against actual sex. As writer Brett Harvey says,

> "Did you ever think about the fact that all the fabrics we wore in the fifties were stiff?" my friend Ronnie once asked me. I hadn't, but the minute she said it I thought: faille, shantung, felt, taffeta, pique. Nothing clung, or fell, or draped — everything was crisp. Fifties clothes were like armor.[27]

Christian Dior's "New Look," a tight jacket over a flared or pencil skirt, worked for fashionistas and slim-figured women, but the Paper Doll look was the signature 1950s style. Invented by New York designer Ann Fogarty, the Paper Doll silhouette was a fitted bodice and a skirt flared out at a precise 45-degree angle, which at the very least gave girls a reason to pay attention in geometry class. The proper profile required layered undergarments. Lace and cotton petticoats were difficult to stiffen. Horsehair was the right stuff. It was rigid enough to remain airborne. (Its itchiness would have satisfied the most masochistic medieval penitent.) Crinoline was more common and also worked well, especially if starched and damp-ironed. Petticoats were hideously uncomfortable and made sitting difficult. (I remember fidgeting in my fifth grade class, trying and failing to attain gluteal equilibrium on my lumpy petticoats.) The only good thing about them was that they disguised big hips — a concern for fully developed women but an irrelevancy for prepubescent girls.

Dress-up occasions were truly special back then. Girls watched their mothers straighten the seams of their stockings, cinch their belts, pull on gloves and grab a "bucket" purse for an evening on the town. Prom was a girl's first opportunity to imitate Mom's fashion maturity. For prom, it was necessary to find not only the perfect dress but a matching evening coat. Camel's hair was fine, but the best was cashmere. A shawl-collared cashmere coat was the perfect wrap, especially with the sleeves pushed up to the elbow. Lacking buttons, it was often called a "clutch coat," and if your walk was just right, you could pull off an entrance into the gym looking like gorgeous Natalie Wood in *Rebel Without a Cause*. If you really wanted to wow your date, a strapless dress, or better still, a scoop-back dress, was the height of womanly fashion.[28]

Clothes were important, but the main driver of the burgeoning teen

"Junior Elegance" dresses with classic paper doll profile advertised in May 1955 *Seventeen.*

market was music. *The Billboard,* a music industry trade paper, reported in 1957, "More than 16 million teenagers will make cash registers ring to the tune of over $9 million next year. This explains why the 13–19 age group has always been looked upon as the record industry's best customer. It also explains why wiser dealers woo this market and woo it hard."[29]

In 1951, Cleveland radio personality Alan Freed began a late-night radio show, playing rhythm and blues (R&B) to an audience of black and white teenagers. He was inspired by a local record store owner who told him about all the white kids who came into his place to listen to African American artists such as the Cadillacs, Chuck Berry, Fats Domino and Little Richard. He told Freed, "The beat is so strong, that anyone can dance to it without a lesson."[30] He was talking about the accented second and fourth beats of a four-beat measure, a distinctly black musical idiom.

Freed's show was so popular that he soon sponsored live shows for his listeners, who were the first to defy the conventions of a strictly segregated society. The premiere in 1952 drew a crowd of 10,000 teenagers, not counting the thousands who were turned away (nearly sparking a riot). Around this time, Freed started describing the music as "rock and roll," a term that was also slang for sex. By 1955, most newspaper reporters started referring to the music as *rock 'n' roll,* crediting Freed with the coinage. That year Freed moved to New York City, where his radio show, *Rock 'n' Roll Party*, once again drew a mixed-race audience. Freed's live New York shows caused teenage pandemonium. Adults, authorities and medical professionals went cuckoo. The way the kids danced was depraved, pathological! One psychiatrist compared the teenage rock 'n' roll dance fest to the "contagious epidemic of dance fury" that had swept through Europe in the fourteenth century. Frank Sinatra, staring into a chasm of fading popularity, complained, "Rock 'n' roll ... is sung, played, and written for the most part by cretinous goons."[31] Freed defended the music: "Rock 'n' roll is really swing with a modern name.... It's the rhythm that gets the kids. They are starved for music they can dance to after all those years of crooners."[32]

A 1950s cream chiffon and satin party dress.

In 1957, the ABC television network gave Freed a show, *Allan Freed's Big Beat*. The show came to an abrupt end when black singer Frankie Lymon pulled a white girl onstage to dance with him. The network "suits" were appalled, or perhaps they pretended to be. Their real concern was the apoplectic response of the network affiliates in Southern states. By airing Freed's show on their local stations, the affiliates had invited Lymon — this black boy — into the living rooms of white viewers. Lymon had repaid them by figuratively soiling the carpet. In the eyes of the affiliates, the gaffe was a heinous breach of decency. The rules of segregation were not to be messed with. Freed and Lymon were out, but rock 'n' roll was just getting started.

Social critics blamed rock 'n' roll for everything from a rising crime rate to crumbling morals. The Reverend Jimmy Snow, son of country singer Hank Snow, said,

> I know how it feels when you sing it. I know what it does to you. And I know the evil feeling that you feel when you sing it. I know the lost position that you get

into and the beat. Well, if you talk to the average teenager of today and you ask them what it is about Rock and roll music that they like. The first thing they'll say it's the beat, the beat, the beat.[33]

Jeremiads notwithstanding, by the mid–1950s rock 'n' roll was an unstoppable force. Record producers saw the business opportunity, but felt uneasy about the music's overtly African American style. They responded by producing white cover versions of black tunes. The primary source of cover versions was Dot Records, a label owned by Randy Wood, who promoted Pat Boone, the whitest of white singers. "The recording directors at the small R&B labels wanted to attract attention to their artists, and the covers expanded the impact of a song," Wood said. "Little Richard, Fats Domino and Chuck Berry were all thrilled because it made it possible for their songs to finally get heard."[34] Wood's sunny assessment was not borne out by record sales or the original artists. Consumers rejected white cover versions, and Little Richard still complains about Boone's cover of his song, "Tutti Frutti." The white cover version trend that began in 1954 died in 1956. The crossover of black-influenced pop music into the mainstream came via two routes: *American Bandstand* and Elvis Presley.[35]

Elvis was a nice, white Mississippi boy who sang black. Pat Boone was boyish and charming, but music fans preferred manly and sexy, which Elvis delivered and then some. As one grandmother said, Boone was a "pale replica" who lacked 'the terrific masculine appeal of Elvis.'"[36] Although his gyrating hips bothered adults at first, "Elvis the Pelvis" soon caught on across demographic lines. He sold records — lots of them — and was simply too profitable too ignore. Owing to Elvis's popularity, rock 'n' roll gained a firm footing in the culture. And he could move almost as well as he sang. Watching Elvis, teens learned that the rhythmic impulse of the music was more important than specific steps. You didn't count, as in "one-two, cha-cha-cha." You just felt the rock 'n' roll "backbeat" and let it move you.[37]

The after-school televised dance party *American Bandstand*, however, had the biggest influence on teenage musical taste and dancing. In 1957, ABC handed over a local Philadelphia show to a former radio disc jockey named Dick Clark whose boyish looks and sincere manner made Pat Boone look like a hipster. Clark's affable on-camera persona belied his penchant for running the tightest of ships. The punishment for gum chewing on camera was banishment; boys had to wear coats and ties; slacks and low-cut tops for girls were *verboten*. The show featured numerous African American performers, but the kids who danced to their music were white. (Black students were eventually allowed to dance on the show, but only with each other.) All of the dancers, recruited from Philly high schools, were amateurs, which was their appeal. *The American Bandstand* dancers were like a cast of prom kings and queens —

the best dancers and most popular kids in school. The regulars on the show became celebrities themselves. Teens wrote fan mail to favorite couples such as Bob Clayton and Justine Carelli; Kenny Rossi and Arlene Sullivan. (Their "Philadelphia collar," a rounded Peter Pan type, caught on, too. It was worn outside a sweater, which, unbeknown to the viewing audience, covered up a Catholic school uniform.)

Within weeks of its first airing, the show drew over 20 million viewers — kids who wanted to know what the latest tunes were and how to dance to them. The *Bandstand* dancers were exemplars of respectable teenage behavior. Their good manners were showcased specifically to calm parents who worried about

Dick Clark, 1961.

the effects of dancing to rock 'n' roll. Clark, dubbed "the world's oldest teenager" as the years wore on, modeled himself as a fount of teenage guidance, publishing advice books designed to keep his young viewers on the straight and narrow. This was his genius: Freed made the career-killing choice to confront his critics, but Clark co-opted them. He and his cast were much less bland than they appeared, but he understood, perhaps earlier than any other TV producer, the power of a carefully crafted image.[38]

On each show, a couple served as "record raters" who scored the tunes on a scale of 43 to 98. The standard review was, "It's got a good beat and you can dance to it." *Bandstand* was a national dance class for teens. Kids all over the country learned the Stroll, the Hand Jive, and the Bop. The Madison Time was a line dance with the steps called out on the recording of the same name. The Fish, not so much a step pattern as the male's attempt to grind his pelvis on the thigh of his female partner, was summarily banned.[39]

American Bandstand and the recording industry provided the play list and the dances for high school proms. They also put live musicians out of business. Band booker Zeke Nicholas said, "We do not intend to sit idly by while the deejays take over. They are taking the livelihood from scores of legitimate performers and variety acts. They force record names to accompany them on these prom dates by using their power as a subtle blackjack."[40]

By the late 1950s, live bands were still popular on college campuses, but high schools relied on recorded music for proms. The kids wanted to hear the songs the way they sounded over the radio, and live bands were too pricey for high school budgets. A "DJ" with a record player and stack of "platters" was far less expensive than a live orchestra. Orchestras at the time played music that didn't suit the kids anyway. As one student complained, "The bands feature too many of their old hits. The numbers are too short and there's too much novelty stuff." In addition to old-fashioned music, some of the "orksters" had a habit of showing up drunk — and not just the leader but the whole ensemble. Many "maestri" were "taken over the coals" in the words of one *Billboard* report, for "being poorly or sloppily attired. One school pointed out that the name crews rarely comply with requests to be dressed formally in keeping with a formal dress prom."[41] Radio stations held promotional "proms," sometimes co-sponsored by a local Kiwanis Club to raise money for charity. Band bookers did their best to compete with DJs by throwing teen dance parties (nice but not formal dress required) for small admission fees, netting just enough to pay the band and maybe contribute something to a local high school.[42] Some bands managed to stay in the prom business for a time by playing at after-parties, but in general dance bands were on the wane. According to *The Billboard*, "The kids explained that the phonograph record is the center of social activity. The disk affords them the best in dance music." The article goes on to say, "In a discussion of social dancing, it was shown that the girls in the teenage set were the pace-setters while the fellows were fairly shy about learning to dance. One of the male students told why: 'Dancing in the old days was an excuse to hold a girl in your arms. Today we're more practical. We get it over with necking sessions. This gives us time for more practical things like playing ball.'"[43]

Teachers and parents took an interest in proms, the former supervising preparations and the latter often serving as chaperones. The venue in the 1950s was the high school gym, and the task for prom was to make the space as un-gym-like as possible. (The imagination reels at the number of trees felled for the production of crepe paper.) Marietta Abell and Agnes J. Anderson's guide, *School Dances and Proms*, spelled things out for the uninitiated, even suggesting guidance in girls' attire:

> As the time for the prom draws near, many high school pupils are doubtful about what to wear.... It would be a good idea to have a joint meeting of the junior and senior girls when some person of authority will talk to them on the subject of dresses for proms. This speaker should certainly be someone who dresses in excellent taste herself and someone who is really authoritative.... A home economics teacher or dean of girls could be asked to do it.[44]

A 1958 ad for GM cars in *Boy's Life* links the products to prom night safety.

According to the writers, participation is the key to a successful prom, and the key to participation is committees. They suggest no fewer than seven: decoration, invitation, music, program, floorshow, refreshment, and social. The series of cross-committee interactions and negotiations they propose would discombobulate the United Nations General Assembly.[45] Above all, a proper prom has to have a theme. Abell and Anderson list a few: "In Chinatown" (with a recipe for chop suey that includes a can of tomato soup), "Puss in Boots" and "Spring in Hellas," to name three. The beauty of their scheme was the high school shop-made sets and scenery — a perfect way to involve the boys and male teachers. Lattice work, arches, Chinese lanterns, Hawaiian sunsets made of construction paper and glue, menus, printed programs, performances — the guide has a project for every student.[46] That said, it's hard to imagine even the most unsophisticated student body going for a Puss in Boots theme, or any other suggestion in the book, which seems more suited for elementary school. (Their advice to keep expenses down is a notable exception.) One senses that even in the relatively innocent 1950s, students were way ahead of parents and teachers in their relationships to school and each other. The redoubtable Miss Manners (Judith Martin) observed, "Chaperons don't enforce morality; they force immorality to be discreet."[47]

Chaperones Marjorie and Rollie Neibauer, Des Moines, 1966 (Mary Anne Erickson).

Chaperones have always been a fixture of high school proms. Grown-ups attend to forestall inappropriate behavior, but it's not the actual prom that's most in need of supervision. It's the potential for after-prom mischief, specifically drunk driving and sex, that has worried parents and teachers for decades, and not without reason. In Creston, Iowa, for example, increased numbers of auto accidents at prom time were a matter of record. A 1953 *Time* magazine article reported that "in the May 1–June 10 periods since 1946, 50 Iowa teen-agers have died on the highways, most of them on prom night." Creston merchants fought the trend by sponsoring an after-party, with stipulations that pleased the students: No teachers were allowed to attend. Adults could serve food and act as chauffeurs but were not permitted to actively chaperone. The after-prom committee staged a Hollywood-style movie premiere at the local theater, complete with searchlights, so the townspeople could line the sidewalk and gape at the students in their prom finery. A late supper featured a cholesterol-laden menu of "hot dogs, half-pound hamburgers, sandwiches and deviled eggs," an attempt, perhaps, to feed the students into a compliant stupor. After supper, a "lady ventriloquist" recruited from far-away Kansas City performed. She was tipped to some student names and peccadilloes, and delighted the audience with jokes written especially about them. More dancing followed, and the gala event concluded with a train ride (complete with a serenading orchestra) to a town twelve miles away. For the adults involved, the peace of mind purchased with the time, money, and effort expended was well worth it. The students responded with a three-column thank-you note in the *Creston News Advertiser* that read, "Thanks to the people of Creston. We had such a good time. We'll never forget."[48]

Rotary Clubs have been particularly active in the post-prom business. In 1958, for example, Rotarians in South Haven, Michigan raised $1,550 for a nautically-themed after-prom bash, free to the students, who numbered in the hundreds. The students selected the theme and did the decorating; the Rotary Club supplied the music, food and entertainment. A college fraternity pitched in by opening its house for the party.[49]

Each prom season, adult anxiety bloomed anew. Wrote one reporter in 1957, "The weeks before the prom ... are at an end for the girl graduate when prom night at last arrives. As she walks out the door on the arm of her young escort, however, in all too many homes in these mixed-up times, parents' worries are just beginning."[50]

Residents of Norwalk, Connecticut were as concerned as any community about the safety of their students, but couldn't quite come to terms on the issue of after-parties. They planned an event for the 1958 prom but failed to obtain a license. Adult-sponsored or not, teens on the street after 1 A.M. were in violation of the town curfew and that, according to the party-pooper police commissioner, was that. The after-party was canceled — a big disappointment, no doubt, because the town had chartered a train to take the students to the Roosevelt Hotel in Manhattan.[51] *Life* magazine reported about a successful after-prom event that lasted well into the following day:

Students at Mariemont High School near Cincinnati came close to the ultimate this year when they put on a "prom" that lasted almost 32 hours. It started with a progressive dinner (spaghetti to strawberry cake), followed by a formal but highly energetic dance. Then the students boarded a riverboat for a cruise and dancing to a jazz combo. Dawn found them somewhat subdued and back at school for breakfast. Sent home for a short rest period, they emerged refreshed and descended on an amusement park. By nightfall half the students had discovered they were mortal and had gone home to bed. The rest whipped up another dance. "It keeps getting better and better," one said, "as I get more and more numb."[52]

It would have been a shame for all that prom merriment to go unrecorded. Fortunately, 1950s prom-goers had the perfect tool for capturing the evening: the Brownie camera. Eastman Kodak's first model (in 1900) retailed for a dollar and put photography in the hands of amateurs. The model 127, introduced in 1952, cost a mere $4.75 — a price well within reach of most teens. With heavy print and television advertising, Kodak sold millions of cameras. Between 1953–54 alone, a quarter million Brownies were imported from the United Kingdom where they were manufactured. Home movie cameras were also very popular. A 1957 TV commercial for a Brownie 8mm camera ($29.95) asserted that "more families than ever are saving their good times with movies." No less iconic a '50s figure than Ozzie Nelson, family patriarch and star of *Ozzie and Harriet*, pitched the camera on his show. The Brownie's ease of operation and affordability made photography a part of the prom night ritual.[53]

Prom-goers in the 1950s were the "good" kids who followed the rules set down by high school deans, Ann Landers, Dick Clark, *Seventeen* and so on. But not all '50s teenagers signed on to the program. Some kids persisted in attending rock 'n' roll shows with a mixed-race crowd. There were chain-smoking boys in peg-legged black jeans and oily duck-tailed hair cuts, big-busted girls in tight sweaters who wore hair curlers under kerchiefs. They wore pink and black, a fashionable combination, but one that in a rock 'n' roll context possibly symbolized the intent to erase the racial divide. "Greasers" were loud, tough and rebellious. Some were vandals, brawlers and car thieves. They hung out on sidewalks and forced adults to walk around them. Newspapers exaggerated the threat of juvenile delinquency (teenage crime rates in the 1950s were actually fairly low) and cops treated minor miscreants like hardened felons because they were everything adults feared about the new teenage culture. But teenage rebellion was inevitable. The popular 1950s model of teen life was only for those who could live it. High schools were in the business of inculcating middle-class values, but what good were those values if you were working class or had dark skin? What was the relevance of *Leave It to Beaver* if the closest you came to a home like that was mowing the lawn? What was the point of a prom if you couldn't afford to go? The mainstream culture promoted an idealized image of American life that was unavailable to large swaths of the population. Even if you were affluent and white, there were commies and the bomb to worry about. The surface of American life was artificially placid; underneath it boiled with anxiety and tension. Ironically, it was rock 'n' roll that provided many teens with a clear-cut choice: to be or not to be a greaser. You could dress and dance nicely or you could

Electric-eye camera
by Kodak... $^{LESS}_{THAN}$ $22

THE SKILL'S BUILT IN—electric eye tells you the correct exposure for each subject.

Brownie Starmeter Camera helps you get a clear shot every shot!

This electric-eye Brownie camera tells you the correct exposure setting for every subject . . . instantly.

No guesswork. It keeps you right—whether the day is cloudy, hazy, or full of sunshine.

And the Brownie Starmeter Camera is such a compact handful! Gets 12 pictures on a roll of film . . . needs no focusing either for close-up or distant scenes.

Waiting for you at your Kodak dealer's now—less than $22. And also see the Brownie Starmeter *Outfit*—a grand gift, less than $28. Check your dealer for exact retail prices.

Prices are subject to change without notice. Many dealers offer terms as low as 10% down.

Brownie Starmite Camera is ultra-compact, and the flash is built in. Less than $12.

Brownie Flashmite 20 Camera with built-in flash, plus adjustable settings. Less than $17.

Brownie Starmatic Camera. Electric eye sets lens opening *automatically.* Less than $30.

...See all the new cameras in Kodak 1961 **Cameraland**—*at stores displaying the Kodak Girl*

EASTMAN KODAK COMPANY, Rochester 4, N.Y.

DON'T MISS "THE ED SULLIVAN SHOW" AND "THE ADVENTURES OF OZZIE AND HARRIET"

Kodak TRADEMARK

Ad for Brownie Starmeter camera, produced in the U.S. from 1960 to 1965.

go the other way. You could embrace the establishment or poke a finger in its eye.[54] Small wonder that pictures of clean-cut teens in '50s prom wear inspire nostalgia.

Americans have turned the 1950s into a national in-joke. The cliché, cartoonish signifiers that decorate '50s-themed burger joints — poodle skirts, circle pins, roller skates — mask the reality of a fearful, tumultuous time. It's not that we've forgotten the Korean War, the McCarthy hearings, the Cold

War with its threat of nuclear annihilation, racial conflict, sexual repression, and all the other problems of the era. But serious issues don't sell hamburgers and TV shows. Even the decade's juvenile delinquents have been denatured in today's popular culture. Jokey characters such as Fonzie from the TV series *Happy Days* and Rizzo from the musical comedy *Grease* are nonthreatening, risible versions of the "JDs" who used to strike fear in the hearts of law-abiding middle-class citizens.

The prom was the era's ritual demonstration that the kids were all right, that adults knew what they were doing. (They didn't name one of the decade's most popular TV shows *Father Knows Best* for nothing.) If some teenagers wanted to wear their hair in greasy ducktails, smoke cigarettes, commit crimes, and reject the scrubbed, happy world of "normal" teens, well, that was their loss. Seeing the "nice" kids all dressed up with somewhere to go made everyone feel, for an evening at least, that any problem could be solved with a snazzy car or a pretty dress. If prom night was the promotion of a beautiful illusion, at least the fun was real. Besides, what's wrong with a good illusion every now and then?

By the late 1950s, teen life in America had come into its own. Adolescents had their own music, dances, clothing, and money. They demanded more freedom and knew more about sex than their predecessors at the beginning of the decade. Prom was a wonderful conclusion to a successful high school career. The 1960s were just around the corner, and things were really fixing to rock 'n' roll.

3. Boomer High

*"I don't know where you were in say, 1964, but I divided my time
between screaming wildly for the Beatles, wearing a cheerleading uniform, scrubbing my face ten times a day with Noxzema, and putting
my hair up in rollers the size of Foster's lager cans."*
— Susan J. Douglas, *Where the Girls Are*

The Sixties. The phrase is practically a Rorschach test. Say it out loud,
and you'll elicit a range of responses from eye rolls to a chorus of "Lucy in
the Sky with Diamonds." How the 1960s struck you depended on where you
stood. If you lived in the vortex of the counterculture — places like New York,
San Francisco, Los Angeles, Ann Arbor or Chicago — you could watch the
decade's changes firsthand. In the Midwest and South, the cultural revolution
was more remote, and the environment was far more conventional. In other
words, '60s proms went on as usual in the so-called Heartland and diminished
in importance on the coasts and big college towns. My friend David, for
example, attended school in Los Angeles (Hamilton High class of 1968). His
prom was canceled due to lack of interest. Instead, he smoked pot with friends
and hung out at Dino's Lodge on the Sunset Strip where they goofed on "the
weird Rat Pack hipsters." Another friend, Bill (class of 1967), went to school
in rural Virginia. He was forbidden to take the girl he liked to the prom, having been busted making out with her in the school library a week prior. He
gamely suited up in a white dinner jacket and endured an awful evening with
a near stranger because in his world prom was more or less mandatory.[1] People
experienced the '60s in all kinds of ways — not everyone was a hippie.
(Although some of us were weekend hippies when we could get away from
Mom and Dad, go to a concert and smoke the ditch weed that college-age
scam artists palmed off on us.) Some watched events unfold in amazement and
hoped the world would be saner by the time we graduated. (It wasn't.) High
school in the 1950s was a terminus for many students. In the '60s it was a
launch pad — students expected to go places after graduation.

A 1960s orange moiré taffeta party dress with brown sash.

If you were a teen in the 1960s, did you prefer Carnaby Street fashion, tie dyes or good old Sears? Rock or folk? Bass Weejuns or Capezios? Nixon or McCarthy? The decade was full of contradictions and bewildering choices. The '60s are actually more of a concept than a decade. It's even hard to define the '60s by date. For many, the decade started in January 20, 1961, with the inauguration of President John F. Kennedy. For others, it was November 22, 1963, the day Kennedy was shot and killed — bookends of optimism and despair. The end of the '60s could be 1969, the year of the Manson "family" homicides as well as the moon landing. It may be that '60s weren't over until 1973, when President Nixon halted combat operations in Vietnam and declared "peace with honor."

College kids were the unlikely movers and shakers of the 1960s. They weren't the only ones participating in the sexual revolution, protesting the war in Vietnam, upending artistic conventions and so on, but they were at the heart of the upheaval, especially those who attended between 1963 and 1968. University students rocked tradition and rolled over tired stereotypes. "The ways we were shaped by the Sixties," says Annie Gottlieb, "depend on how old we were when they hit."[2] Teens who started college before 1965 were the most transformed by the decade. Those who were born later watched the first wave of Baby Boomers go off to college, learned from them and adapted.[3] High school students didn't have as much opportunity for participation in the rapid societal changes as their older siblings, but their eyes were trained on them as they transformed college campuses into social laboratories. There were proms in the 1960s, but they weren't as important as in prior years. Boomer kids had a lot of distractions.

As Hine says, "The very term 'baby boom' connotes an explosive phenomenon, though it lasted for two decades and still continues to shape American life."[4] Just like the '60s, the Baby Boom is hard to pin down. Depending on the source, the Baby Boom began in 1943 or '46 and lasted until 1960 or '64. Any way you slice it, that's a big spread. By 1969, the world was a vastly different place than it was at the beginning of the decade. The Boomer cohort itself was viewed differently from one end of the decade to the other. Strauss and Howe in their definitive study, *Generations,* write, "In 1965, *Time* magazine declared teenagers to be 'on the fringe of a golden era.' — and two years later described collegians as cheerful builders who would 'lay out blight-proof, smog-free cities, enrich the underdeveloped world, and no doubt, write *finis* to poverty and war.'"[5] We all know how that prediction turned out. Nevertheless, there are a lot of Boomers, and sheer numbers make them influential.

Suburbs teemed with Baby Boom kids, and there were plenty of them in cities and rural areas, too. Wherever they were, they shared a frame of reference produced and disseminated by mass media. Television producer Joel Westbrook says of moving to Los Angeles as an adult, "Absolutely nothing about L.A. was foreign to me. Riding around L.A. was pure geographic déjà vu. Remember, I was a child of TV; I'd already spent half my life in L.A."[6] The Baby Boom generation was the first to have a common culture shaped more by the years in which they were born than the locations.[7] If you didn't live in a place with a sports team, for example, you could still watch a game on TV at the same time as the people in the stadium. A shopping mall in Minneapolis had the same chain stores as one in Denver. That's old news now, but Baby Boomers were the first cohort to be knit together by big commercial entities with a national reach.

Boomer kids loved to shop, taking in marketing messages with their baby formula. A 1948 *Time* article referred to the 2.8 million new souls in the country as that many more "consumers" than the year before, a description as accurate as it is cold-blooded. Boomer kids were relentless consumers, the first generation to be plunked into high chairs in front of the "tube." They had as much interest in the commercials on *Howdy Doody, The Mickey Mouse Club* and *Sky King* as the shows. Frances Horwitch of television's *Ding Dong School* (known to her kid audience as "Miss Frances") told an advertising conference in 1954, "[A child] has brand loyalty and the determination to see that his parents purchase the product of his choice."[8] Boy, howdy.[9] Parents indulged their kids because Dr. Benjamin Spock told them to. His book, *The Common Sense Book of Baby and Child Care* (first published in 1954, now in its seventh edition), was read by more than half of all new parents, according to some polls. Spock counseled patience, attention and oodles of whatever little Susie wanted. Unlike her grandparents, who would have paddled Susie's rebellious bottom for failing to clean her room, her parents held their noses and waited until she was in the mood.[10]

Adults railed at the teen culture of the '50s, but by the time Boomer babies were in high school, they had given up the fight. Retailers considered teens far too profitable a market to alienate. "Rebels or not, baby-boom teenagers demonstrated an unprecedented ability to open their parents' wallets, and that made all the difference in the world of adult commerce," says author Grace Palladino.

Boomer teens had advantages their parents could not have imagined. Alfred E. Neuman, the fictional cover boy and mascot of *Mad Magazine*, summed it up best: "What, me worry?" The sunny skies of the '60s were marred, however, by the specter of mushroom clouds, to name just one fear of the decade. Anxiety supplanted the country's postwar swagger. Psychologist Daniel Goleman says,

> The boomer generation grew up having routine A-bomb drills. You may remember if you're of [a] certain age, that every few weeks, we would stop what we were doing and get under our desk and put one arm over our eyes and the other behind our neck, to protect ourselves from nuclear annihilation. If you grow up with that as a routine part of your reality, I think it forces you to consider deeply where we're going in this world.[11]

White middle-class high schoolers were insulated from adult concerns to some degree. Low-income minority students, however, had problems of their own. White flight caused inner cities to crumble, bringing schools down, too. Outdated structures were only one problem. Public high school was invented to give every student a good education, but the curriculum was designed with the middle-class Anglo-American student in mind. Educators assumed that all students would have the same orientation to language and learning, but that wasn't the case. For example, the well-developed verbal skills of working-class and minority students did not offset curricula weighted toward reading, an academic strength of the white population. The difficulties of jamming square pegs into round holes resulted in unfortunate, erroneous stereotyping of large groups of people. Minority and low-income kids have been set up from the get-go to struggle with poorly designed curricula, inadequate funding and hide-bound administrations.[12] It's probably fair to say in the '60s, prom was not uppermost in the minds of students in strained circumstances.

By the 1960s, public high schools served the majority of American teens, but quickly became victims of their own success. Moving big numbers of students through a K–12 system requires a bureaucracy, which treats people impersonally. School days are set up to eliminate all but the most cursory interactions between adults and the teenagers they teach. High school students are essentially powerless except in one area: socializing. In high school, friends are paramount. Philip Cusick, who studied a Midwestern high school in the late 1960s said, "One just did not hang out with anyone, or eat with anyone. He talked to, walked with, ate with, and spent as much time as possible with his few friends and literally did not pay attention to those who were not in his group." As one student said, "You can't go to high school without friends."[13] Classes were an afterthought. The real action took place in parking lots, hallways, locker rooms and lunchrooms.

School administrations categorize students, but they're amateurs at labeling compared to kids. Teenagers jump into the hopper and sort themselves with machine-like efficiency. They form alliances, better known as cliques. Jocks, burnouts, soc's (pronounced *sō-shes* for *social*), drama nerds, just plain nerds, goths, druggies, band geeks; every school has its own designations. In one school, unfortunate loners whose solitary ways kept them out of the middle of the halls were dubbed "wall huggers."[14] In the '60s, the clique became as regular a feature of high school as cafeteria "mystery meat." The importance of the senior prom was in direct proportion to the status of one's clique. If popularity was your game, you and your friends probably attended the dance. If not, nobody really noticed your absence. You stayed with your school of fish and swam around the others without so much as a glance.

Cusick and others discovered to no one's surprise that there are "power cliques," groups who run student councils, homecoming and prom committees year after year. "In that class of 364 members," he writes of the school he studied in the late '60s, "there were about fifteen to twenty students who seemed to get elected to whatever office happened to be available and who seemed to run whatever there was to run."[15] In most schools, the leaders are the athletes, cheerleaders, and the shiny few who with little effort ascend to that rarefied group, Most Popular. Charismatic types tend to know who they are and assume their rightful place in the hierarchy without resistance from the lesser lights among them.

A '60s prom was the culmination of a K–12 social career. By the time senior prom rolled around, students had years of practice making their way through the social maze. High school students created societies so insular and complex that academics and others set out to study them as if they were a group of Margaret Mead's Pacific Islanders. Some, such as Cusick, were up front about their research, but there were also occasional spies. Lyn Tornabene, described by *Life* as a 36-year-old "childless" housewife, enrolled as a junior in a Colorado high school to get the lowdown on teenagers. The result was her book, *I Passed as a Teenager*, published in 1967.[16] Tornabene found that girls' preoccupations were the same as hers at that age: dating, hair and clothes. She managed to pass muster with students and teachers because she avoided making friends and kept a low profile. "That's the No. 1 truth about teenagers," says Tornabene. "They're running the economy, controlling the airwaves, taking over the highways. But nobody ever looks them in the eye."[17]

In the '60s as in every decade, teens eyed each other. If you wanted to attend the prom, you had to have a date. If you were a girl, you waited to be asked, and if you were a boy, you paid for the evening. That custom resembled earlier decades superficially, but uneasiness with the dating game had begun to percolate under the surface. On the one hand, *Playboy* magazine promoted a vision of pipe-smoking, perpetually pajama-clad men, who paused for a shot of single-malt scotch when they weren't listening to jazz and bedding buxom blondes. Sex, we were told, was for fun, but in publisher Hugh Hefner's world, sex was still very much a man's prerogative and women were rated by bra size. On the other hand, as early as 1962, *Harper's* identified a trend it called "crypto-feminism." Betty Friedan called it *The Feminine Mystique*. Her book, published in 1963 got the feminist ball rolling, calling into question the cult of housework, motherhood and female passivity that was the hallmark of the 1950s.[18] Helen Gurley Brown's *Sex and the Single Girl* (1962) urged unmarried women to go right ahead and have a sex life while remaining independent.[19] High school students viewed the whole enterprise with confusion and began to regard the opposite sex with suspicion. Sex was great, one imagined, if you happened to be, say a Vegas lounge singer or had some fantasy job at a New York fashion magazine, but everyone knew that a double standard existed in real life. Single girls who went all the way were still in danger of unwanted pregnancy at worst and a bad reputation at best. "We used to get together to talk about virginity," said one cheerleader in 1965. She and her friends discussed their dates so they all would know which boys pressured girls for sex. Years after graduation, she acknowledged being sexually active in high school, but at the time, "nobody admitted to losing their virginity."[20]

"Sex is the biggest topic in high school and you can't tell me it isn't," one teen told a *Newsweek* reporter in 1966. Although sexual messages permeated advertising, adults were in denial about teenage sexual activity. Sex education, when it occurred at all, was the presentation of a short film about the mechanics of sex and pregnancy that avoided all other aspects of the topic. Teenagers were left to sort out the relationship part for themselves. Girls knew boys wanted sex and maybe wanted it, too, but didn't want to go steady or get married. They certainly didn't want to get pregnant. So what, exactly, was the point of dating? If sex was supposed to be free and easy excepting when it wasn't, how were teens supposed to behave? If girls didn't want to be judged by their physical appearance, wasn't it equally unfair to judge a boy by how much money he spent on a date? Girls in the early 1960s went along with the old program, but those who graduated late in the decade couldn't shake the feeling that a date meant being rented for the evening. In the 1950s, an "ideal" date, according to a *Senior Scholastic* article, was predicated on expense. Dinner, dancing, flowers, snacks; the heroic boy who ventured into the world of dating had to open his wallet. The prom was the main event for living large, but even an ordinary date comprising dinner and a movie was costly. A boy with a steady girl was expected to take her to "every stated teenage function," and was as financially obligated as "a father of eight with a mortgage."[21] By the mid–'60s, the old dating arrangement seemed absurd. All of those issues and more complicated the high school dating scene, but nothing affected boy-girl relationships more than the Pill.

The birth control pill was developed in the 1950s and certified for use in 1960. First prescribed only for married women, it soon filtered into college life and ultimately down to high school. By 1965, the Pill was the most commonly used form of contraception. It was easy to get. You could go to your family doctor if you trusted him not to rat you out to your mother. If not, most big cities had a chapter of Planned Parenthood or other clinics where a girl could get a prescription in confidence.

The pill enabled teenagers to have sex at far higher rates than their predecessors in the 1950s, but it still behooved a young lady to keep her mouth (if not her legs) tightly closed about it afterward. Whether prom night was especially active sexually in the '60s is an open question because secrecy was still the order of the day. It may well have been, though. If you hadn't lost your virginity by prom time, that was as good a night as any.

Prom night was still a formal affair in the 1960s. In more affluent areas, proms relocated from high school gyms to commercial venues such as banquet halls and hotel ballrooms, lending a more adult, sophisticated cast to the evening. Getting there, in the words of the old advertising slogan, was half the fun. Boys borrowed the family car, or drove their own if they had one. The car of choice for young men was the Ford Mustang. Introduced at the New York World's Fair in April 1964 (two months after the Beatles' appearance on *The Ed Sullivan Show*), the car was designed by Lee Iacocca and his team with the growing Baby Boomer demographic in mind. The "pony car," with its running horse logo on the grille, was an immediate hit. Ford ran commercials on all three TV networks prior to the car's debut. Twenty-two thousand car enthusiasts swarmed showrooms and bought a Mustang on its first day on the market. Ford sold almost 1.3 million of them in two years.

If a prom date included dinner, a '60s restaurant often had beef Wellington, fondue or steak Diane on the menu. Foreign food gained currency, but in Americanized versions: Swedish meatballs, Chinese short ribs with ketchup

Val Air Ballroom, a popular prom venue in West Des Moines, Iowa (Mary Anne Erickson).

or lightly spiced Mexican food. Beef stroganoff was a favorite dish of the Kennedy White House and was served at dinner parties, political functions and restaurants country-wide.[22] Prom-goers on a budget had a wide range of options. McDonald's, Burger King, Arby's, Kentucky Fried Chicken, Howard Johnson's, Long John Silver's Fish and Chips, Red Lobster and Domino's Pizza all took off in the '60s.[23]

Boys wore white dinner jackets or simple tuxes (no cummerbund). Girls wore floor-length gowns with plain pumps. Skirts were poofy in the early '60s and slimmed down by mid-decade. Many formal gowns were cut in the empire style. (Those in the know pronounced it "om-peer.") Bras were contoured to more natural-looking shapes as the pointy armored look of the 1950s mercifully disappeared. Dresses contained new synthetic fibers such as Lycra. Hair was teased and sprayed in the early '60s into bouffant hair helmets and gave way to somewhat looser styles by mid-decade. In 1965, a new synthetic fiber, Dynel, was pinned to female heads in the form of falls and wigs, used to supplement thin hair, prop up a mound on top, or conceal dirty hair altogether. The "flip" was a favorite mid–'60s look, often worn with a bow at the part.[24]

Mary Anne (Neibauer) Erickson in empire waist gown and elaborate evening coiffure, Des Moines, Iowa, 1966 (Mary Anne Erickson).

At the beginning of the decade, Paris still held sway over the fashion world, and a prom dress was a school girl's interpretation of haute couture. Dior was supplanted by Audrey Hepburn's fashion muse, Givenchy, and Jackie Kennedy's favorite designer, Oleg Cassini. Let us now praise Jackie Kennedy. Before the '60s, women dressed like matronly Mamie Eisenhower. Jackie was a cool breeze who blew away old-fashioned prints and fussy collars. She wore three-quarter sleeves or no sleeves at all. Under Jackie's influence, skirts flattened to a pleasing A-line, used in everything from formals to knee-length school wear. Suit jackets often had one big button near the neck, not the waist. The pill box hat topped the whole pulled-together look.

After Jackie left center stage, fashion was somewhat adrift. Then along came Mary Quant, the English "bird" who invented the mini skirt and revolutionized the fashion industry. Before Quant, knees were thought to be ugly. Mary Quant showcased those lowly joints and several inches of thigh as well. Teens couldn't wear minis to school, but they paged through fashion magazines dreaming of the day they could dress as they pleased. Paired with go-go boots, first introduced by French designer Courrèges, minis became a symbol of the swinging '60s. Quant emphasized bold colors, freedom of movement and fun in everyday wear, and accelerated the inclusion of junior departments in clothing stores. Her simple, clean lines were evident everywhere, even at the prom. Many girls wore knee or cocktail length dresses to the prom because of Quant's influence. The look was completed with white eye shadow, black eyeliner, false eyelashes for formal occasions and pale lipstick. Teen girls

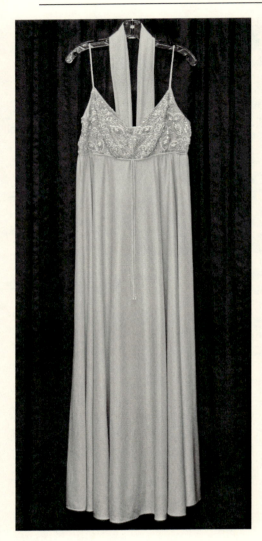

A 1960s powder blue empire gown with beaded bodice and sash.

longed to look like Twiggy (Leslie Hornby), the stick-thin model who wore a mini skirt like nobody else. Twiggy, the patron saint of flat-chested girls, popularized the gamine look. Few of us could match her slenderness, which was a travail for the adipose inclined but a blessing for the "underdeveloped."

School dress codes were the norm during the '60s. Most required boys to wear tucked-in shirts with belted slacks and forbade pants for girls. Principals noticed a connection between clothing and behavior and enforced dress codes with all the disapproval they could muster. The biggest challenges to their authority came from boys with Beatles haircuts. It's hard to overstate how exercised adults were by the introduction of this hairstyle. Not since the zoot suit was a fashion statement regarded with such fear and loathing. The GI and Silent Generations equated masculinity with short hair. Bangs were for girls. Beatles cuts occasioned much hand-wringing by adults who thought the entire male teenage population had gone "queer."

Quite the contrary. Boys liked girls. (And in the '60s, homosexual boys pretended to like girls, too.) Girls liked the Beatles. Boys got the message and knew that in the absence of an actual rock star a classmate with a Beatles cut would suffice. The surfing craze, reflected in the music of the Beach Boys, was another trend that popularized long, tousled hair. As one California student said, "I couldn't see how something like my hair could be considered disruptive. But when they told me to cut it, I felt it wasn't a reasonable thing for them to ask."[25] Many a prom escort attended the dance with his hair hanging over the collar of his dress shirt.

The Beatles were emblematic of the '60s, as everyone knows (or ought to). Rather than add to the mountain of printed pages devoted to the Fab Four, I'll just say that teens danced to their music at parties, school dances, and of course, the prom. (Theorizing about Beatlemania has become a publishing genre all its own.)[26] The '60s was a wonderful, evolutionary decade for music. For the sake of this discussion, I'll divide the music into two categories: danceable and non-danceable. Teenagers danced to rock 'n' roll with a strong back beat (including "British Invasion" bands such as the Rolling Stones), soul music (e.g., Sam and Dave), girl groups (Ronettes, Shirelles, et al.), Aretha and Motown. They listened to folk, acid rock (Jefferson Airplane, Jimi Hendrix), Dylan, the Byrds, Buffalo Springfield and other musicians with a message. There was a tremendous amount and variety of music in the '60s, far too much to describe here. But one song, first aired in 1960, deserves a mention. It was called "The Twist." It wasn't a particularly good song, but it forever changed the way people approach social dancing.

The song was originally recorded by Hank Ballard in 1959. In the summer of 1960, Dick Clark observed an African American couple "doing a dance that consisted of revolving their hips in quick, half-circle jerks, so their pelvic regions were heaving in time to the music." Clark hit the ceiling, screaming at his producer to "keep the cameras off that couple!"[27] His commercial instincts quickly overcame his moral outrage, and he realized that those dancers might be on to something marketable. He found local Philly singer Chubby Checker (Ernest Evans), snatched him from the obscurity of a job plucking chickens and hired him to cover "The Twist" for Clark's Cameo Records label. Clark played the song on his show until the song hit number one on the charts. Viewers of the show got a two-fer: the song and a dance lesson. Rock critic Lillian Roxon says, "You put one foot out and pretend you're stubbing out a cigarette butt on the floor with the big toe. At the same time, you move your hands and body as though you're drying every inch of your back with an invisible towel. That's the twist."[28] The Twist was a continuation of African American dance. As one writer notes, "This movement was used in dances from decade to decade so really one dance was just an extension of another."[29]

Cultural historian Richard A. Long says, "The Twist was the first break from couple or tea dancing. In the Twist, everyone could go for broke on his own, which is very African."[30] "That song changed the whole world," says Checker. "People started dancing apart."[31] Teenagers took up the Twist enthusiastically and adults followed suit. It was liberating to move without having to lead or follow a partner. For the first time on America's dance floors, many white people discovered their hips. The Twist allowed dancers to turn their focus inward, feel the music and just let go. The style arrived at the same time as the civil rights movement and removed one more brick from the wall that separated blacks and whites. It broke down notions about the "right" way to move and gave physical expression to the rebellious youth culture. "Before the sixties there was no consciousness of certain things as being dance," says choreographer Trisha Brown. "I think the Twist helped a lot.... Rock dancing was a bridge between your daily life ... and your classroom life." The usual outcries about overly sexual, black-influenced dancing ensued. One visiting English journalist wrote in 1962, "I'm not easily shocked but the Twist shocked me ... half Negroid, half Manhattan, and when you see it on its native heath, wholly frightening.... The essence of the Twist, the curious perverted heart of it, is that you dance alone."[32] The Twist gave teenagers a reason to question the necessity of a date for the prom. Girls usually danced better than boys, anyway. Sometimes it was more fun to dance alone or with other girls.

Proms weren't terribly popular in the '60s, but dancing was. By 1965, there were 5,000 dance venues in the United States called discotheques, where the most danceable singles of the day were played at top volume. Many popular dances originated in Baltimore, owing to a local Dick Clark–type named Buddy Dean. His TV show launched the waddle-waddle, the Madison (reintroduced in the '60s as the Bus Stop) and a teen version of a Puerto Rican dance called "La Bomba." Social dance was democratized in the '60s: Black, white, brown, young or old — anyone could follow the instruction to "Shake it up, baby. Twist and shout."[33]

By 1970, the national mood was bleak. The decade started badly. On May 4, panicky National Guardsmen opened fire on student anti-war demonstrators at Kent State University in Ohio, killing two girls on their way to class and two others, including an ROTC cadet. Campuses all across the nation exploded in rage. More than 400 shut down until the protests blew over. In 1973, President Nixon halted combat in Vietnam, diffusing antiwar fervor and refocusing attention on himself. By the time he resigned in 1974 under the mounting pressure of the Watergate scandal, the exuberance of the early '60s was a distant memory.[34] The shocks to the collective system during the eleven years between the Kennedy assassination in '63 and Nixon's resignation in '74 reverberated at every level. As if our domestic troubles weren't enough, the world economy underwent drastic changes in the early '70s, owing to the rising influence of the Organization of the Petroleum Exporting Countries (OPEC) and the importance of "petro-dollars." When the United States supported Israel in the 1973 Arab-Israeli war, oil producing nations such as Saudi Arabia retaliated by imposing an oil embargo. The price of gasoline skyrocketed; lines at gas stations stretched for blocks. In addition, cold war tension between the United States and the Soviet Union intensified. Interest rates went through the roof, and inflation was out of control. For the

Homemade prom gowns from the 1970s in forest green velvet and chiffon (left) and royal blue velvet (right).

first time since the end of World War II, the economy contracted. As market researcher Daniel Yankelovich says, "In a matter of a few years we have moved from an uptight culture set in a dynamic economy to a dynamic culture set in an uptight economy."[35] These were not issues that teenagers thought about necessarily, but they had a direct impact on the lives of all U.S. residents. In the '70s, the brash, youth-oriented culture of the '60s was as faded as a well-worn madras shirt.[36]

High school students in the '70s were among the last wave of Baby Boomers, or "Shadow Boomers," as historian Steve Gillon calls them. He further clarifies the difference between older and younger Baby Boomers:

> What I call Boomers are those born between 1945 and 1957, when the birth rate leveled off— this leading edge of the generation was the group that changed the country. "Shadow Boomers" are those born between 1958 and 1964, maintaining the momentum of the Boomers but not changing its impact. Certainly the life experiences of a child born in 1946 were very different from one born in 1964. The early generation of Baby Boomers grew up with rock and roll, the Mickey Mouse Club, prosperity, crew cuts, the idealism of John F. Kennedy, and the social struggles of the 1960s. A child born in 1964 confronted a world of oil embargos, stagflation, Watergate, sideburns, and disco balls. Older Baby Boomers spent much of their lives trying to reconcile their youthful idealism with social reality. Younger Boomers, raised in an age of cynicism, had less idealism to compromise.[37]

High school students in the 1970s weren't apathetic; they cared about the world no less than any other generation. They were cautious, however, and wanted to use their time and resources wisely and enjoy high school while it lasted. One thing that still rankled students was the omnipresent school clique. In the '70s, while the boy/girl dynamic had loosened up — a girl might have felt comfortable asking a boy to the dance — it was prudent to confine invitations to one's social circle.

Speaking of social circles, nothing upset the apple cart as much as school busing, which was specifically designed to bring disparate groups together. School desegregation began in the 1960s and was bolstered by several court rulings in the 1970s. The humble yellow school bus was at the center of the controversy. "Forced busing," mandated to accomplish integration, created tremendous anxiety and resentment. Black kids spent the most time each day on buses, traveling long distances to schools with white populations; many white kids' parents, especially in the South, wanted nothing to do with these black interlopers. In some schools that met the technical requirements for desegregation, classes and extra-curricular activities (proms in particular) were separated by race. Proms were often cancelled to prevent white and black students from socializing. Desegregation was the law of the land, but de facto segregation was still the overarching reality.[38] An even bigger problem in the '70s was the high school dropout rate: 13.2 percent for whites and 27.9 percent for blacks.[39] Between 1974 and 1978, a whopping 45 percent of all New York City public school students dropped out before graduation.[40]

For those who stuck it out, high school went on as usual. Prom planners had a wonderful range of music from which to choose. The Federal Communications Commission (FCC) ruled in 1966 that AM radio stations in major markets had to have FM stations, too. By the early '70s, FM stations were all over the dial providing listeners with eclectic play lists: Southern rock (e.g. the Allman Brothers), progressive rock (Pink Floyd), glam (David Bowie), and metal (Led Zeppelin) to name a few.[41] That said, prom music tended toward the usual Top 40 hits. The sentimental ballads of the Carpenters made for good slow dancing. Singer/songwriters such as Joni Mitchell, Carly Simon and James Taylor were popular. The California sound included Jackson Browne, the Eagles and Linda Ronstadt. Berry Gordy's Motown label provided dance music for the

A sampling of 1974 prom memorabilia from Oconto Falls High (Wisconsin).

R&B and pop markets. If the Jackson 5 and James Brown didn't get you up on your feet nothing would. The suburbs were a world away from the inner cities, but the proverbial mountain came to Mohammed in the form of funk, a purely black, urban-influenced sound, exemplified by the funkiest musician of them all, George Clinton. Funk was so infectious that white groups such as Wild Cherry and Average White Band got in on the act.[42] The music was disseminated on radio, of course, and on the black *American Bandstand*, better known as *Soul Train*. The show was produced by Don Cornelius in 1971 out of WCIU, a small UHF station in Chicago. *Soul Train* copied the *Bandstand* format. It was an instant hit in the African American market, scoring good ratings in cities such as Atlanta, Detroit, New York and Philadelphia. The following year, the show moved to California and was syndicated in thirty-three markets. *Soul Train* was unabashedly black, lively and loads of fun. It introduced three of the most popular dances of the '70s: the lock, the breakdown and the Scooby Doo. Millions of teens watched *Soul Train* to learn how to dance.[43] Funk led to disco, the iconic music and dance of the '70s.

Adults' traditional objection to teen music and dance was its blackness. Disco gave them a double-whammy — it was black and gay. Disco started in underground black gay clubs in New York City in the late 1960s. It went mainstream in 1974, primarily through the efforts of Gamble and Huff, the Philadelphia record-producing team responsible for such hits as "When Will I See You Again" and "Love Train." The music went from dance clubs to AM radio to proms, and created a new type of pop star: the DJ, who kept parties jumping with well-chosen play lists. In 1975, a song called "The Hustle" gave a name to a dance that was already popular. Invented by New York City Puerto Ricans, the hustle was the first Latin dance invented in North America and the first to go mainstream. By 1977, the disco fad was fading. It was revived by the movie *Saturday Night Fever*, which added a few years to the disco craze and made TV actor John Travolta (*Welcome Back, Kotter*) a movie star. (His rhythmic strut down a Bay Ridge, Brooklyn street to the Bee Gees' "Stayin' Alive" is one of the greatest opening credit sequences in film.) Many a prom king wore a white suit with wide lapels and a black shirt unbuttoned to the chest in imitation of Travolta's character. For many, however, disco was too loud and too gay. By 1979, discophobes banged the "disco sucks" drum every chance they got. Disco's association with drugs as well as sexual and criminal activity at clubs was more than some people could stand. Casablanca record promoter Kenn Friedman says, "There's a big cultural difference between rock and disco, and it's gayness. Some people don't like to talk about it, but it's true."[44] Historian Bruce Schulman adds, "It obviously threatened suburban white boys who found it too feminine, too gay, too black."[45] Hatred of disco was so intense that on July 12, 1979, the Chicago White Sox baseball team sponsored a "Disco Demolition Nite." The price of admission was a disco record destined for destruction.

Early 1970s powder blue tux jacket with pin stripes and black piping (author's collection).

Not everybody hated disco because it was black and gay. Some people hated it because of its monotonous electronic beat and simplistic, repetitive lyrics. It was also overmarketed. Dozens of products were disco-themed. There were disco weddings, fashion shows, bar mitzvahs and endless disco proms. Giorgio Moroder, producer for singer Donna Summer says, "Disco killed itself. Too many products, too many people, too many records jumping on this kind of music. A lot of bad records came out. It became — what's the word? A cuss-word."[46] Disco accomplished one very important thing, however. It restored "touch" dancing. You needed a partner to boogie down on the disco floor and a rudimentary knowledge of dance steps. Because many proms in the '70s and early '80s were disco-themed, one had to have a date to participate on the dance floor.

Once again, it was Travolta to the rescue! His dance performances in the 1980 movie *Urban Cowboy* started the line-dancing fad. Anyone could join in the tush push or the boot scoot. Line dances were the savior of dateless prom-goers everywhere. If you did have a date, the two step was a simple, romantic dance for couples.[47]

Men at discos were resplendent in high-heeled shoes, polyester leisure suits and jewelry. For formal occasions such as proms, tuxes were outlandishly colored — anything from pastel blue to traffic cone orange. Dress shirts often sported ruffles. On the other hand, prom dresses in the '70s made the wearer look like an extra from the TV show *Little House on the Prairie*. For a decade so sexually open, '70s prom dresses were remarkably chaste. Makeup was minimal, and hair was often worn parted in the middle, shoulder-length and perfectly straight or with the sides blown back in imitation of actress Farrah Fawcett. Covered from collarbone to ankle in "granny gowns" often made of Laura Ashley prints, female prom-goers were the picture of modesty.

Men wore jeans and cowboy hats to country line dances, which brings us to the subject of denim. According to textile expert Beverly Gordon, the "jean-ing" of America occurred in the 1960s. Invented for physical laborers by Levi Strauss in 1850, jeans were a distinctly déclassé garment until rebellious beat-niks, hipsters and bohemians donned them in the 1950s. The breakout year for Levis sales was 1962, when sales doubled and then quintupled a few years after that. Jeans were "the common anti-fashion denominator" standing for rebellion, classlessness, democracy and youth. By the end of the 1960s, jeans were ubiquitous and customized. As Gordon says, "Soon counterculture youth were glorifying their jeans," personalizing them with beads, sequins, bells, feathers, indeed anything that could be applied to denim. It wasn't until the 1970s, however, that girls could wear them to school. The loosening of school dress codes elevated jeans to an unofficial school uniform, making the contrast between everyday wear and prom night all the more vivid. By the late '70s, designer jeans had hit the racks. "Couture denim filtered down to the ready-to-wear market," says Gordon. There were even denim prom gowns.[48]

By the end of the 1970s, the age of the teen Boomer was over. Muscle cars lost out to leaded gas and high prices at the pump. Disco gasped its last breaths. The sexual revolution was no longer revolutionary. Life went on, and proms did too as a new cast of characters waited in the wings.

4. Like, Totally

If you attended high school in the 1980s and missed your prom, no problem — you can still go. If you went and had a lousy time, you can have a do-over. Find your old teasing comb because '80s proms are back, complete with big hair, shiny dresses and bouncy, danceable music. Party companies all over the country are sponsoring '80s-themed "prom" gatherings for corporate events, reunions and fundraisers. The high school students of the 1980s are the parents of today's high school students, and they're ripe for a wave of nostalgia. They'll tell you that back in their day, proms were really something. Even if the prom king's severed head ended up in a pool of blood on the gym floor, '80s proms were awesome! Okay, that last part is a scene from the 1980 movie *Prom Night*, but that's the point. In the ironic '80s, kids didn't take things too seriously.

The 1980s were a second golden age of proms. After the rebellious 1960s and '70s, when proms were in decline, the 1980s saw a resurgence of conservatism in all areas, including teen culture. High school students accepted the idea of proms and attended enthusiastically. According to social critics at the time, however, students had little reason to feel like dancing. Public school test scores were dismal. Drop-out rates and drug use soared. Variously dubbed Gen X, Baby Busters, New Lost, Caretaker, Boomerang, and Nowhere Generation, teens born after the Baby Boom faced many problems, including bad PR.[1] Adults piled criticism on teenagers, regarding the entire cohort as a bunch of know-nothing slackers.

Grownups were in a grumpy mood. The optimism of the post–World War II years and early Boomer era was long gone in the wake of the Vietnam War, the Watergate scandal and the 1979 capture of American hostages in Iran.

During the 1980s, the United States spent an enormous amount of money in the arms race with the Soviet Union while slashing funding for social programs. Inner cities suffered the crack cocaine epidemic. The Iran-contra scandal and savings and loan debacle ensued. By 1980 the economy had contracted, the national mood was bleak and teens had to fend for themselves. "Latchkey" kids were home alone while parents worked long hours. The Gen X group is the "onliest," according to writers Howe and Strauss, "their families the smallest, their houses the emptiest after school, and their parents the most divorced."[2] A high divorce rate made single-parent families increasingly common, with women bearing the economic brunt of the "feminization of poverty" that occurred during the decade. Teen girls got pregnant and dropped out of school in greater numbers.[3]

Generation X came of age with high gas, interest and unemployment rates. If you were poor in the 1970s, your lot in life probably didn't improve in the 1980s. Young urban professionals, or "yuppies" did just fine, however, as the nation's wealth flowed to the most affluent fifth of American households.

The economy picked up in 1982, followed by years of frenzied acquisition for those who could afford to buy. The 1980s are sometimes called the "decade of greed," or the "gimme decade."[4] As the character Gordon Gekko (played by Michael Douglas) said to an approving crowd in the film *Wall Street*, "Greed is good!"[5] If the Boomer experience depended on location, the Gen X experience depended on one's location on the socioeconomic scale. It was an age when the rich got richer and the poor sank even lower. Scores of family farms went under. Homelessness was rampant. Not since the Great Depression were so many families pushed into poverty.[6] For teens who didn't make it to their senior year, prom was a non-issue. But for those who completed high school, prom was a must.

A 1980s charcoal party dress.

The 1980s were a hard-partying decade in which the rich flaunted their wealth. Rich women have always dressed expensively, but in the '80s, no amount of consumption was too conspicuous. High fashion was for anyone who afford it or fake it. Women in the upper echelons of society displayed their wealth with wardrobes that would have beggared the French court at Versailles. Tom Wolfe lampooned the sartorial extravagance of the rich in *Bonfire of the Vanities*, writing about one character's dress with "short puffed sleeves the size of Chinese lampshades" and a skirt "like an aerial balloon." As he noted, "This season no puffs, flounces, pleats, ruffles, bibs, bows, battings, scallops, laces, darts, or shirrs on the bias were too extreme."[7] The trend Wolfe described originated with designers such as Christian Lacroix, whose bright colors and theatrical designs were instantly popular. English designer Vivienne Westwood, who drew inspiration from pirates, royalty and rock stars, was also influential. High fashion usually makes its way from European and New York City runways to the closets of the wealthy and famous, eventually manifesting on American department store racks in versions suitable for mass consumption. A high school girl would not have spent $30,000 on a Lacroix gown, but a hot pink J.C. Penney prom dress was a good enough imitation. The look was completed with dyed-to-match shoes and big hair. Owing to the invention of hair mousse, '80s hair styles achieved impressive altitudes. Bangs were curled under and mousse-stiffened away from the face.[8] Ponytails were fastened on the side of head; hair was teased, crimped, bleached and permed — the natural look was not for the '80s girl. Even boys treated their hair as a sculptural medium. The two oddest male styles of the '80s were the mullet (short-cropped in front, long down the back of the neck) and the mohawk (shaved except for a cockscomb of hair from nape to forehead).

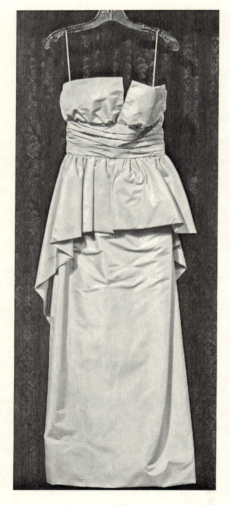

Strapless emerald green gown with peplum from 1980s.

Two examples of late 1980s clothing and hair. Veronica See, Moreau Catholic, Hayward, California, class of 1988 (Veronica See Bryce).

The decade was marked by a crass emphasis on money and power. TV shows like *Dallas* and *Dynasty* featured characters who wore designer gowns to breakfast. Costuming on the shows was a middle-class interpretation of high fashion, and prom dresses were an interpretation of the clothing on the shows. A girl may not have had a remote chance of living like a character on *Dynasty*, but she could act out the fantasy on prom night. Even Barbie dolls in the 1980s had furs and jewelry safes.[9]

The designer who most influenced men's formal wear was Giorgio Armani. Before Armani, the tailored suit was the uniform for the board room. Armani transformed it into a symbol of self-assured sexuality. Gender roles were somewhat blurred in the 1980s. Armani made it safe for men to be admired for their clothing. Featured in the film *American Gigolo* (1980), Armani suits signified casual, expensive elegance. The title character (played by Richard Gere) had a closet full of Armani suits. In one scene, he lays out his wardrobe on the bed with more tenderness than he treats his clients. According to one critic, the character's "shopping trips provided the film's true sexual excitement."[10] No wonder men became interested in fashion. Boys on the cusp of adulthood dandied themselves for prom with an eye for fabric, cut and fit.

First Lady Nancy Reagan would probably like to be known for her "Just Say No" (to drugs) campaign, but her wardrobe was memorable, too. Mrs. Reagan was a clotheshorse who often borrowed gowns from designers James Galanos, Adolfo, Bill Blass and Oscar de la Renta. Her personal style did not directly affect the look of prom dresses, but she helped usher in an era of dressing up.[11] Prom dresses were often made of satin and adorned, as in Wolfe's novel, with puffed sleeves, frills, lace, smocking, netting and sequins. The romantic look was in.[12] Westwood's clothes exemplified the style, but Diana, Princess of Wales, was the Englishwoman who influenced fashion more than any other. Lady Diana Spencer charmed the world on her wedding day in 1980 in a gown that made her look like a walking mound of whipped cream. As a *Vogue* reporter wrote, "Five foot ten and long-legged like her mother, it is rather as if a charming young giraffe had wandered onto the royal enclosure." Princess Diana and *Dynasty* had an enormous impact on the way ordinary people dressed, especially for formal occasions. Many a prom dress sported ruffles and ornamentation owing to those influences.[13]

Physical fitness was important in the '80s, and that also had an effect on design. Formal dresses were often form-fitting and revealing; the woman (or girl) underneath the dress was supposed to supply the proper shape for draping the garment. As one catalog noted, "For the first time in the history of western fashion, woman's body, which fashion had always sought to modify by dis- simulating or deforming it, played an interactive role in the form of clothing.

This fashion which shocked at the beginning of the eighties is now completely accepted."[14]

As Gen X grew into the 1990s, supermodels such as Claudia Schiffer, Cindy Crawford and Christy Turlington set the standard for beauty. These leggy, muscular girls embodied the "aggressive eighties."[15] They earned spectacular salaries and were worth it because they got consumers into stores. Slender Kate Moss was another popular model, but her extreme thinness was thought to send a "dangerous message" to weight obsessed teens. The grunge and waif looks worn by Moss were mercifully short-lived, and by 1993 "hardcore glamour" was back in style.[16]

Madonna had the biggest influence on teenage girls' fashion sense. In collaboration with designer Jean-Paul Gaultier, Madonna literally turned fashion inside out with bras used as outerwear. In a deliberate attempt at gender-bending, the self-styled "Material Girl" put bras and fishnet hose on her male dancers. Diane Rafferty, writing for the *Village Voice*, noted, "Now we feel there is nothing wrong with dressing ourselves as a prostitute, provided that this costume is chosen with deliberate humor and irony.... That is what clothing is all about."[17] For prom-goers, that meant dressing as one pleased. The '80s were an age of conformity, but in a different way than the 1950s. Individuality was important theoretically, but in actual practice, teen girls tended to dress like each other.

The rules for dating in the '80s were as wide open and sexually ambiguous as fashion. As writer Beth Bailey noted, "Can you say today what it means if a middle-class girl in Middle America picks up the phone and calls a boy?"[18] The term *dating* actually fell out of use among teenagers. The trend away from dating began in the 1970s with the last wave of the Boomer generation. As one teen remarked in 1972, "We don't date. A date means you don't like the person enough to want to get to know him better, you're just using him to get out of the house.... 'May I take you to the prom' is just a big joke."[19] Gen X teens simply got together and did, as they might have said, "whatever." A favorite hangout was the mall, a self-contained space complete with food, hallways, cliques and spectators. For teens, the mall was an extension of high school devoid of pesky classes and adult supervision. You didn't need a date to have fun at the mall. You just had to show up. In the 1950s, high school was the social locus for teenagers, but socializing was secondary to academics. By the 1980s, the emphasis was reversed as far as students were concerned. Senior year was the last best chance to achieve a high level of social status among one's peers, and prom was the ultimate opportunity to flaunt it.[20] The prom was something of a throwback in terms of dating; many schools required students to attend with a date of the opposite sex, a de facto exclusion of singletons and homosexuals. (A pair of lesbian students successfully sued their

Salinas, California, school in 1986 for the right to attend prom together, but their lone suit was far from a movement.[21])

In the more conservative regions of the country, especially the South, the dating and rating system hung on. The boy did the asking, and the girl's part of the bargain was looking pretty. In other places, dating customs were in flux. It was theoretically acceptable, if not common practice, for a girl to invite a boy to the prom, share expenses and provide transportation. This newly egalitarian approach was far from clear-cut, however. According to a 1986 issue of *Seventeen*, girls inviting boys was "one of the more pressing and controversial teen issues these days." As one girl said, "Today, unless a boy calls you up and says, 'I'm taking you out on a DATE,' you don't know if you're supposed to pay or not."[22]

Perhaps one reason proms were popular in the 1980s was the opportunity they provided for conspicuous consumption. Pre-prom dinners, professional photo sessions and limousines came into vogue. All-night after-prom parties gained acceptance, although the many instances of drunk driving and accidents were a big concern for parents.[23]

Prom night was sexually active for many Gen X teens. According to a 1988 study, half of all teenage girls had lost their virginity, in contrast to the 35 percent who were sexually active in 1973. Gen X did not accept the sexual double standard of previous generations. Sex was seen as an integral feature of high school. As one girl remarked, "Kids are never going to stop having sex. Our parents fought for that right in the '60s and now it's our reality."[24] A loss of virginity was no longer tied to a loss of respectability. If anything should have put the brakes on teen sexual activity, it was the AIDS epidemic, which was raging in the 1980s and early '90s. "You'd think AIDS would be a deterrent, but it's not," said a health teacher in a New York City school. In the midst of a worldwide pandemic, sex education still consisted of clinical discussions of anatomical parts, with little or no emphasis on consequences. If the emotional and physical health issues were raised, the message was decidedly mixed. As sex educator Sol Gordon noted, "There's something wrong with a country that says 'Sex is dirty. Save it for someone you love.'"[25] One 16-year-old girl remarked, "I get confused when I hear everyone saying, yeah, go ahead and do it. So long as you're careful it's okay. Then others are saying no, don't do it at all. So it's very confusing to figure out what you're supposed to do about it."[26]

In some cases, condom use increased owing to dissemination of AIDS prevention information, but many teens had unprotected sex with multiple partners. Teens worried about sexually transmitted disease and unwanted pregnancies, but they didn't necessarily do anything about it. A 1988 study reported that a third of teen boys always used condoms. Teen girls were less likely to get pregnant in that year than in 1982, but since more girls were having sex, the pregnancy rate was unchanged. Nonchalance about sex extended to virgins, too. According to one girl, at her school "there is no pressure [to have sex] at all. Some people do and some people don't."[27] Another girl remarked, "There are more virgins in high school than people think. It's just that virginity isn't the gossipy subject that sex is. Nobody's going to come to school on Monday morning and say, 'Hey, guess what I didn't do Saturday night!'"[28]

In any case, Gen Xers were determined to make their own rules. As the last wave of them entered high school in the early 1990s, the cohort could best be described as having "attitude." Mistrustful of institutions and authority, Gen Xers went to prom or not, had sex or not and dressed up or down as they saw fit. As one young lady remarked, "There's our 'attitude,' a coolness, a detachment. There's the way we dress —'mock' turtlenecks, way-too-big suits. And the way we speak: ironic, flip, uncommitted, a question mark at the end of every other sentence."[29] Gen Xers took a dim and often condescending view of Boomers' political activism. As one young woman said in 1982, "I think your generation was very sweet to be outraged by Vietnam and Watergate. Incredibly innocent, dumb, stupid, and naïve. But very, very sweet."[30]

One could chalk up Gen X apathy to mass cynicism, but an alternative explanation might be that popular culture during this time provided many distractions from the issues of the day. Teen culture was disseminated as never before with the introduction and rapid expansion of cable TV. In 1981, MTV was launched, bringing a 24-hour schedule of music videos and commercials aimed directly at teenagers. By 1983, the channel had 14 million daily viewers. The marriage of arresting visual images and music made the careers of Madonna and Michael Jackson, whose music was eminently danceable and often played at proms.[31] As RCA marketing director Laura Foti noted, "There isn't a national radio station. That's where MTV comes in ... showing everyone this new band." English singer/songwriter Joe Jackson said of the new emphasis on videos, "Things which used to count, such as being a good composer, player, or singer are getting lost in the desperate rush to visualize everything."[32] The Boomer generation said, "I heard that song on the radio." Gen Xers said, "I saw that song on MTV."[33]

MTV also ran a heavy rotation of videos by Van Halen, Bon Jovi, Def Leppard and Mötley Crüe, whose "pop metal" brand of rock and roll was popular. In the 1980s, Top 40 play lists (the usual music for proms) comprised a wide range of styles. At the softer, "easy listening" end of the spectrum were such artists as George Michael, Debbie Gibson and New Kids on the Block. Artists such as Janet Jackson, Prince and Whitney Houston supplied many popular dance tunes. (Bruce Springsteen, also known as The Boss, did very well in the '80s, but not so much with teens. Springsteen embodied the hopeful romanticism of Boomers.) Country rock artists such as Dwight Yoakam and Travis Tritt appealed to listeners in the so-called heartland. Michael Jackson was the most popular '80s singer by far. Seven songs from his *Thriller* album alone reached the top ten singles.[34]

Disco was falling out of favor in the early 1980s, but it hung on with some crowds who enjoyed dancing with a partner. It was still played at proms — actress Jamie Lee Curtis performed a lengthy disco number in *Prom Night*. By the 1980s, however, the electronic disco beat was employed in other pop styles, and people went back to dancing separately. The Electric Slide was one 1980s dance among many with colorful names such as the Alf and the Chinese Typewriter.[35]

Camaros and Mustangs were still favorite cars for boys. Economical imports such as Datsuns were also popular. A boy might have taken his girl for a meal of blackened fish — Cajun food was in.[36]

Teens who had an interest in "classic (Boomer) rock" could hear it on audio cassettes played on the Sony Walkman, a portable tape player that racked up $6.7 billion in sales in 1981. The old vinyl LPs were nearly pushed into extinction with the Walkman, and the Walkman was rendered obsolete a mere decade later by high-quality digital recordings on compact discs (CDs).[37] Video cassette recorders (VCRs) provided an alternative to cable and broadcast television. VCRs boosted sales of camcorders, enabling prom-goers to record their festivities with ease, especially after 1990 when cameras were lighter and had longer playback times.[38]

In the early 1990s, the economy contracted again, and the national mood followed suit. Dour youth found their voice in the Seattle grunge movement, exemplified by the band Nirvana, whose music comprised elements of hardcore punk, metal and oddly, Beatles-like melodies. Stone Temple Pilots and Pearl Jam were also part of this scene. The dominant sound of the '90s was rap and hip-hop, which started in New York City in the '70s and was initially influenced by disco and African oral tradition. Passing through various phases such as "old school" and "gangsta," hip-hop eventually found a wide audience with suburban white teens.[39] Followers of grunge and hip-hop had signature wardrobes. The former wore loose-fitting jeans and plaid flannel shirts often tied around the waist. The garb for hip-hop listeners was oversized pants, shirts, shorts and sneakers. As white suburban kids adopted hip-hop style, black teens brought back the preppie look purveyed by the Gap, Tommy Hilfiger and Eddie Bauer. Girls showed off bra straps and midriffs. Boys displayed the band of their boxer shorts. Khakis were as popular as jeans with girls and boys.[40] Crop tops and baseball hats worn backward, Aerosmith and Mariah Carey — '90s fashion was as varied as the music. Comfort and individual expression were the values of the early '90s, perhaps inspired by corporate culture, which had instituted "casual Fridays." Soon, every school day was casual Friday. In the 1990s, the contrast between everyday dress and prom wear was very stark.[41]

Prom wear in the '90s was simpler than in the 1980s. Dresses had a long, slim profile. Many girls opted for black. Halter tops became fashionable. If a dress required a supporting garment, the Wonder Bra, a modern version of the push-up bra, was deployed for extra heft. Lingerie retailer Victoria's Secret was a first stop at the mall for many prom-going girls. No prom outfit was complete without a startling coat of metallic green, purple or magenta nail polish. Tuxes were worn with wide ties or none at all. Movie stars popularized the plain-neck shirt with a small stand-up collar, a look often copied at prom time. Hair styles became far more conservative; teasing, crimping and "big" hair styles for girls went out with the '80s, although trends tended to lag in the middle and Southern regions of the country. Boys wore their hair long, short or even shaved. Braids and cornrows were in for black students.[42]

Clothes were less adorned in the '90s, but bodies were decorated. Gen

A 1990s black slip dress.

X took to tattooing and skin piercing as a marker of individuality. Although tattoo parlors in most states require customers to be eighteen or older, younger teens got tattoos when they could get away with it. Some teen girls may have been inspired to ink their skin by Cher, who displayed multiple tattoos in the 1970s and '80s. Boys may have taken their cue from the illustrated arms of Guns N' Roses frontman Axl Rose. Formerly associated with sailors and bikers, in the 1990s tattoos were seen on the shoulders and ankles of middle-

Cream Versace tux from the 1990s.

class white students. Piercing was common and easier to hide. Piercing is also regulated by state law, but underage teens got around the prohibition by doing it themselves. Pierced ear lobes were in vogue for boys and girls, as well as pierced noses, ear cartilage and belly buttons. "Don't be surprised when Barbie starts sporting a belly button ring," said Paul King, a writer for *Piercing Fans International Quarterly*.[43]

Nothing affected teen life in the 1990s more than the ubiquity of computers and the Internet. Personal computers had become de rigueur by then, and teens took to them as if they had been born with a mouse in their hand. Providing privacy from parental intrusion, the Internet allowed teens to converse silently and constantly. Before cell phone texting supplanted email, teens used the Internet to make friends in chat rooms, play games, gossip, flirt and ask each other to the prom. This mode of communication was for those families who could afford computers and Internet servers; low-income teens often could not. Teens who were online had a very different experience from those who were unable to join the virtual party.[44]

The recession of the early 1990s was a sobering experience for teens and adults. The free-spending student of the 1980s gave way to the careful shopper of the '90s. Price-conscious and looking for bargains, late Gen X teens spent their part-time job money carefully, often making several trips to several malls before deciding on a purchase. Teens spent $57 billion of their own money in 1992, up 16 percent from the previous year.[45] Merchants were often annoyed by teens who tried on clothes but seldom bought. Nevertheless, "mall rats" were an important part of the economy and became even more important as the decade and the new millennial generation took center stage.

5. Everyone Gets a Trophy

"Ladies and gentlemen, your 2011 prom queen, Kurt Hummel."
— *Glee*, season 2, prom episode

Baby Boomers, who dictated popular culture for decades, have been elbowed aside by their kids, the Millennial generation, born between 1980 and 2000. Numbering 76 million, native-born Millennials (so called because they're coming of age in the twenty-first century) are the biggest generation in American history. If you count young immigrants, their numbers approach 100 million.[1] That's a lot of prom gowns and tux rentals, and marketers know it. Teens spent $208 billion in 2010, not counting the influence they exerted on family purchases.[2] "Mom and Dad are coming to them saying, 'What kind of computer should I buy?'" says advertising executive Mark Swanson. According to market researchers Yankelovich Partners, the teen market is more important than ever.[3]

The first wave of Millennials hit the dance floor in 1998. Some of the older Millennials are already parents to the next generation. Sometimes called Gen(eration) Y, Gen Next, the Boomlet or Echo Boom Generation, Millennials are experiencing adolescence in a whole new way. They are the digital generation, who have never known a world without computers, cell phones and instant, constant connectedness. Boomer kids stared passively at the tube, but Millennials make active use of the Internet, spending far more time online than they do watching television.[4] They're team players who would just as soon attend prom in groups than with a date. Unlike fractious Boomer teens, Millennials "rebel by being upbeat," according to demographers Howe and Strauss. Modern teens stay close to their parents and look to them for guidance. And why shouldn't they be fond of the 'rents? They're the most wanted and watched-over kids ever. "They were raised to feel special and worthy," Strauss says. "The culture treated them that way."[5]

As Howe and Strauss note, "During the Gen X child era, planned parenting almost always meant contraceptives or abortions; during the Millennial childhood, it often means a visit to the fertility clinic."[6] Gen Xers were the "great unsupervised generation. But Generation Y was the great oversupervised generation."[7] Rebellious Boomer teens matured into hovering "helicopter" parents, lavishing time and attention on their kids to ensure a high level of self-esteem. If a kid is a washout on the playing field, he or she will receive a trophy just for showing up. There's no such thing as a loser in Millennial land. Just to be clear: The kids are not conferring trophies for attendance on themselves. It's Boomer parents who can't stand to see little Dylan go home empty-handed. We all grew up hearing the motto, "It's not whether you win or lose, it's how you play the game," but the Millennial generation lives it.[8] Competition is fine as long as no one's feelings are hurt. *Cooperation* is the Millennial by-word. A modern-day prom is an opportunity to plan and execute a group project — a really expensive and overhyped one, but what's prom without financial pressure and teenage angst?

Although many aspects of the Millennial prom are the same as they've always been, this modern cohort is redefining the prom and adolescence itself. Millennials enter adolescence early. Business consultant Bruce Tulgan calls age 12 the new 19. Marketers call the phenomenon KGOY, or "kids getting older younger." Girls are tired of children's clothing at age eight and want to dress like their teenage sisters. Teenage girls want to dress like adults, which in their minds means sexy.[9] The upshot is that at prom time Millennial girls frequently dress as if they were in a Vegas revue.

Millennials remain adolescent longer, often living with Mom and Dad for years after high school graduation. They want their own families, but they're in no rush to start. A mere one-fifth of the cohort is married, compared to twice that number for their parents at that stage of life. They might as well take their time. Boomer parents aren't eager to become empty nesters.[10] The generation that was raised according to Dr. Spock has taken indulgent parenting, or "positive tolerance," as psychologists call it, to a whole new level. Material goods are a part of the scene, but the real currency of parenting these days is praise and acceptance. As Tulgan sees it:

> In the short time between Generation X and that of Generation Y, making children feel good about themselves and building up their self-esteem became the dominant theme in parenting, teaching and counseling. Throughout their childhood, Gen Yers were told over and over, "Whatever you think, say or do, that's okay. Your feelings are true. Don't worry about how the other kids play. That's their style. You have your style."[11]

Placing a high value on self-expression, Millennial teens have absorbed the Boomer axiom "Do your own thing." Paradoxically, they see themselves as members of a group — they're well aware of the power of their numbers — but they want everything in their personal lives to be customized. Everything from sweatpants to prom gowns has to represent the wearer. Ideally, the prom as a whole should be an expression of a senior class's collective personality.

Millennials value peers as much as family. For many, friends are an extension of family. Yet pressure is not a word they associate with peers. According to one study, when asked how pressured they felt to smoke, take drugs or have sex, well over 70 percent responded "not at all."[12] Millennials, objects of constant attention, have been studied and quantified from birth, so here are a few more statistics: nine out of ten describe themselves as happy, confident and positive, a statement that is supported by studies indicating that teen suicide rates have fallen. They trust government, follow rules and respect their parents. Millennials are spiritual but not religious; they customize their inner life, often cobbling disparate elements of various schools of thought into a personalized belief system.

They're the most racially diverse cohort in history. As of 2009, among ages 13 to 29 in the United States, 18.5 percent are Hispanic, 14.2 percent are black, 4.3 percent are Asian, 3.2 percent are mixed race, and a record low of 59.8 percent are white. Racial diversity has transformed the suburbs, which for the Boomer cohort was almost exclusively white. Fully 41 percent of suburban public school kids are now nonwhite. Increased diversity is evident in Millennial relationships: 83 percent see no problem with interracial dating, a remarkable change from the 36 percent approval from the Silent Generation. Jennifer Twitty, who was 16 in 1997, said at the time, "The dating scene has changed dramatically at my school in the last year. At first only blacks dated blacks and whites dated whites, and interracial kids had to choose. You now see blacks dating whites and males and females coming out and saying they are bisexual or gay, and interracial kids saying they won't choose a race."[13]

Millennials see themselves as the generation that will do the most for the environment. They may be all about peace, love and understanding while "greening" the planet, but these kids aren't hippies.[14] Most of them want to be rich and famous. To that end, they are their own best press agents. Three-quarters of them have a profile on a social networking site, and one-fifth have posted videos of themselves. Eager to be well known, their lives are on digital display. Social networking sites such as Facebook and Twitter enable teens to craft public personae and project them into cyberspace with frequent updates and modifications. No modern prom is complete without posting photographs on Facebook, even as the event unfolds. Most online activity occurs via cell phone, a device employed by the vast majority of American teens. Cell phones are bridging the digital divide between the affluent and the less privileged. Low-income teens, particularly African Americans, are more likely to access the Internet on a cell phone.

Teens talk on the phone to parents and other adults, but the preferred mode of communication with each other is texting. They are so adept at thumb typing that they can literally do it blindfolded. In fact, texting is so pervasive (sending and receiving hundreds of messages a day is not unusual) that the practice is reshaping relationships. Teens text about everything — school work, social activities, their personal lives. Nothing is so intimate that it can't be reduced to a few dozen characters and IM'd (instant messaged) or tweeted in the blink of an eye.[15] New York Governor Andrew Cuomo says of his 16-year-old twin daughters, "It is a generational issue, the texting. They are on that telephone device all the time. It's all the time."[16] "I didn't get your email" or "My mother didn't give me the message" are no longer plausible excuses. The majority of teens see the cell phone as the key to their social lives. The band-width they consume is in direct proportion to their popularity, and the kind of phone they use is a more definitive marker of status than clothes or jewelry. "[Texting] is in essence a reflection of how teens want to communicate to match their lifestyles. It is all about multi-tasking, speed, privacy and control," says Joseph Porus of Technology Group, Harris Interactive.[17] What bedroom princess phones did for Boomer teens, cell phones do for Millennials, and so much more.

Teens also use cell phones for information and entertainment. Dress shopping, coordinating prom night activities, photographs, music play lists, gossip in real time and even rides home from disastrous proms are all facilitated by cell phones. Cars revolutionized dating by providing physical privacy. Cell phones provide the privacy contained between one's ears. Cell phones are a big part of teen sexuality. Many young people engage in "sexting," sending sexual messages and photographs. Owing to their portability, cell phones are always available. Teens are so attached to their phones that most of them sleep with it in or by the bed.[18]

The U.S. Postal Service is impossibly slow for most teens, who hardly ever mail letters. Teens are in a hurry and expect to be in constant touch with each other. Messages are often brief, in shorthand or coded. Acronyms (e.g., LOL, OMG) abound. Texting may lack romance, but it comes in handy for planning group events, such as coordinating logistics for a group date to the prom.[19] Which brings us to prom dates in the twenty-first century.

Facebook lists "It's Complicated" as a designation for one's relationship status, an apt description of modern dating, if the word *dating* even applies. Many Millennial teens forgo dates altogether and attend prom in groups. It's only natural that Gen Next should want to stick with the herd at such a fraught time as prom. Millennials spend most of their childhoods in closely supervised groups and are used to doing everything en masse: team learning, team sports, church activities, volunteer organizations and school dances. The senior prom is the penultimate opportunity (before graduation) to share

Chris Kaiser and Liz Anderson, Los Alamitos High, 2010. Prom clothes have become less formal and more "dressy casual."

a group identification with classmates. At Mary Institute Country Day School in Missouri, headmistress Louise Morgan estimates that 75 percent of students attend prom in groups rather than as couples. "They have definitely slid away from that feeling of 'I don't have a date, I can't go,'" says Morgan. "The going-in-groups trend has allowed it to be more fun, more relaxed."[20] Group dating eliminates the hassle of coordinating outfits, buying corsages and handling rejection. "I'm really happy that I'm going with a group of friends," Kayla Mosberg said of her 2010 prom. "It's awkward to get asked by a person you're not interested in, and it's even more awkward asking the person you would like to go with!"[21] For some girls, going in a group is both a political statement and a rejection of a custom that's barely within their frame of reference. "The way it used to be, when I've seen it in movies, is that the guy takes care of the girl and is expected to pay for the girl's ticket," says Adrienne Alair, a student at Northwest School of the Arts in Charlotte, NC. "I'm into the whole feminism thing," she adds. "We buy our own ticket, go with a group of friends, and if you don't get a date, you can have fun anyway and not worry about it being a popularity contest."[22]

Some prom groups are so large that a bus is the only conveyance that can accommodate them. In some cases, schools require students to travel to the venue by bus. Such rules are designed to prevent drunk driving but are often resisted by students, who would prefer to drive themselves or rent a limo. Ally Stevens of Palo Alto, California, says, "I don't really want to ride on a school bus dressed in a nice outfit," an understandable sentiment, but not one that held sway with her school district.[23]

For some students, a dateless prom is an oxymoron. "If I were going to prom, I would much rather go with a date, because it makes you sound awkward and pathetic when you just go with friends," says Diana Damian of Mechanicsville, Virginia. "I mean, that's pretty much the purpose of prom, to go with someone."[24] Some opt for the failsafe approach of going with a good friend. "I'm going with a friend as a date," says Sydney Sprenkle, also of Mechanicsville, "because friends are more important to me and I think you can have more fun with a friend." Sprenkle adds that a friend was less likely to ridicule her "strange, funky dancing" than a conventional date.[25]

Not that teenagers know what a date is anymore. Between hanging out, going out, kind of going out, seeing each other, and hooking up, the permutations of modern high school romance practically require a thesaurus. "The social ladder at my age is incredibly complex," says Mike Babb of Seattle. "There are about 10 million unwritten rules and codes of conduct for dealings with the opposite sex."[26] Some of the rules are familiar: Nerds go with nerds, the pretty ones pair up, jocks and cheerleaders are a perennial duo. But the term *dating* is as old-fashioned as a polyester tux, and no particular term has replaced it. One boy laments the vagueness of "all this talking about 'are we seeing each other, or just talking, or going out, or not really going out?'"[27]

"It would be so weird if a guy came up to me and said, 'I'd like to take you out on a date,'" says Irene, a high school senior. "I'd probably laugh at him. It would be sweet, but it would be so weird! There's a few people I know who date, but most of us are like, 'There's no one good to date, we don't need to date, so why date?'"[28] The scene is so free-wheeling that a subgenre of publishing has sprung up to explain it. One such book is *The Date Book: A Teen Girl's Complete Guide to Going Out with Someone New*. As its author, Erika Stalder, writes in the chapter "What Exactly Comprises a Date?":

> So, what exactly is a date? Is your after-school ice-cream run with the hottie from fourth period a date? And what about that football game where you met up with your crush after making loose plans via text? You guys had a great time, but you're not sure what the next step is. How can you possibly know how to proceed? Sometimes a girl needs to play detective to figure out whether an outing is date-ish or just friend-ly.[29]

Stalder cites the "wonderfully clear-cut days of Johnny asking Betty to the drive-in, but those dates are now as rare as drive-in movies themselves." She notes that today's custom of young men and women hanging out as friends is probably a good thing overall, but the scene is also fraught with ambiguity.[30] Here's how one teenage girl categorizes teen relationships:

> Hooking up: "This is the most casual term. Two people very casually see each other once or twice and mainly just make out."
> Going out: "When you move into this stage you stop seeing other people and start to see each other exclusively. This stage can still be casual with group dates, or it can be serious and very exclusive."
> Just talking (via cell phone) and/or dating: "Comes after hooking up but before seeing each other. Dating is more serious than hooking up, but less serious than seeing each other."[31]

Liz Anderson of Los Alamitos, California, says that roughly half of her 2010 high school class dated and were in relationships; the other half hung out or hooked up.[32] *Hooking up* is a catch-all phrase, which seems to be a deliberately vague way of describing a brief sexual encounter that does not lead to more involvement. It can be anything from making out in a broom closet to having sex in a bedroom, depending on whom you ask. "Ambiguity is the key to hooking up," say Andrea Lavinthal and Jessica Rozler, authors of *A Single Girl's Guide to Living It Up*. "We've heard it defined as everything from making out to full-on sex, but for most people it's somewhere between a peck on the lips and some grinding with your hips."[33] Then there's the category of "friends with benefits," or a pal with whom you have regular hook-ups but share no commitment. According to MTV market researcher Nick Shore, "Millennials are running the bases backwards," or having sex "before the first date."[34]

If relationships are confusing for teens, they're even more confusing for the people who study them. Depending on the source, teenagers are either restraining themselves sexually or going hog wild. Teen pregnancy, sexual activity and abstinence rates fluctuate every year and with every study.

Depending on the researcher, girls are either becoming more assertive about drawing sexual boundaries or they're as passive and subject to pressure as ever. One area of controversy is oral sex. According to the *Journal of Adolescent Health,* oral sex is a commonly used "work around" to avoid pregnancy and sexually transmitted disease.[35] On the other hand, Laura Lindberg of the Guttmacher Institute says that for teens sex is sex, oral or otherwise. "If they're having oral sex," she says, "it's likely they're having sexual intercourse."[36] It's also likely that if a Millennial teen is sexually active, the loss of virginity occurred well before prom night, and if one's virginity is intact, prom is not the designated time to lose it. As Anderson notes, "Losing their V card on prom night is extremely cliché."[37] The prevalence of prom night deflowering may be something of a myth. According to the *Journal of Marriage and Family,* teens who lose their virginity do so mostly in June, when school and prom season are over.[38]

Some reports say that for teens, oral sex has become as casual as a handshake and doesn't even count as sex. As one girl said when asked to define "hooking up," "Well, first you give a guy head and then you decide if you like him and he decides if he likes you." She goes on to say that sometimes relationships devolve into hook-ups, which she views as a good thing. "It's nice because you don't have to worry about hurt feelings. I have a friend who broke up with her boyfriend and now they're just friends with benefits. At our age, we're supposed to be having fun."[39] For Millennials, the definitions of both *fun* and *sex* are open to interpretation. Like everything else in their lives, their sex lives are a matter of personal design.

Many adults and students are alarmed about casual teen sex. "Sexually active girls and boys continue to be treated very differently," says psychiatrist Lynn Ponton. Referencing an ongoing double standard, she says, "The girls I see both in my clinical psychiatric practice and the pediatric clinics are very concerned about what others will think if their sexual activity or even interest is discovered."[40] Teenager Katy Montague agrees that a double standard still exists. "On the night before the prom, a guy gets a pat on the back from his parents and a credit card: 'Here, go get a hotel room.' A daughter is told to 'Come home, be safe, don't do anything stupid.'"[41]

Whether virginity is making a comeback, as one Centers for Disease Control and Prevention study suggests,[42] or whether teens are going at it like bunnies in springtime, according to a Guttmacher Institute report,[43] one thing is clear: teen pregnancy no longer carries a stigma. The MTV series *Teen Mom* and *16 and Pregnant* are big hits for the network and have turned its young mothers into reality TV stars.[44] Pregnant high school girls used to be shipped off to what were quaintly called "homes for unwed mothers" and kept safely out of sight of embarrassed families. Now they stay in school and go to the prom. As one teacher reports, "One of my students told me that her pregnant friends, one of them seven months along, wore basic black [to the prom] 'because it is slimming.'"[45]

The ins and outs of high school romance come into sharp relief at prom time, when some schools still require students to attend with a date of the opposite sex. If you're a dateless girl in Bismarck, North Dakota, call Mike and Yancy, two enterprising hospital orderlies who moonlight as rent-a-dates. For $100 each, they escort two single girls to the prom. The fee covers the tuxedo rental, corsage and dinner. They'll even wait in the living room and make small talk with parents. "We're not looking to make a profit," says Mike. "We'll treat the girls nice, just like we asked them out ourselves."[46]

Girls who want to attend with a classmate are no longer expected to wait for an invitation. These days it's acceptable for a girl to ask a boy. That's a step toward equality, one supposes; girls are now exposed to all the preinvitation anxiety and crushed egos that were formerly the lot of teenage boys. In her prom guide for girls, *This Is Not Your Parents' Prom*, writer L.A. Galloway devotes an entire chapter to "popping the question," an early 20th century turn of phrase that conjures up a marriage proposal on bended knee. The mixture of feminist moxie (taking the invitation into one's own manicured hands) and fin-de-siècle male gallantry is presented without a trace of irony. Offering a detailed system for analyzing one's chances with a prospective date, as well as suggesting a variety of strategies for popping said question, Galloway implies that the process of securing a prom date is a do-or-die campaign.[47]

Many teen boys eschew the cell phone at prom time and adopt the old-fashioned approach with a Millennial twist. It's the grand gesture — an elaborate invitation that often includes music, flowers, stunts and a video camera, all the better for posting on YouTube. Jason Pitts, a senior at Santa Monica High School, serenaded his lady love in class (with the approval of his teacher), backed up by a chorus of a cappella singers and a video camera operator. Pitts posted the video clip on the social news site Reddit, where it was picked up by TV host Ryan Seacrest and posted on his Twitter feed. Producers from the ABC program *Good Morning America* saw Seacrest's post and featured Pitts on their show. Justin Chung jumped off the diving board into the school pool during team practice fully clothed with a rose in his teeth. Chung's invitation drew a half-million views on YouTube. His soggy stunt was for the benefit of Jessica Kim, who had received a prior invitation in the form of a large banner carried onto the field during a football game. Ft. Lauderdale student Taylor Hecocks sang to his girl and posted the clip on YouTube, drawing 1.2 million hits. When James Tate was banned from prom for posting an unauthorized invitation sign on the school wall, 200,000 people came to his defense on Twitter and Facebook. The school reversed its decision owing to the "international

Kaelan White and Greyson Miller enjoying some preprom photo session clowning, Spokane, Washington, 2011 (Thomas White).

notoriety" the case had garnered.[48] For Millennials, anything worth doing is worth doing publicly. The "promposal" as it's come to be known, is a by-product of reality TV, according to Jesse Drew, director of Technocultural Studies at the University of California, Davis. "We're in a fame-based culture," he says. "Everyday [people] doing mundane things become superstars. For many people, this is one of the most dramatic acts they will have performed in their life up until that point." Marriage proposals are frequently posted online, and promposals are following suit.[49] In this respect, teens are part of a larger phenomenon: As of 2011, 71 percent of Internet users log on to video sharing sites such as YouTube and Vimeo, up 5 percent from the previous year.[50]

Whether an invitation is made public or not, "the worse thing you can be is unoriginal," says Baltimore student Paul Ballas.[51] During the 2011 pre-prom season, boys were inventive indeed, dropping roses from an auditorium catwalk onto the lap of a prospective invitee, crafting a gigantic papier-mâché duck in an homage to a rubber ducky collector, delivering a frosted cake (during class) with the query written in icing, sealing a note inside a piñata, posting a 30-foot sign on a school fence, stuffing fortune cookies with the all-important question and much more. "You really want to make it hard for her to say 'no,'" says Jacob Taylor. "The whole prom event is just over the top and this just adds to it."[52] History teacher David Harley says, "Back in my day [the 1960s], it was hard enough to screw up the courage just to ask a girl. The pressure has increased extremely."[53]

Relationships are customized like everything else in Millennial Land. Teens are doing whatever works for them at prom time. Michael Brownlee took his mother to the Central Dauphin East High prom in Pennsylvania. She missed her own senior dance, and Michael wanted her to have the prom experience. Brownlee, for the record, is a popular kid—he was a member of his school's prom court.[54] Lem Jefferson of Decatur, Alabama, took his single mother, Annie, "not because it's sweet," he says, but because "I want to show her what it's like." Jefferson missed her own prom because she had to drop out of school to go to work. "Everybody treated me like everybody else," she said. No one ridiculed Lem, a 5-foot-11, 275-pound defensive football tackle.[55]

Securing a date is important, especially for girls, but finding the right dress is practically a matter of life or death. If you're stuck going to prom with your cousin, a really great dress can make up for that. If your date is the cutest boy in school, the dress had better measure up. Prom night is the end result, but preparations for the big night comprise most of the project. Shopping has long been a favorite pastime for teen girls, and Millennial teens approach the search for a prom dress like seasoned pros. Teens visit over 20 stores per year, and when it comes to retail, they know what they're doing. Here's advice from one young lady on how to get proper service: "If you have something like a Louis Vuitton wallet or coin purse, take it out and check your money. Do not go to the counter and ask for help. The sales employees are there to serve YOU, not you serve them."[56] The hard-to-please bride, or "Bridezilla," now has a little sister, "Promzilla," who goes to great lengths and expense to get what she wants:

Leslie, eighteen, of Charlotte, North Carolina, found her dream dress online and then convinced her mom to drive two and a half hours to buy it. The straight dress with bold pastel prints and a crisscross of sequins down the back cost more than $500. "When my mom saw the dress I wanted, she was like, 'What are you thinking? You're only going to wear it once,'" Leslie said. "But she knew it was the one I wanted. When something like the prom comes up, you just want to go all out."[57]

Prom spending increases every year. According to retail experts Kit Yarrow and Jayne O'Donnell, prom spending nearly doubled between 2003 and 2007. It's now a $6 billion industry.[58] Shopping for a prom dress is one way teen girls try on identities. The dress is a costume that helps them "get into character." A revealing dress or a modest one lets a girl see a preview of the adult she may become, and many spare no expense on this experiment. Prom dress designer DeBora Rachelle sells dresses in the $250 to $600 range, but has custom designed gowns for as much as $11,000. It's always been important to look great on prom night, but Millennial girls are especially image-conscious.[59]

Girls with means wear designer gowns. Colby Jordan of Chicago's Latin School wore a John Galliano dress with matching Dior pumps in her junior year. For her senior prom, she's "doing a chartreuse Roland Mouret gown with purple snakeskin YSL Tribute sandals." Jordan will change into another gown for the after-party, just as many actresses do for the Academy Awards. She's eyeing a white Herve Leger dress with silver heels by Azzedine Alaïa. Girls like Jordan may not be the norm, but they're not unusual. Trends in prom dresses are influenced by TV shows such as *Gossip Girl*, which references designer clothes, and by celebrity culture in general. "I'm a total stalker of celebrities online," says Sara Weiss, a senior at Pope High in Marietta, Georgia, "and will see what they wear to red carpet events."[60] If a designer gown is financially out of reach, a girl can still have the luxury shopping experience, all part of modern prom preparation. At Neiman Marcus, the salespeople "are so accommodating," Weiss says. "They bring you water, there's space in the dressing room, it's just a nice experience," she said as she shelled out $530 for a dress she plans to wear again at college sorority formals.[61]

Fashionistas on a budget go to the used designer dress website Rent the Runway, where a dress can be had for a night for a tenth of its retail price. Quincy Childs, who attends the Hotchkiss School in Lakeville, Connecticut, rented a $2500 pink strapless Matthew Williamson gown for $250. The dress was seen on four different celebrities and showcased in the *US* magazine feature "Who Wore It Best?" "I'm more excited about getting ready for prom than prom itself," she said — a summation of the Millennial attitude toward prom.[62]

Fortunately for the rag trade, prom wear is recession-proof, even in areas of the country hardest hit by economic downturns. Mothers of prom attendees are determined to see that their daughters are satisfied with their dresses, even if they have to sacrifice necessities. Marlin Cortez did without new shoes for herself so that she could help pay for her daughter's $400 prom dress. "Yes, we are in a recession," says Tampa store owner Georgette Diaz. "But [moms] are going to forgo other things to make sure their daughter goes to prom."[63] Not every mother is so accommodating. The price of dresses has sparked some intergenerational conflict. "I've had girls go out of here in tears when their mothers won't buy them something that they liked," says Pam Funderburk, manager of Dar-Lynn's Bridal and Formal Wear in Matthews, North Carolina. "I'm sure it had something to do with the economy."[64] Generally, however, prom clothing is moving off the racks at a good clip. Even boys spend at prom time during recessions. Clifford Pearl, owner of Cardita Formalwear in Port St. Lucie, Florida, says that boys spent $150 to $160 on tux rentals in 2009, up from $120 to $135 the previous year. Pearl estimates that 80 percent of his customers tell him, "I want to go all out."[65]

Truly savvy shoppers look no further than their older sisters' closets. Fashion trends used to take 30 years to come back into style; now they make a comeback in 10 or 20. Dresses from the 1990s are already back in style, but not owing to nostalgia. Bridget Foley of *Women's Wear Daily* says that the '90s aren't back — they never left. "I don't think we can draw a divide. I don't have a clear mental image that distinguishes the '90s from the 2000s," she says.[66]

Owing to our increasingly casual lifestyles and the Millennial insistence on self-expression in all things, anything goes for prom wear: long flowing dresses with floral prints, halter tops, spaghetti straps, no straps, mini-dresses and cocktail length are all on view. Preferences often vary by region. Frilly, pastel, ultra-feminine gowns are popular in the South and suburbs, whereas more sophisticated, fitted dresses in black and dark colors are popular in the cities. To avoid wearing the same dress as another girl, many prom shoppers use the Internet to find something unique. The search phrases "prom dresses" and "prom hairstyles" typically make the list of top 50 search terms. Best-promdresses.com racks up thousands of hits per day, and traffic grows yearly. Internet shopping is especially useful for girls who live in small towns. "I've been looking and looking, and there's nothing here," says Jennifer Morriss who lives in Statesboro, Georgia, a four-hour drive from Atlanta. She found a black matte jersey sheath with a plunging neckline and a train for $189 at prom-dress.com. "I was nervous it wouldn't fit," says Morriss, "but it was perfect. And I know no one else is going to have this dress."[67] Internet shopping is driven by the technical proficiency of Millennial teens and the demand for one-of-a-kind dresses.

Girls also post photographs of their dresses on the Internet to ward off copycats. The Facebook group "West Hill Prom Dresses" read, "No one wants to see someone with their dress on prom night! So this group is basically so you can add a picture of your dress." Acknowledging the value of a dramatic reveal, the site goes on to say, "I know ppl [*sic*] will not want to add pictures BUT, you can give a description of your dress. The colour, length, style etc. The store that you bought it from, so people are aware." And if that doesn't make the case, the site says in 16-point type, "JOIN THIS OR YOUR NIGHT COULD BE RUINED!!!"[68] There are many Facebook pages with names like "Don't Steal My Dress." Even with such preventive measures, girls sometimes buy identical dresses, a breach of teen etiquette that is simply not to be borne. "You're paying how many hundreds of dollars to look nice? You want to look original and pretty — and you don't want to be standing next to someone in a picture wearing the same dress," says Lauren Wagner, a classmate of Collette Dong, who created a Don't Steal My Dress page. In spite of Dong's efforts, another girl bought a dress just like hers and refused to exchange it for another. "My friends are like, 'Oh my God, you have to be so mean to her, she can't do that,'" Dong says. "She asked if she could come on the same bus as us. The girl in charge of the bus was like, 'No, you can't be on our bus. Are you crazy?'"[69]

Girls who are hard up financially can often find a group that donates prom dresses. Millennial teens are inclusive and don't want the lack of a dress to keep a girl from her Cinderella moment. Alexandra DiSanto, a recent graduate of Trinity High School and Girl Scout Troop 2270, created a prom dress drive to earn a Girl Scout Gold Award. DiSanto collected 200 dresses, set up a temporary "store" in a local shopping plaza and enlisted women from the Friendship Senior Center to do alterations. "I wanted something intergenerational," DiSantos says. "And I think my project did that. The older ladies helped the girls try on the gowns and would hem them if needed. The girls who got gowns left with big smiles. It was awesome."[70] Many such give-aways are organized each year.

Prom wear has become more adult over the years, to the dismay of many parents. Nancy Wolf commented, "It's not so much the school clothes; it's what they wear when they go to dances. I call it the pre-prostitute look. They go to a place called Bebe and they buy something that is very short. They look like hookers with prison shoes, those shoes with the big stack heel. They girls think they look swell. The boys look like babies compared to them."[71] Some of girls' male classmates agree. "What girls wear is just out of control," says Ari Goldberg of Boca Raton, Florida. "You see just everything. It is unbelievable. If I had a daughter, I wouldn't let her out of the house."[72] In spite of protests from parents, "revealing dresses are flying off the racks," according to *Teen Vogue*:

Dubbed "slutty chic," the new trend has many young girls purchasing dresses that, well, are leaving them practically bare with up-to-there leg slits, plunging necklines and provocative cut-outs — sometimes all in one dress! Pushing the boundaries at Prom is one thing, and of course, showing a little skin can be sexy, but many feel these dresses are taking it too far."[73]

The magazine goes on to offer an "ultimate prom guide ... guaranteed to get you lots of attention — the good kind!"[74]

"When clothes get skimpier and skimpier, moms get angrier and angrier," says Dannah Gresh, organizer of an evangelical Christian group for tweens.[75] In a 2008 study, market research firm BIGresearch found that 64 percent of respondents age 18 and up agreed with the statement "Fashions for young people have gotten too provocative." Dress manufacturers and retailers may be responding to a consumer demand for more modest clothing. Nordstrom added a "modest" category to its website, and Macy's has added modest apparel to its line.[76]

For every girl who dresses for maximum sex appeal, there's another with an altogether different style. "If there's peer pressure," writes reporter Kathleen Schuckel, "it's to conform not to one look, but one of a dozen looks."[77] Every high school has its goth kids with pale faces and black lipstick, latter-day hippies in tie-dyes, faux Rastafarians in dreadlocks, disco divas, preppies and anything else you can name.

The same goes for hair styles. Long, straight hair for girls is prevalent lately, but anything goes. Girls love to go to salons for a special prom up do, but often leave disappointed by the effect. Celebrity hairstylist Oscar Bond offers a tip for avoiding "prom hair": don't go to the salon with your mother. "Come in with your mother, you'll leave with her hair," he warns. He goes on to say that an elaborately knotted up do with "those lame curly tendrils" don't necessarily look formal. And the golden rule? "No hair spray!"[78] Some girls choose "bought hair" for maximum glamour and a big change in their looks. Popularized by such celebrities as Halle Berry and Tyra Banks, hair extensions or weaves are locks of hair affixed to the head by various methods and are a growing segment of the hair product industry. Two to three million pounds of human hair are imported into the United States every year, and the demand goes across all races. Paris Hilton, Britney Spears and Jessica Simpson frequently sport extensions or weaves. Stylist Angela Stone says, "Wanting to have options with your looks is not about being white. The best part of my job is watching women with low self-esteem and low self-confidence leave on top of the world when we add the hair."[79] Shalinda Williams of Dorsey High in Los Angeles spent $500 for hair extensions to make her look like Beyoncé Knowles. "I love the way Beyoncé looks so different each time, and it's the hair," says Williams. "I couldn't lose 30 pounds or get a nose job before the prom, but I knew I could add some hair to make me look amazing."[80]

Hair can be modified, but tattoos are trickier when it comes to dressing up. Whether to ink is not the issue — one in three Millennials has a tattoo. However, whether a dress should reveal a tattoo can pose a quandary depending on the size and location of the image. The website promdressesdirec tory.com offers guidelines: "What exactly is it? Skull and crossbones or a devilish Betty Boop with red eyes and horns may not go well with a sweetheart bubbly pink cocktail dress. Little charm tattoos strategically placed, like on the inside of your ankle, can add a hint of personal flair. Treat your tat as an accessory if elegant enough. If not, cover it up."[81] Piercing and tattooing started as a form of rebellion, but with so many people doing it, it's now a mark of conformity. "Long hair in the 1960s was kind of rebellious," says sociology professor Barry Markovsky. "But millions of people were doing it and so it was somewhat conforming. And that's what you have with tattoos and piercing — it's becoming more accepted."[82]

Tanning is another skin alteration favored by Millennial girls. Indoor tanning salons are especially busy before prom time when teen girls want a dose of "healthy color" to enhance their appearance. The Indoor Tanning Association (ITA) promotes their service as a vitamin D booster, but adolescent girls absorb enough of the "sunshine vitamin" during the course of a normal day according to medical doctors. Furthermore, dermatologists say there is no such thing as a healthy tan. "A tan is an injury to the skin. It's a reaction by the skin to protect itself," says Dr. Henry Lim, dermatology department chair at Henry Ford Hospital in Detroit.[83] Nevertheless, indoor tanning has become a must for many girls at prom time, despite warnings from the medical profession about the risk of skin cancer. Nearly half of white American teens use ultraviolet tanning beds regularly, and many girls start hitting the salons heavily in January to ensure a deep bronze skin tone by prom night. Brittany Lietz thought her skin was too pale to look good in her white prom dress, so she went to a tanning salon in Annapolis, Maryland. What seemed like a good idea at the time turned into a 20-minute-a-day compulsion. "I became a 'tanorexic,'" says Lietz. "You know how an anorexic never thinks she's thin enough? I never thought I was tan enough."[84] Lietz developed a melanoma at age 20, and now works with dermatologists on public service campaigns to warn teens about indoor tanning. It's an uphill battle. "A lot of these places set up shop close to schools and place ads in school newspapers," says Dr. Scott Fosko, dermatology chair at St. Louis University School of Medicine.[85] Teens, as is their wont, think of themselves as invincible. "A lot of people tell me I do it [tanning] too much, blah, blah, blah," says Alex Lloyd of Campbellsport, Wisconsin. "But I just don't care."[86] If the threat of cancer doesn't keep teens away from UV tanning beds, vanity may eventually do the trick. "People get the same thing from us that they get from the sun," says ITA executive director John Overstreet. "They get wrinkles."[87]

Girls often begin prom preparations months in advance, but boys wrap it up in an afternoon. "Cut and tux, that's pretty much it," said Shameal Taylor as he settled in to a barber chair. Within 30 minutes, he had a haircut and razor-trimmed eyebrows, mustache and beard. All that was left was a quick trip to the tux shop to pick up his suit.[88]

Teens of any era love to dance, and that goes for Millennials as well. In the age of easily acquired, downloadable music, teen tastes run the gamut: pop, hip-hop, alt rock, heavy metal, country, classic rock, '80s tunes; DJs play all kinds of music at proms. School authorities and chaperones have no problem with the music, but the way teens dance often causes great consternation. Variously known as grinding, booty dancing, freaking and dirty dancing, the moves require a willingness to gyrate your naughty bits on someone else's, front to back, back to front or face to face. As one reporter notes, "Honor roll kids do it. Church-going kids do it. In fact, almost anyone can do it. Freak dancing takes little coordination and even fewer skills, which makes it all the more appealing to kids who formerly shied from the floor. And you don't need a boyfriend of girlfriend: Strangers freak strangers. Girls freak girls."[89] Short of dousing students with ice water, school administrators are stymied when it comes to halting what they view as explicit sexual behavior. They deploy chaperones with walkie-talkies, make prom-goers sign no-grinding pledges, serve up lectures on appropriate behavior, expel offenders, blow whistles, shine flashlights, physically separate dancers and ban songs like "Back That Thang Up," all to little avail. Kids often form tight clusters around a grinding couple to shield them from chaperones.

"[Freaking] sets up a climate that people's bodies are sexually available to other people's," says Deborah Roffman, author of *Sex and Sensibility: The Thinking Parent's Guide to Talking Sense About Sex.* "The idea that kids can go up to whoever they want and bump them with their pelvis, after we just spent 10 years teaching them about sexual harassment — that's a very dangerous thing."[90] Teachers at Cleveland High in Portland, Oregon, were so offended by grinding that they refused to chaperone the 2010 winter formal, forcing the principal to cancel the activity. "There's a certain amount of genuine bewilderment on the faces of kids when we talk about it," says Cleveland special projects coordinator Jan Watt. "They can't figure out what's wrong."[91]

Predictably, teens reject the notion that freaking is sex or will lead to sex, citing the 1960s furor over the Twist. "I've never gone out afterward and had sex because of the way I dance," says Mark Hines of Anderson Township, Ohio.[92] "We just think it's fun," says Cleveland student Zoe Koss. "It's a generational thing."[93] Portland parent Susan Hall remembers her parents "hating the Beatles. They thought all their songs were about drugs. But at a dance, we just danced ... far apart."[94]

Not all teens are fans of freaking. "Some girls are gross when they dance," says teenager Keri Francois. "They exploit themselves, and it's not meant to be that way."[95] Other students dance in a more restrained fashion, or if they really don't like freaking they stay home. Washington, DC, principal Art Bridges thinks the fad will pass, just like all other teen dances. Like many other school personnel, he doesn't worry about the way kids dance. "Dancing is so far down on my list," says Ronald Ross, school superintendent in Mount Vernon, New York. "I think if you asked 1,000 urban principals, dancing would not be a problem. There are just so many other things we're dealing with."[96]

One of the things administrators deal with is the prevalence of prom night drinking. According to the National Institute on Alcohol Abuse and Alcoholism, 5,000 underage drinkers die each year, and booze is a factor in nearly half of fatal car crashes involving teens during prom season.[97] "Some kids were literally staggering off buses and limos and into proms," says Roger C. Bogstead, Nassau County commissioner.[98] Educators are cracking down, which is why sales of breathalyzers are up. "We get a lot of orders from principals before proms," says breathalyzer distributor Charles Lee.[99] Despite objections by the American Civil Liberties Union about civil rights violations, many schools won't admit kids to school dances unless they blow a clean breath at the door. But kids are inventive and not always in ways that benefit them. Favorite smuggling devices are flip-flops with zippered heels containing alcohol and flasks disguised as cell phones. Determined drinkers have become so crafty that limousine companies won't transport prom-goers unless their parents sign off on promissory notes to cover damage and liability.[100] Alcohol isn't the only problem substance. Kids swipe medications from their parents' and grandparents' medicine cabinets and find mood-altering products on the Internet. "Kids have gotten to be devious little animals," says substance abuse expert Barbara Keller.[101] Educators and lawmakers are using every tool they have to combat the problem. Limos are inspected, assemblies are held, kids sign no-drinking pledges, chaperones lock attendees in to prevent a quick tipple in the parking lot. One school dramatizes fatal car crashes with fake blood, hysterical faux family members and firemen with the jaws of life, who carve up autos to pull "victims" out of the wreckage. "Young people think they're invincible," says Harris Blackwood, director of the Georgia Governor's Office of Highway Safety. "We're trying to convince them otherwise."[102] Administrators at San Marcos High in San Diego take no chances. They book their prom at marine base Camp Pendleton. "There are military police all around," says prom coordinator Bill Singh. "What else can you say?"[103]

Some schools schedule prom on a weeknight and expect students to be in their first period class on time the next day. That's a fun-killing move in the eyes of many students, who then skip prom altogether. "Honestly, it just seems pointless," says Bridget Mathis, a student at Pearl River High. "When you're thinking about having a good time, you're not thinking about going out on Wednesday night."[104] The Pearl River PTA, in an effort to soften the policy, serves breakfast the morning after prom and hosts field day events until noon — then it's time for class. Parents don't much care for the scheduling, either, but the policy stands.[105] In Westchester County, New York, authorities take no guff from students or parents. If the district attorney finds that any adult has supplied alcohol to a student before, during or after a prom event, they could be sued or held liable for any infraction of the law committed by a minor. "They'll come after you, your insurance, your house — they'll garnish your wages," says assistant DA Bruce Kelly. "That usually gets their attention."[106]

There's no surefire way to safeguard a prom, but parents and teachers of Millennial students are determined to try. Millennials may be more Internet-savvy than their elders, but they are still kids with a lot to learn about good judgment. Parents and teachers don't want to ruin prom night, they just want to make it safe. The kids want to dress up and dance. Some things don't change.

6. Everybody Dance! (Or Not)

"Maybe the issue is not [teen] sex but adults' response to it: the harm we do trying to protect teenagers from themselves."
— Judith Levine, *The American Prospect*

On the face of it, prom is a straightforward matter. You obtain a dress or a tux, buy a ticket, find a date or a group of friends, and go. If you're black in a small Southern town, however, or gay in any conservative place; if you're Muslim or Southern Baptist; home schooled or in special ed classes — that's where prom can get tricky. Generally speaking, the Millennial cohort is fine with interracial dating, homosexuality and self-expression in all its forms. But when it comes to prom, old habits die hard. In some Southern towns, black and white students have separate proms. In many schools, gay couples are not allowed to attend. Muslim students are often forbidden by their parents to attend school dances, and in certain Christian schools, no dances are held at all. Students who don't match the local template of adolescent normalcy find themselves in an awkward spot at prom time. Determined to experience high school their way, Millennials are balking at the older generation's prom rules. So when gay students, for example, are refused attendance to their school's prom, they do the creative thing: they hold their own. When special ed students feel sidelined by their disabilities, compassionate classmates hold a prom just for them. For better or worse, the twenty-first century has seen the rise of niche proms — dances for self-identified groups — and increasingly inclusive proms in which students who would have been excluded in prior years now take part. Niche proms are often initiated by students; others are dictated by local custom. In other words, some barriers are being constructed, and some are coming down.

In 1954, the Supreme Court held in *Brown v. Board of Education of Topeka, Kansas,* that separate schools for black and white students are unconstitutional.[1] School integration did not automatically follow. Some Georgia schools, for instance, didn't integrate until the 1970s. In the twenty-first century, almost

50 years after *Brown*, some parents in certain Southern high schools are still aghast at the thought of black and white students mingling socially. As historian Susan K. Cahn writes,

> High schools and dance floors had two things in common. Each constituted a shared physical space that teenagers — black and white — had claimed as their own.... As sexually charged physical spaces, the high school and the dance floor threatened to undermine another kind of southern place — the place each southerner occupied on the social and economic ladder of southern society. Southerners customarily spoke of "knowing one's place," referring to one's social status and its expected behavior.[2]

The resistance to mixed-race proms is as old as the antebellum South. Nothing horrifies some white Southerners more than the thought of sexual contact between an interracial couple, particularly a black boy and white girl.[3] Proms are culturally loaded to begin with, and in the rural South, a school dance is as charged as an electric fence. If prom is the populist debutante ball, a Southern prom is the night for white girls to be that quintessential deb, Scarlett O'Hara, and a chance for black girls to cast off any perceived hint of Scarlett's servant, Prissy. A prom dress is more than a means of enhancing one's appearance; it's a declaration of self-worth. Dancing isn't just fun. It's an expression of sexual ardor, and in some towns, if you express that ardor with a dance partner with a different skin tone than yours, trouble ensues.

In 1957, three years after the seminal *Brown* decision, Barbara Baker, a white student at Fort Wayne's Central High, and James Bowie, a black classmate, were sent to jail for dating each other.[4] In the twenty-first century, that would be unthinkable. Today, opponents of racial mixing employ more subtle means of separating interracial teen couples, such as segregating proms. Integrated proms are becoming more common in the South, but in some small towns, resistance to mixed-race dancing is as solid as a Georgia pine. Separate black and white proms are so entrenched in some locales that when a school integrates the dance, the event makes the national news.

Turner County High School in Ashburn, Georgia (population 4,400) held its first integrated prom in 2007. Until then, the community sponsored two unofficial separate proms for whites and blacks to avoid violating any laws. The first school-sponsored integrated prom was such a momentous change that ABC's *Good Morning America* covered it. In Ashburn, the railroad tracks, known as "the line," separate black residents from white. Some people regarded the mixed prom with a marked lack of enthusiasm, so much so that a group of white students held a private prom at a local marina. Mixing is a class issue as well as a racial one. "The black kids and the 'normal' white kids, we're all for the prom," says Mandy Alberson, a Turner County High student. "It's the upper-class preppy kids that don't want it together."[5]

The administration at Montgomery County High School in Mount Vernon, Georgia, is up front about the racial divide. The ballot for prom queen circulated in everyone's home room has a slot for "black girl" and one for "white girl." Two proms are held, and skin color determines attendance, an easy call when the town had little diversity beyond African American and white. In recent years, however, immigrants from the Middle East and Asia have moved to town. White Montgomery County student Julie Rich says, "My best friend is Egyptian. What prom is he supposed to go to?"[6] When Julie's sister, Anna, stopped by the black prom to have her picture taken with her boyfriend, Lonnie, she was promptly shown the door. Anna and Lonnie had a friend snap a picture in the parking lot. A Mount Vernon student who goes by the street moniker "Slim Dirty" says, "We ain't never gonna have an integrated prom. Never. They [school officials] said part of it was a music issue, but you go into any white person's car in this school — they all got a rap CD!"[7] As an *Ebony* article notes, "the provocative point here is that Black youth culture has become, in a strange way, the youth mainstream, and that White youths, and White adults, are integrating into a multi-ethnic cast."[8] But not everywhere.

Montgomery County High School in Charleston, Mississippi, had always held "the white folks' prom" and "the black folks' prom" until actor Morgan Freeman offered to sponsor one prom for everybody in spring 2008. His offer was accepted, which is the basis for the HBO documentary film *Prom Night in Mississippi*. Without Freeman's sponsorship, the event would most likely not have occurred. "Most of the students do want to have a prom together," says Terra Fountain, a white girl who graduated a year before Freeman showed up. "But it's the parents who say no. They're like, 'if you're going with black people, I'm not going to pay for it.'"[9] Judging by the film, the dance was a big success. Black and white students danced together to R&B songs and country line dances. Sadly, the following year the school failed to sponsor an integrated prom, and the community reverted to privately sponsored black and white events. Cracking jokes about the white prom, one black girl said, "Half of those girls, when they get home, they're gonna text a black boy."[10]

For those who want racially segregated dances, the real issue is sexual tension. As Freeman remarked, "We've avoided talking about the sexual aspects of this separation, but that separation is primarily black boys and white girls."[11] Writer Eugene Kane puts a finer point on the problem:

> If you think the idea of an "all-white" prom has to do with different styles of music, dress, slang or anything other than white parents deathly afraid their fair-skinned daughter might dance too close to a black male, it's time to take your head out of the sand. Interracial sex is one of the great hidden secrets behind America's struggle with race. Although there are more relationships across the color line than ever before,

for some narrow-minded folks, it is still the greatest taboo. In an age where so many pay lip service to America's way of life being vastly superior to everyone else's, it's awfully hard to hear about an all-white prom held on purpose somewhere in this great nation and not wonder what the hell is going on.[12]

Proponents of segregated proms cite "tradition" as the rationale for continuing the practice. "It's just the way it's always been, a tradition," one student at Taylor County High in Butler, Georgia, told a reporter in 2003. "But there's going to be black people catering there, so it's not racist," another student offered.[13] As one blogger quipped, "Thank heavens we had the foresight to break away from the 'tradition' of slavery, the 'tradition' of prohibiting women from voting, the 'tradition' of living without electricity."[14] Progress is slow, but fewer towns hold segregated proms each year. "Everybody says that's just how it's been," says James Hall, the African American senior class president at Turner County High. "It's just the way of this very small town. But it's time for a change."[15]

In 1979, Fred Stephens, the principal of Lincoln High School in Sioux Falls, South Dakota, gave a gay student permission to bring a male date to the prom. "My belief is that people need their rights protected," Stephens said. "Homosexuals have rights. You have to accept that." So the student had his way, but only because the school district couldn't find a way to stop him. "We've discussed this with our attorney and we have no legal basis to keep the kid away," said John Harris, superintendent of schools, implying that unlike Stephens, the school board would have kept the kid away if the law allowed.[16] In that same year, Rhode Island student Paul Guilbert was barred from bringing a male date to the Cumberland High prom. He wanted to sue and tried to enlist the American Civil Liberties Union (ACLU) in his cause, but his efforts failed. Guilbert's parents did not support him, and without their backing the ACLU felt the case would not succeed. Guilbert not only missed the prom, he endured tremendous abuse from his classmates.[17] In an editorial about Guilbert, the *New York Times* said,

> There is a sensible alternative: have dances but not dates. At schools where that is the custom, students seem to have a fine time. That would not, of course, eliminate Guilbert's problem. He would still court his father's displeasure and probably the derision of fellow students if he stepped onto the floor with the date of his choice. But it would at least be a gesture toward treating social events as a treat, not a trauma, and dealing with teenagers the way they deserve to be dealt with — as individuals.[18]

If school boards had followed the paper's advice, they would have saved a lot of bad feeling and litigation. But in the ensuing decades, the issue of gays at the prom has vexed students, parents, and school administrations across the land. As recently as 2011, the first Gay-Straight Alliance (GSA) chapter was founded in conservative St. George, Utah, over the strenuous objections of parents, administrators, and even the state legislature. Opposition to the "gay lifestyle" is so strong in communities like St. George that a same-sex couple at prom is completely out of the question. Gay students in Utah forgo school proms and attend annual queer proms sponsored by the Utah Pride Center in Salt Lake City and held in various locations around the state.[19]

Gay proms are popping up everywhere. In Winston-Salem, North Carolina, local PFLAG and GLSEN[20] chapters throw an annual "alternative" prom at open-minded Trinity Presbyterian Church. Everyone dances with a "blatant disregard for gender roles and dates' rights," according to reporter Bob Moser. Anyone can attend. "I'm not gay, but I'm having a helluva time," shouted one "square-shouldered jock."[21] As fun and freeing as the event is, many attendees go without the knowledge of their families, employing the usual cover stories for teenage misbehavior: band practice and play rehearsal, a movie, a trip to the library or the church youth group.[22]

The Boston Gay, Lesbian, Bisexual and Transgendered Youth prom bills itself as "original and largest LGBT youth prom." The 2006 prom was held at Boston City Hall and drew 1,200 participants. Daniel McCarthy wore an emerald-green dress with a padded bra and high heels. His mother, Joyce, helped him dress. "I don't know what's wrong with some parents who don't understand," she said. "Live life the way you want to live it."[23] A mother of another gay teen says, "We're making up the rituals. Of course he's not going to take a girl to the prom; he's going to take the cutest guy to the prom. Who's going to stop him? If they do, we'll have our own prom."[24]

As commentator Gabriel Rotelle notes,

> There are actually two gay prom movements, both important. One is the demand by lots of gay, lesbian, bisexual and transgendered kids to be allowed to bring same-sex dates to their traditional proms. Things have improved so much that these days it's bigger news when schools refuse to allow same-sex couples to attend — though that certainly still happens. But just because gay kids are allowed to take their same-sex dates to the prom, it doesn't mean they want to. High schools remain hotbeds of homophobia, and straight kids in black ties can be just as mean as those in jeans and backpacks. So the other big prom story is the growing movement to create alternative proms where same-sex couples are the norm.[25]

Public and secular private schools policies have to conform to antidiscrimination laws, but religious school policies do not. Gay couples at Catholic school proms are a nonstarter, which is why lesbian student Rosanne Strott was not permitted to bring a female date to the 2007 Bishop Feehan High prom in Attleboro, Massachusetts. "We're not looking to have trouble at our prom," says George A. Milot, superintendent of schools in the Fall River diocese. "Having boys bring boys or girls bring girls opens the door to all kinds of scenarios that could lead to problems. We're not willing to open the door."[26] Lest there be any confusion, the diocese spelled out the policy in a press release from its Office of Communications:

> It is the policy of the school that a student may bring one non-class member guest of the opposite sex, if he or she desires. Along with helping to maintain a traditional prom experience, this policy has been helpful in limiting the number of non-class members who are present and minimizing issues that arise when former or would be girl or boy friends — who are not members of the class — attend as well.[27]

The diocese does not specify the issues they wish to minimize, but their usage of "guest of the opposite sex" and "traditional prom experience" is clear: prom is for straight kids. Single students are permitted to attend, which may be stretching the diocesan concept of prom tradition. You can be a homosexual at the Bishop Feehan prom — Strott attended solo — but you can't behave like one.

Marc Hall was banned from inviting a boy to his Catholic school prom because the church does not condone the "homosexual lifestyle," or so he was told. "I'm sorry, but I don't have a lifestyle," Hall says. "I have a life. The school board uses this expression because they really do not accept and support gay students."[28]

Brother Kenneth Hoagland, principal of Kellenberg Memorial High in Uniondale, New York, canceled the prom in 2005 because he's not a fan of teen sex in any form. "Common parlance tells us that this is a time to lose one's virginity," Hoagland wrote in a letter to parents. "It is a time of heightened sexuality in a culture of anything goes. The prom has become a sexual focal point. This is supposed to be a dance," he adds tartly. "Not a honeymoon."[29] Hoagland also cites a culture of excess in his decision to cancel the prom, decrying the money spent on clothes, limos, and so on. The cancellation sparked a national debate. The *Chicago Tribune* editorialized in favor of Hoagland's decision, not for the principal's reasoning or even his conclusions but for starting a conversation about "prom night activities and about parents and educators who don't do their jobs." Parents countered by saying it's the few indulgent parents who ruin things for everyone.[30]

Constance McMillan sparked a high-profile controversy when she enlisted the ACLU in her fight to bring her girlfriend to the Itawamba County (Mississippi) High School prom. A federal judge agreed with the ACLU's contention that McMillan's rights were violated by her school's ban on same-sex dates.[31] The school board responded by canceling the prom and told parents to sponsor private parties. "That's really messed up," McMillan says, "because the message they are sending is that if they have to let gay people go to the prom that they are not going to have one. A bunch of kids at school are really going to hate me for this, so in a way, it's really retaliation."[32] As McMillan predicted, many of her classmates shunned her, and she did not receive an invitation to a private party. She did attend an LGBT prom (straight kids welcome) called Mississippi Safe Schools Coalition's Second Chance Prom. McMillan subsequently appeared on Ellen DeGeneres's day time TV program and has advocated for gay students' rights.

Maureen Costello, director of Teaching Tolerance, a project of the Southern Poverty Law Center in Montgomery, Alabama, says that acceptance of gay students is a long way off in her part of the country. "You have to have a critical mass of students willing to declare themselves gay," she says. "That's very unlikely in the South, where everyone is expected to conform to a cultural norm."[33] Nevertheless, there are signs of change: Principal Michelle Masters of the high school in Bleckley County, Georgia, okayed a same-sex date for student Derrick Martin in 2010. "You don't have the right to say no," says Masters. "As a principal, I don't judge him. I'm taught not to judge. I have to push my own beliefs to the background."[34]

Gay, transgendered and cross-dressing students continue to test the limits of their communities' tolerance. The results are mixed. Kevin Logan was turned away when he showed up at his Gary, Indiana, prom in 2006 wearing a fuchsia gown and heels.[35] Derrek Lutz, on the other hand, a self-identified cross-dresser, not only went to his 2010 prom in an evening gown but was crowned prom king.[36] That same prom season, two males, Charlie Ferrusi and Timothy Howard, were crowned prom king and queen at Hudson High School in New York state. The pair was inundated with interview requests from media outlets such as MTV, *Huffington Post* and Fox News. The head of Hudson Pride Day, Victor Mendolia, says, "People need to look and see if King and Queen are proper nomenclature for these kinds of awards." He questions the appropriateness of enshrining a custom based in gender identification.[37]

Andrew ("Andii") Viveros is a transgendered student who ran for prom queen and won in a south Florida school in 2011, triumphing over 14 girls for the title. According to the NBC affiliate in Miami, Viveros is the first transgendered student in the nation to achieve the honor.[38] Stephen Boyer, who came out to his classmates in 2011, his senior year, was crowned queen of the Blacksburg (Virginia) High School prom. He donned a blond wig and a gown à la Lady Gaga. "This was as much a social experiment as a fun thing to do," says Boyer. "This prom queen thing sort of became a manifestation of 'all right, this is who I am. It's time to show it off.'"[39]

Every year more gay students petition their school to take same-sex dates, and they're winning. "It's exploding," says Alice Leeds, a spokesperson for PFLAG. With the backing of supportive organizations and occasional legal help from the ACLU, gay couples at prom are becoming more common, although there's still a lot of resistance. Kevin Jennings of GLSEN says, "Prom is the central social ritual of high school life, and anyone who goes to high school knows that. For [nonstraight] students, it's an important symbol of whether or not they're really part of a community. They don't want a 'separate but equal' prom. They want to be part of the main prom, too."[40]

Gay students are in demand at prom time for another reason. As Seattle-area high school student Frank Palva says,

> Lately I've become wary of the question, "Frank, what are you doing next Saturday night?" In the month of May, it can only mean one thing: I'm going to yet another prom. And no, I'm not doing a cousin a favor. Cousins are out. I'm this century's new answer to the last-minute prom date: the gay best friend.[41]

Center Place Restoration School is a Mormon K–12 school in Independence, Missouri, that holds a senior prom in accordance with its particular behavioral standards, which differ in some ways from those of mainstream Latter-Day Saints (LDS). Profiled in the 2002 documentary film *Prom Night in Kansas City*, the school selects its prom king and queen from those who exhibit "Christian values — courtesy, kindness and brotherly love." It's not clear how those attributes are quantified or who does the measuring, but that's only one way the school's prom differs from most. For starters, there's no dancing. As one female student says, "We totally respect that and we're fine with that. It's a different kind of fun. It's clean fun. Or whatever."[42] The school board issues "guidelines for modesty," which are evidently for the sake of female students: no exposure below the collarbone and no spaghetti straps or strapless dresses. Instead of dancing, Center Place students attend a "formal" dinner at a cafeteria-style banquet hall and enjoy a limo ride to nearby Kansas City (Missouri) where they meander about in their finery and eat some more.[43]

The mainstream LDS church has taken to sponsoring formal dances for its students who find the music and dancing at public school proms offensive. "People were hardly wearing anything. It was gross. I stayed for like five minutes and left," says Lytal Morgan of her Waubonsie Valley High school prom in Illinois.[44] She and a friend came up with the idea of a Mormon prom, and the event soon took shape. Dancing beneath a banner that read "Reflecting Eternity 2007," Morgan and her friends were supervised by adults from their church who carried spare ties for boys who neglected to don the required neckwear and shawls for girls with bare shoulders. They also ensured that all couples danced a *Book of Mormon* width apart. Printed tickets for the event spelled out the dress code: *Sunday dress or better*, a well-known reference that means an absolute minimum of exposed skin. The DJ was a church member who played songs with acceptable lyrics: no overtly sexual references or curse words.[45]

The 2007 prom held by the LDS Grand Blanc Michigan Stake Center drew a large crowd of kids from around the state who were eager to meet new people. Adult volunteers and youth committees pitched in as caterers, parking valets, security guards and photographers to make the evening fun, safe and inexpensive. For modest prom wear, girls added sweaters to borrowed dresses, made their own, went to thrift shops and repurposed musical theater costumes. "Here the guys say, 'You look beautiful,' not 'You look hot,'" says Tiffany Morris of Bloomfield Hills. "It seems like a real compliment."[46] LDS wards provided pre-prom instruction in ballroom dancing. "We dance kind of old-fashioned, and I like that," says Amanda Rosenhan of the Grand Blanc ward. Her friend, Andrea Brown, adds, "It's a good chance for us to realize that we can have fun together and still keep our standards."[47]

The Dallas LDS prom grows bigger by the year. Over 1,000 teens attended in 2009. "When you go to a high school of over 2,000 where there are only a dozen members of the church, it is nice to see that you are not alone," says prom chairwoman Joanne Poulsen.[48] In Texas, no party is complete without a mechanical bull, so there was one at the prom. The prom sponsors provided hospital scrubs for the girls so they could have a go at the critter without flashing anyone. The bull operator commented, "I have never seen so many people having so much fun, and no one is drinking!"[49]

At Heritage Christian School in northwest Ohio, a fundamentalist Baptist school, proms are strictly off-limits. Dancing, hand-holding, kissing and rock music are "part of the counterculture which seeks to implant seeds of rebellion in young people's hearts and minds," according to the school's handbook.[50] Principal Tim England says, "When the school committee ... set up the policy regarding dancing, I am confident that they had the principle of fleeing lustful situations in mind ... should a Christian place themselves at an event where young ladies will have low-cut dresses and be dancing in them."[51] Nevertheless, student Tyler Frost attended his girlfriend's public school prom and incurred the wrath of his school board, which suspended him and barred him from graduation exercises. "In life, we constantly make decisions whether we are going to please self or please God," England says. "[Frost] chose one path, and the school committee chose another."[52]

Many fundamentalist Christian blogs and message boards are full of concerns about prom. As Brother Todd Clippard, a preacher at Burleson Church of Christ near Hamilton, Alabama, writes, "While the word 'prom' is a shortened version of the word 'promenade,' it might as well be a shortened version of 'promiscuity.' Dancing is an inherently sexual art form and as such incites lust." Posing a series of questions such as "Would you invite Jesus as your guest to the prom and do you think he would dance with you?" Clippard concludes, "I believe any honest person can clearly see that Prom is no place for a Christian teen."[53] His article circulated widely on email and was posted on several blogs.

Many practitioners of Islam of are fine with dancing, but not doing so with the opposite sex, hence the growth of Muslim all-girl proms. Arriving at venues in dresses covered by jackets and with heads covered by hijabs (head scarves), girls reveal strapless gowns and halter tops when safely ensconced behind closed doors. They eat, laugh and dance until midnight to music played by female DJs. At the 2007 prom at the Minneapolis Al-Madinah Cultural Center, Sabrina Wazwaz said, "I think it's really nice how they thought of the Muslim girls who can't go to the American prom, so they made this for us."[54]

Prom presents problems for Muslim boys, too. Imam Khalid Fattah Griggs says, "We're not even supposed to be sitting among people doing Haram (forbidden) things and so the environment is just pregnant with acts we're not supposed to be involved in — from the music that is being played to the Islamically inappropriate interactions to the drinking. It's just a very un–Islamic atmosphere." The imam recognizes the commercial aspects of the event, saying, "Prom isn't about North American society wanting its youth to turn into well-adjusted people via grad night. This is a multi-million dollar business of selling clothes, accessories, make-up, limousine services, food, alcohol, condoms. You need to realize what this is all about."[55]

Some North American–born Muslims see no problem with mixed-gender dancing. Media consultant Raheel Raza says of her son's public school prom, "They are forging an identity as Muslims and want to celebrate with their peers in the North American cultural system. It's a very important passage in their life. Why should they feel left out?"[56] The range of opinion on proms varies widely in the Muslim community; the Islamic website SoundVision.com is squarely in the antiprom camp, offering pages of advice to parents on how to discourage attendance. Their objections to skimpy dresses, racy music, lustful dancing and postprom booze and sex would be familiar to many Christians.[57]

Home-schooled students have proms, too. A cursory online search yields dozens of sites for planners. As one site says, "Home school doesn't mean students have to miss out on memorable high school experiences. Homeschoolers all over the country are taking part in an age old tradition by attending home-schooling proms. You can attend a home school prom in your area by contacting local support groups and home school organizations, or by gathering a group of friends and planning one of your own. Here are some tips for planning homeschool proms."[58] The site offers advice on all the usual prom considerations, such as budget, location, decorations, dress and behavior codes, theme, music, food and photographers.

Scott Mann knows how to dance the Hustle, the Macarena and the

Electric Slide. He had a great time at his prom, first dining at a restaurant in Collierville, Tennessee, then having his picture taken and dancing in a tux. He and other special needs students from all over Shelby County enjoyed the event sponsored just for them. Students in wheelchairs were spun around the floor by their dates. Kids with disabilities of all kinds were accommodated at the event. "Everybody needs these memories, no matter what disability they have," says Southwind High special ed teacher Genita Bell, who brought six students to the dance. Several students not in special ed participated to help out and keep the party going.[59]

Physical and mental challenges often keep special ed students away from activities that able-bodied students take for granted. In New Iberia, Louisiana, that reality has been recognized for decades. The special needs prom is a tradition there, and every effort is made to include all the disabled students in the parish. Over 300 kids with disabilities such as blindness, deafness and autism attended the 2010 "Hot Time in the City" dance. Helped by students in a peer tutoring program, disabled prom-goers do everything nondisabled students do at the prom, including crowning a king and queen. Peer tutor Erica Olivier said, "It's much better than our prom," as she Cupid Shuffled onto the floor with a large group of kids.[60] Events like this occur countrywide, often with the assistance of peer tutors or organizations such as the Rotary Club. "You learn that everybody's the same," says peer buddy Tammie Miranda of Elsinore High in Riverside County, California. "These kids are no different than any other kids."[61] Special ed kids who are mainstreamed needn't fear the prom these days. Autistic student Justin Amandro was crowned prom king at his 2011 public school dance, and the kids at Loveland High in Ohio crowned two Down syndrome classmates. "I imagined that she would be snubbed and made fun of," the girl's mother says. "What I imagined for her turned out to be the exact opposite."[62]

When students are too sick to go, friends bring the prom to them. With the help of nonprofit organizations such as the Embrace Kids Foundation, Santa's Foundation, kind nurses, hospital staff and others, disco balls and corsages are in evidence in hospitals that want to help teenage patients have one normal night of teenage fun. Ashley Riemer is one such patient. The 17-year-old had been battling cancer at Walter Reed Army Medical Center when her friends from Mount Vernon High and Rose Hill Baptist Church descended on the hospital with a juke box and a red carpet. Resplendent in a turquoise gown, Ashley had a wonderful time, dancing and eating snacks. "These kids with cancer grow up fast and lose some of that innocence," says third-year pediatric hematology/oncology fellow Jacob Wessler. "How do you go back to school? How do you relate to friends? This prom is a way to give back some of that normalcy."[63]

Kids who want nothing to do with the prom also have a niche. An "Anti-Prom" is held yearly at the New York Public Library, and anyone who feels like an outsider or objects to school proms on principle can celebrate that. The web page for the dance says, "Anti-Prom provides an alternative, safe space for all teens who may not feel welcome at official school proms or dances because of their sexual orientation, the way they dress, or for any other reason."[64] The 2011 dance drew 600 people, dressed in everything from skate park clothes to what might be described as bride of Frankenstein meets Cruella de Vil. "You get judged in high school," says 16-year-old Clare Early of Manhattan. "You come here and you don't get judged. Everybody is the same, everybody's equal, everybody's awesome," which may be the best description of the Millennial prom yet.[65]

7. Rituals, Signifiers and the Meaning of It All

"It's just a temporary metamorphosis. They change back. Midnight and they all turn back into pumpkins."
— Anonymous Philadelphia high school teacher

Crystal Hughes of First Colonial High in Virginia Beach began her prom preparations three months in advance, coordinating plans with five other students who attended as a group. "From all the planning on rides, dates, restaurants, dresses, tuxes, boutonnieres, corsages, appointments, and all that jazz, we spend so much time preparing for something that lasts about four hours," Hughes says. "It's all of this craziness that makes the experience all worthwhile."[1] Happily for Hughes, she enjoyed her prom. Results tend to vary, however, and after all the money has been spent, the food eaten, the dances danced, the photographs taken, the tux returned and the dress stored in a garment bag, what is prom all about? Filmmaker John Hughes (no relation) wrote a monologue in *Pretty in Pink* about a woman who always feels like she forgot something because she missed her prom. The speech is quoted widely as proof that prom is a must, but do the words of a middle-aged male screenwriter resonate because they're true or because they were in a movie?

If you ask students about the purpose of prom, the range of responses is as varied as the individuals themselves. According to one researcher's sample, prom is

"An evening away from my parents."
"A night I can stay out 'til morning."
"Being able to look and feel like I'm rich."
"A hassle. Stress."
"Money, time and let-down."
"Drinking and naked time."
"A popularity contest."[2]

In another study, many students described the prom as "just a fun time" and refused to assign to it any other significance, as if fun and meaning were mutually exclusive.[3] That's the inherent contradiction of the prom: it exists in a culture that prides itself on rational thinking, but it's the holy grail of high school, often described in terms bordering on rapturous: "The most magical experience I could possibly have!"[4]

Rite of passage is the phrase most commonly used to characterize the prom. Like many axioms, the term is employed so often that it's accepted uncritically and then repeated all the more. Rite of passage is an easy way to describe proms, but it's not very accurate. As one student says, "Some people say like [the prom is] some type of rite of passage. Into what? This is not what adult life is like. You don't wear tuxedos all the time and spend all kinds of money. It's just another event!"[5] Rites of passage comprise specific components, and although prom may resemble those rites in some ways, important elements are missing.

Anthropologist Arnold van Gennep coined the phrase *rite of passage* in 1909. Ever since then, academics who study initiation processes have employed the term.[6] Here are the basics: A rite of passage, according to experts van Gennep, Victor Turner and others, is a ritual that takes the participant from one stable state of being to another from which there is no going back. Rites of passage are transportation into a permanent, widely recognized change of status. Marriage qualifies as a rite of passage. You can get a divorce, but once married you cannot be never-married again. A bar or bat mitzvah also qualifies. The Jewish ceremony that formally ushers adolescent boys and girls into the community of adults is a bell that can never be unrung. High school graduation certainly qualifies. After a literal passage from one side of a stage to the other, the high school graduate possesses documentation of altered status — a diploma — and is considered officially fit for the workforce. After twelve or thirteen years in the grasp of one bureaucracy or another, the high school graduate is given a ceremonious shove out the door and expected to take responsibility for his or her own Monday through Friday schedule.

Rites of passage, as defined by Turner, typically involve mentoring and close supervision by adults who oversee every aspect of the ritual. Rites of passage can involve special costumes, periods of isolation and severe physical trials. The sexes are often separated.[7] Participants have different roles, rights and responsibilities after the rite is concluded. In some rites, one's sexuality is recognized and stamped with a seal of community approval. Rites of passage can also include the acquisition of new skills in preparation for adulthood.[8]

So how does the prom stack up? Let's start with the easy part, the myth that losing one's virginity is a prom rite of passage. If having sex is part of the total prom package (and that's debatable),[9] it's the thing that most adults don't want to happen. It's true that a loss of virginity is a permanent change in one's condition, but so is reaching puberty or the extraction of wisdom teeth. Prom night sex does not take place under adult supervision, obviously. Quite the opposite — it's concealed from adults, who actively discourage it. If anything, adults present teens with a tricky contradiction: they sequester the most hormonally revved-up segment of the population in their most attractive clothes, and then tell them to dance together but refrain from overt sexual contact later. It's an exercise in frustration, perhaps, but not a rite of passage. Sex may seem infused with ritual magic when you're seventeen years old, but at that age, so does driving a car. In any case, two randy teens doing the deed is hardly a rite. And so much for the part about separation of the sexes.

When adults are not explicitly discouraging prom night coupling, they're refusing to discuss it all. Preprom assemblies tend to focus on other types of unwanted behavior, such as drunk driving. Discussions about prom night sex are practically taboo in Catholic schools, and they hardly ever occur in public schools, either. In twenty-one Philadelphia public school prom assemblies, sex was mentioned only six times. As researcher Felicity Paxton observes, "Drugs and alcohol and car crashes are not the only dangers of prom night, but they are the only ones the schools seem willing to address."[10] It likely wouldn't matter much whether a sex lecture is part of the preprom assembly. As previously mentioned, prom-goers who have sex on prom night have probably been sexually active well in advance of the occasion.

Adult supervision at the prom is a touchy issue in general. Prom is promoted as a night for teens to do their best imitation of adulthood. Why else would a teenage boy submit to donning a tux if not to appear more mature than in mufti? Yet adults control or attempt to control every aspect of the evening. Deemed old enough to dress like adults but not mature enough to behave like them, teens are discouraged and often prevented from driving on prom night, consuming intoxicants, coming and going from the venue at will, and so on. Many schools require the signing of contracts that specify prohibited behavior under the apparent assumption that responsible behavior must literally be spelled out. Although strict supervision is a component of most rites of passage, prom contracts are a weak attempt at best and focus only on preventing bad behavior as opposed to coaching and rehearsing approved behavior. Students sign prom contracts because they want to attend the event, but they often have no intention of keeping their part of the bargain. "You're signing it in jest," says Scott, a senior at Woodrow Wilson High in New York state. "I saw a kid who changed the Prom Promise into the Prom Compromise."[11] Adults supervise the prom, but are not expected to interact with students except to stop or forestall inappropriate activity. As Paxton notes, "Whatever fun is to be had is to be had within rigidly enforced spatial and temporal boundaries."[12] Adults are involved in the prom, but only up to a point. That point is intrusiveness, and when prom-goers feel that adults are breathing down their necks, they simply stop spending time at the event. Paxton says,

> The most unwanted consequence of the new surveillance is that the heavily policed prom is one that students show less and less interest in.... Many make the briefest of stays, remaining just long enough to be seen and collect their proofs of attendance: the prom pictures and favors. For these students, the prom is little more than a drop-by photo shop. The true magic of prom comes later and takes place far from the watchful eye of school staff, chaperones and hotel security.[13]

Parents are permitted to photograph and cheer on the participants outside the venue but are not permitted entry.[14] Family members are relegated to supporting roles on prom night: caterer, set decorator, personal shopper, lady-in-waiting, photographer. They enjoy the night by proxy; the kids are supposed to have enough fun for everyone, while parents look on wistfully and wait at home like Cinderella before her fairy godmother materialized. In that respect, prom resembles a rite of inversion — a time when the master serves the servant, a medieval European carnival custom that allowed peasants to blow off steam and heap ridicule on the lord of the manor with impunity. Adult participation in prom preparations, typically dress and tux shopping, can be fraught with conflict. There are no established customs for how much input a parent ought to have. It's every mom and dad for themselves, and that includes giving advice or laying down the law on curfews. The tension between mentoring and letting go is common and unresolved. Writer Michael Riera advises parents to "wedge yourself into the event."[15]

Attending a dance in formal clothes is supposed to introduce teens to adult social life, but the onus for propriety, according to some advisors, is apparently on the shoulders of girls:

> The whole purpose of prom, or any school-sponsored formal, is to give young people the chance to develop their social skills. Somehow that always gets forgotten. That's why it's important to remind your daughter that prom is really an opportunity for her to practice the social behaviors that will benefit her for the rest of her life. She needs to learn how to walk, talk, dress, and act appropriately in formal situations. The more you can help your daughter understand the purpose of prom, the less likely she is to inflate prom into something it was never meant to be.[16]

Is it possible for one event to inculcate behaviors that "will benefit her for the rest of her life"? If the purpose of prom is the cultivation of social skills (and that's not necessarily the case), segregating attendees, often to the point of locking down the facility, is an odd way to go about it. A real rite of passage might be a dinner dance for the whole community, where teens could practice their social skills in the company of actual adults instead of approximating grown-up behavior with each other. The young people dancing in fancy clothes have been together for years, so how different are their interactions likely to be on prom night? The way proms are really organized reinforces the notion that teens should socialize only with their own age group because they're not ready for the pleasures and privileges of the adult world (imminent graduation notwithstanding). Isolating teens on prom night may actually encourage immature behavior. Reports of prom night juvenility such as food fights, chewing bubble gum and running around in bare feet are common. Many students approach dressing like adults with studied irony, costuming themselves in parodies of formal wear: oversized tuxes, exaggerated 1950s beehive hairstyles, or pairing athletic socks with high heels.[17]

For some low-income students, prom is a chance to see how the other half lives. As one inner-city Philadelphia teacher says, "They may not have ever been in a hotel before. Even looking down at the people in the restaurant or in the bar — all kind of business people are down there, professional people are there — is a learning experience for them. All this elegance below them, and they love it, it's transforming."[18] At Evander Childs High School in the Bronx, many students are immigrants. For them, the prom is a potent symbol of assimilation and achievement. "Some of these kids have made it over enormous obstacles," says Principal Richard Urovsky. "Yet in spite of everything that they see, everything they endure, they came to school every day and made it."[19] Patrick Welsh, an English teacher at T.C. Williams High in Alexandria, Virginia, sees prom as the great equalizer. "When I've gone to proms, I've always been moved by the amazing array of nationalities, religions, races and socioeconomic groups celebrating together," he says. "For one night, impoverished Third World refugees, children of millionaires and kids whose families have lived for generations in public housing are all made equal by their tuxes and fancy dresses."[20]

If clothes make the man, then a prom dress makes the woman — or, they make the girl feel like a woman, if only for one night. One raison d'être for prom is the buying and wearing of a fancy dress. Teen girls have fetishized the prom dress in recent years. Little else matches its importance in the creation of the "perfect" prom night, not even the boy for whom the dress is ostensibly worn. Welsh says, "Maybe it was typical male naiveté, but it took me a long time to realize that for girls, the dress is infinitely more important than the date."[21] Unlike a ritual garment in a true rite of passage, however, the selection of a prom dress is the bailiwick of the teen girl, who may receive guidance and support from an elder, but usually makes the final choice on her own. She may spend a period of solitude in her room before revealing to her date and her parents how well she cleans up, but whatever ritual ablutions she performs are limited in their transformative power. Her makeup will go down the drain at the end of the night, and the temporary princess will be an ordinary girl in sweat pants come the dawn.

Prom dress shopping is a rehearsal for buying a wedding gown, if TV shows like *Bridezillas* are any indication. Fussed over by store clerks and focused on by friends and relatives, girls try on dresses with the concentration of a neurosurgeon and the self-absorption of an A-list movie star. Worries over the cost, whether another girl will wear something similar, buying the right accessories — indeed, the whole ritual of assembling the prom costume is a run-through for wedding consumption. If prom is a preview of things to come, the anxiety generated by its preparations ought to discourage anyone from attending the prom and walking down the matrimonial aisle. Instead, it seems to amp up anticipation.

All of that is to say that prom dress shopping is a rite, but what kind? Sociologist Amy Best suggests that prom formally inducts girls into the adult consumer class: "Proms epitomize the expansion of a distinct youth culture and the spending power of youth. The process of being schooled can no longer be separated from commodity culture."[22] Best's book was written over a decade

High school seniors shop for prom at Nordstrom, Tigard, Oregon, 2011.

ago, however, and today's high school girls are experienced consumers well ahead of prom night. In many cases, such as online shopping, they are far more savvy consumers than their mothers. As one columnist quipped, "Teenager-hood as preparation for life makes no sense when the life being prepared for is the one you've been living all along."[23] What sets prom shopping apart from an ordinary trip to the mall or a web site is the price of the garment and the desire to stand out. The prom dress is a high school girl's ultimate oppor-tunity to demonstrate her worldliness. A really great dress signifies economic level, good taste, womanly sophistication and *je ne sais quoi*. In short, the dress plays a dual role of status symbol and marker of the wearer's true identity. The young naïf shuffling down the high school corridor, lo these many moons, has been in disguise all along! The real girl is this womanly creature in tulle and satin. She is, in other words, Cinderella, at least in the prom of her imag-ination. This high school senior's concept of prom is fairly typical: "As a little girl, I always fantasized about this famous night where I would resemble Cin-derella in my gown."[24] In the minds of modern teenage girls, the perfect prom dress is a talisman. To the rest of us (with the possible exception of the girl's mother), it's just a pretty dress. But the quest for the perfect prom dress has taken on greater import in recent years. One young lady mentioned that she tried on "probably twenty-five dresses," as if that were the lazy approach to prom shopping.[25] The problem with the rite of passage construct is that the girl who wore casual clothes for most of her life is the same girl underneath the prom dress. There is no garment that can perform the transformation that a prom gown is supposed to achieve. Prom is marketed as the fulfillment of Hollywood red carpet or supermodel photo shoot fantasies, but it's a tough illusion to sustain, especially on an amateur level. Professional makeup and hair styling can alter one's appearance only so much, and no physical imper-fection can be Photoshopped away in real life. As "supermodel" Cindy Craw-ford once remarked, "I wish I looked like Cindy Crawford."[26] But that doesn't stop legions of ordinary high school girls from trying to look like the models they see in print and electronic media. Prom shopping is the culmination of years of social conditioning. Writer Murray Milner says, "Perhaps the thing that secondary education teaches most effectively is the desire to consume." Teens live within a context of consumer capitalism, and capitalism survives partly on teenage consumer demand. Our culture in general and prom culture in particular comprise a two-way street. Milner goes on to say, "The status systems of high schools were and are a contributing factor to the creation and maintenance of consumer capitalism."[27]

If we each had a dollar for every time a girl says, "I want a princess dress for prom," we could all buy a prom dress for every day of the year. Wanting to look like a princess is a notion firmly embedded in popular culture and reinforced by retailers. Prom magazines use the words *princess* and *Cinderella* repeatedly to inflate various aspects of prom, and primarily to describe the dress. The irony is that when every girl wants to be a princess but "doesn't want to look like anyone else," as teen shopper Lauren Gallo of West Des Moines declares,[28] they wind up looking exactly like each other to the casual observer.

The prom as junior wedding is a subset of the Cinderella fantasy, albeit a wedding that's all about the bride and her dress. "All they need is a really great dress," says boutique owner Kari Smith. "The date will come next."[29] For promzillas, like bridezillas, the date (or proxy groom) is something of an afterthought. He's a prop, an accessory; he's there to complete the picture. *Teen Prom* magazine goes so far as to title an article, "Arm Candy: If he looks good, you'll look good, right?"[30] *Seventeen Prom* is similarly straightforward, subtitling an article "Your guy is the best accessory — show him off!"[31] Prom is a female competition for the prettiest dress and best-looking date, but no one seems to know how to identify the winner or what prize, if any, she takes home.

The girl who fantasized about her Cinderella dress goes on to describe her dream date as "my Romeo-type boyfriend that showers me with flowers and compliments me the whole night through. Nothing would go wrong on prom night and *perfect* would be the only way to describe it."[32] The conflation of Shakespeare and the Grimm Brothers is silly, but it's understandable considering the consumer culture that promotes that sort of thinking. Shakespearean tragedy, fairy tale — *whatever*. Everything in the Western canon can be subsumed into marketing campaigns, and prom is nothing if not a festival of consumerism. It's not clear what is meant by "Romeo-type boyfriend" (she's probably not referring to the knife fight part of the story), but the young lady likely had to settle for a specific high school boy with human flaws as opposed to a Romeo or any other generalized ideal of a person. Chances are that neither he nor the evening were "perfect," if perfect means the absence of bodily functions, awkward moments, frustrations, delays, mishaps and all the other things that go along with real life and impossibly high expectations. Nor does she suggest how the young man (whoever he may be) might benefit from spending a night with *her*. It's clear that this typical prom aspirant has absorbed images and concepts from the culture at large. The prom is the teen apogee of romantic love — a kind of moony dream world where no one's dress shows sweat stains, and teenage boys look like the illustrated hunks on the covers of romance novels. Unlike a real relationship, fantasy prom requires no quid pro quo. In the make-believe prom that goes on for months ahead of the real event, the prom princess is the passive recipient of admiring, non-sexual attention and prized for her ability to model a dress — much like Cinderella, who was never much of a conversationalist. Still, there is something heady about dressing up and mingling in a beautiful setting, and even teen boys can be vulnerable to that allure. Fortunate is the girl whose date plays along with the fantasy:

> I remember commenting that night that I felt like a princess and that I wished I got this type of treatment all the time. It is only one of the nights where the guys actually seemed to care if you are having fun or not. Everyone should feel that special. Those nights are some of the only nights where girls are treated like ladies.[33]

A prom is deemed successful according to how well the evening matched the princess narrative.[34] Prom is the play-acting of the adolescent romantic ideal, which is a version of the culture's emphasis on traditional gender roles. Those roles are signified by clothing. Researcher Elizabeth Hegland observes that "Gender signification in prom dress for males and females is notably more potent than is their school-day dress."[35] Hegland says that traditional male apparel "tends to be tailored with angular or square shapes, dark and monochromatic, plain in style and made from fabric which is often coarse, stiff and heavy." In other words, a tuxedo. Feminine attire is "non-tailored with rounded and flowing shapes, lighter in color and polychromatic, elaborate and complex in style, and made from materials that are soft, fine and light-weight,"[36] which is a good description of a prom dress. Girls who never wear makeup layer it on for prom night. Boys who normally give no thought to their appearance consult the mirror and role-play the gallant suitor, however awkwardly.

For many young people, prom is the first and perhaps only time they will be on public display. In schools with small enough enrollments to accommodate it, the promenade still takes place. Parents, grandparents, siblings and teachers gather to ooh and ahh at the pretty young people in their finery. Names are announced as if couples were entering a nineteenth-century European court. In Racine, Wisconsin, prom is a community-wide event. The entire town turns out for the promenade, even if there's no personal connection to a student. Couples compete to arrive in the most outlandish conveyances; everything from tractors to fire trucks, indeed, anything that rolls makes its way to the Kleig-lighted red carpet. "It's good for the city," says one town elder. "They rent all kinds of things."[37] The Academy Awards is obviously the template for the Racine prom, and the big to-do is televised for those who can't attend.

At promenades everywhere, parents discuss who's with whom, who didn't get a date, the beauty of a particular dress, the hideousness of another, the tragedy of a fallen hairdo. The public promenade is the opportunity for adults to devolve into high schoolers themselves. The spotlight, although much anticipated, can be withering, however. Under the intense scrutiny, students

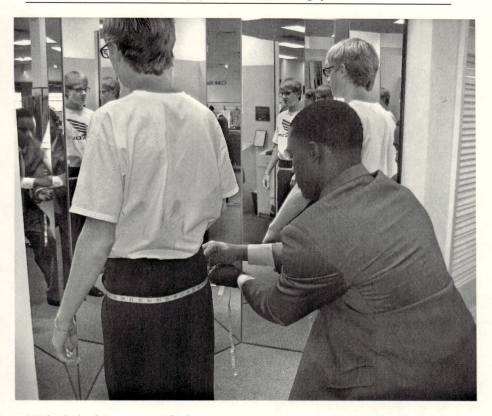

Michael Sheck is measured for his prom tux, a senior year ritual, Northridge, California, 2011 (J. Malone).

flush with self-consciousness as they tug bodices, adjust cummerbunds, totter in high heels and attempt to be graceful while walking arm in arm.[38] Kids don't want chaperones to hover, but they do want to be seen in their good clothes. "When I first started teaching, I stayed away from proms, assuming that kids would want as few teachers around as possible," says Welsh. "But I discovered that the opposite is true. The kids are disappointed if their teachers don't show up." Welsh's colleague, Carolyn Lewis, agrees. "They love for you to see their outfits, especially the girls."[39]

Prom is the endorsement of heterosexual romance, which is why some schools still insist that prom-goers attend with a date of the opposite sex. That said, the mere appearance of heterosexual romance is all that's required. Almost any stand-in for a boyfriend is acceptable if he looks good in a prom photograph, even a blood relative. Best reports about one girl who attended with her brother:

She relayed to me that she had wanted to go with her older brother because he was taller than she; she thought it would look better. She ended up going to the prom with her younger brother who, though shorter, allowed her to maintain a particular construction of the prom as a heterosexual event, and herself as legitimately feminine.[40]

Prom is a marker of acceptance as well as a final reminder of one's place in the school hierarchy. Students are powerless, except, as Milner says, "in their evaluations of each other. The kind of power they do have is status power; the power to create their own status systems built on their own criteria."[41] All of the labels that adhered during a K–12 career are on display at the prom. The popular kids will glow a little brighter than the rest; the nerds will herd up, and so on. It's also the last time that high school labels matter. Soon after prom night comes graduation, and then the pecking order dissolves faster than an aspirin in a glass of Coke. "The good news for all of us," says writer Alina Tugend, "is that once we leave high school, there are far more ways to flourish than in the narrow confines of adolescence."[42] For what it's worth, the lions have their problems making their way through the jungle, too. "Even if you were popular," says psychology professor Joseph A. Allen, "you still had experiences of being left out and rejected. No one goes through unscathed."[43]

Michael Sheck, all set for the Sierra Canyon High prom, Northridge, California, 2011 (J. Malone).

Girls sweat securing a prom date because they believe (erroneously) that doing so is predictive of future success in the mating game.[44] As one student says, "They hear people planning for it; talking about it like in January or December. They start thinking, 'Oh, everyone's gonna go!'"[45] A prom date is a signifier that one is not a loser in the tournament of heterosexual attraction, even if one's date is a ringer, and even if one is not heterosexual. In that sense, prom is a rite of conformity, a springtime mash-up of Valentine's Day and Halloween when everyone wears essentially the same costume. The group date and increased acceptance of gay couples has softened this dynamic to a certain degree, but the concept of prom as a marker of desirability persists. The idea that prom is a stamp of attractiveness is so powerful that prom-goers project it into the future: "One of the reasons that I am willing to pay big bucks to go is so that I can tell my kids that I went. It almost says I wasn't a dork and I was beautiful in my young years."[46] Many single teens refuse to attend without a date and show up later at postprom activities, where the dress is casual and the pressure to have a date is nil.[47] One girl opines, "I definitely don't think you should go to prom with someone unless you're going out with them. It's too romantic!"[48]

Prom is about the creation of memories, at least according to another well-circulated meme. The making of memories boils down to one thing: photography. The Hollywood-style red carpet is a regular feature of the modern high school prom. Students not only expect their parents to photograph them as they swan about in their tuxes and gowns, they expect selected students to role-play paparazzi and entertainment reporters as they enter the venue. "In the past, this would have been seen as intrusive," remarks a school's cable access advisor. "Now it's just a regular part of their lives. They want to be on television all the time. They want *everything* videotaped!"[49] No surprise there; a Pew Research Center study shows that fame and money are the two top Millennial goals.[50] Prom may be a drain on money, but it's a definite boost in the fame department, if fame can be measured in cable access showings and YouTube views. Researcher Montana Miller says, "The new age of participatory media has turned the prom into a fast-emerging vehicle for teenagers' self-conscious displays of stylized drama."[51]

Filmmaker Hali Lee says, "We're told that prom is going to be memorable, so we start shaping our memories of it long before it happens."[52] Girls photograph each other on dress shopping excursions and photograph themselves getting ready. Parents photograph their children before they leave the house, and sometimes organize preprom events so that groups of parents can photograph prom-goers en masse. Seeing their children in formal wear and on their best behavior is a moment that simply must be captured.

> The vision of a daughter or son groomed and dressed to perfection, at the threshold of this night of legendary romance, seems irresistible for many adults; one might speculate that those who regret missing their own high school proms perhaps buy into the mythology with even more zeal. For some parents, striving to recreate a fairytale ideal becomes a sort of competition, as though the child's perfect prom night is a reflection of the parent's success.[53]

The truly prized photographs, however, are taken at the event by a professional photographer who sells packets of photographs so kids can exchange them later like baseball cards.[54] Students take copious amounts of pictures and videos during the prom. Photographs tend to capture iconic prom moments: exiting a limo, standing like the couple on a wedding cake, posing next to a decorative set piece. Prom is recorded in a way that signifies conformity: the people in the picture are on board with the establishment program.[55] On an emotional level, prom photographs are far more important than the high school diploma. Many people have a prom photograph in their wallet, but you'd be hard-pressed to find someone who carries their certificate of graduation.

Prom night is fraught for a number of reasons, not the least of which are the conundrums it presents to girls: Dance but don't sweat; look hot but not cheap; be sexy but don't have sex; pair up, at least for the photograph; bond with classmates but outdo each other in appearance; and the most insidious one of all — look great by negating the body. Feeling good about yourself by slimming down has been an article of faith for teen girls since the 1920s, when arms and legs were bared as never before. Ever since the flapper era, girls have viewed their bodies as projects — the body is a beast to be tamed, or starved into submission if necessary. Losing weight as the solution to all adolescent problems is a concept that's been passed down by several generations. Corsets and girdles used to rein in unruly flesh. Now girls control their shape from the inside out by dieting.[56]

"The most pressing concerns of teenage girls are diet and weight," says Rachel Lynne Levine, an El Paso teen. "I believe this is because of the unrealistically thin bodies shown on television and in magazines." Kristen Keeler of Indianapolis agrees: "Look through the magazines. You can't find anybody who weighs more than 120 pounds."[57] Magazines cultivate the fear that every girl's body is inadequate. *Your Prom* magazine issues the directive, "Start dieting!" as if every reader were overweight.[58] Prom probably doesn't cause eating disorders, but for any girl who has an issue with her weight, prom is a lens that magnifies the issue a hundredfold. The Centers for Disease Control and Prevention has identified adolescent and childhood obesity as a growing problem,[59] but prom does not often inspire healthier regimens. Girls go to unhealthy extremes to fit into the smallest dress possible, skipping lunches for weeks before the event, or eating nothing but one item, such as pretzels. For many girls, altering the body is as important as finding the right outfit: "You have to diet before to fit in your dress!"[60] Veteran chaperones marvel at the girls who "literally change shape" as prom night approaches. Once at the prom, the refusal to take nourishment persists; girls eat next to nothing while boys chow down.[61]

If there's anything worse than feeling fat on prom night, it's a bodily eruption. Prom elevates the importance of girls' bodies, but in a fearful, adversarial way. "Prom trauma," as magazines like to call physical mishaps, usually has something to do with unruly effluvia (heaven forbid you should have your period on prom night), gaseous emissions, an errant breast (colloquially referenced as a "nip slip") or a spill on the precious garment (justification for not eating). Displaying the body as beautifully as possible while keeping it under conditions of martial law is the ultimate paradox of prom night. In Part Two, we'll see how magazines and advertisers use the anxiety they create about the body to cash in.

8. Does This Magazine Make Me Look Fat?

"Find Your Dream Dress Inside! Flat Abs and Killer Legs By Prom Night! Amazing Hair Ideas, Flirty Makeup Tricks, Clear Skin Secrets! Win the Ultimate Prom! Are You a Promzilla? Find Out!"
— *Seventeen Prom,* 2011 cover

The April 1962 edition of *Seventeen* magazine asked "What was the biggest headache before the prom?" Their answer: "Decorations."[1] Boy, have times changed. Decorations wouldn't even make the list of today's prom night worries. The main source of prom anxiety for today's teen girls is their appearance. Prom night has become a competitive festival of "looking amazing," as teen magazines like to say, and that boils down to purchasing and using products, but not just any old stuff. It's imperative to buy all the right things, which is why retailers and advertisers have swarmed over prom season like flies at a hog farm.

A study conducted by Visa in January 2011 estimated that the average American family would spend $800 that year on the prom.[2] It used to be that a girl just needed a dress and possibly a new pair of shoes, but those days are long gone. Prom is now a full-fledged spending season. The Promgirl.com "prom guide" for 2011, to cite one example, lists four categories of products for the construction of a presentable prom body: tanning (salon or self-tanning cream), hair removal (electrolysis or waxing), manicure/pedicure (at a salon or at home) and hair accessories (barrettes, flowers, tiaras). This array of products and services (six are listed for a home pedicure alone) is in addition to a dress, undergarments, makeup, hair styling, shoes, jewelry, purse, wrap, limousine, prom ticket, boutonniere, dinner, photographs and afterparty.[3] No wonder the final tab runs into the hundreds. How did prom night evolve from a simple high school dance into a spending spree that rivals the Christmas shopping season? It's been a long time coming. Teens are immersed in a culture of consumption. A full study of teens and consumer culture is outside the scope of this book, but for the purposes of understanding prom spending, a few influences are worth noting, particularly *Seventeen* and other publications for teen girls.

Teen magazines come and go,[4] but *Seventeen* has hung in there as the bible for high school girls since the first issue hit the newsstands in 1944. The magazine's debut coincided with the apparel industry's realization that girls wanted clothing lines just for them. Retailers, with a push from *Seventeen's* editor, Helen Valentine, installed "junior" and "sub-deb" departments with clothes designed for young ladies whose bodies were larger than preteens but slimmer than college women. Sociologist Kelley Massoni says, "By the early 1940s, retailers had identified a new consumer group (girl teenagers) and a corresponding market (teen girl clothing) and *Seventeen* emerged as a vehicle to bring the two together."[5] *Seventeen* was an early promoter of the importance of the teen consumer. "After all," writes historian Jon Savage, "as its prelaunch ad copy advised, American youth had an estimated spending capacity of $750 million: untold riches awaited those who plugged into this still virtually untapped market."[6] From its inception, *Seventeen* was determined to be the most important conduit to the female teen pocket book.

Seventeen was the brain child of Valentine, a middle-aged editor who persuaded publisher Walter Annenberg to tap into the teen girl market. The first issue featured celebrities (Harry James and Frank Sinatra), a Hollywood gossip column, dating and etiquette advice, and of course, ads for products, primarily clothing. Saks Fifth Avenue jumped on board immediately, promoting its "Young Circle" fashions. The magazine was an instant success. Within six months, the initial print run grew from 530,000 to almost 650,000.[7] That accomplishment marked a sea-change in the fashion and magazine industries. "Stores didn't recognize this age group as a viable consumer group," said Estelle Ellis, *Seventeen* promotion director. "They didn't want them. They felt that these kids were getting in the way of serious buying by older people."[8] It took some doing, but Valentine and Ellis broke through retailers' resistance to young shoppers. Valentine worked with clothing manufacturers to make garments for the teenage body that "reflected the way of life, the style of life, the time of life that teenagers represented." She approached cosmetic manufacturers with ideas for adolescent girls. Flame-glo lipstick and Beaux Catcher perfume were two early results of that effort. Valentine promoted the magazine relentlessly, and within sixteen months, circulation topped the one million mark. Valentine sold teenage girls to advertisers and the advertisers' products to her readers. She had a big hand in creating the teenage girl consumer.[9]

To persuade advertisers to place ads in *Seventeen*, Valentine used market research, a practice that was almost unheard of at the time. Her statistical guru

July 1954 *Seventeen* (Hearst).

was Eugene Gilbert, an entrepreneur twenty years her junior. Gilbert not only pioneered market research, he was the first to recognize the untapped power of the teenage buyer. In his seminal book, *Advertising and Marketing to Young People*, he writes, "Girls begin selecting their own clothing at rather an early age, and by the time they reach their teens they do a major part of their own shopping and much of their family's."[10] That's a nonstory today, but in the

1940s and '50s, it was groundbreaking. Gilbert and Valentine were a philosophical and commercial match. Their success was intertwined from the start, and they continually referenced each other's publications in their pitches to clients.

Teen readers were thrilled with the magazine, writing such encomia as "We are proud of SEVENTEEN because it does not distort our outlook on things, baby us, or make our habits seem ridiculous to adults."[11] Applying makeup, wearing a gown and dating have been highlights of adolescent life since high schools were invented. Valentine and Gilbert recognized that teenage girls dreamed about life after high school. Dressing up and going to dances was a rehearsal for grown-up socializing and even a chance to snare a mate. Girls who could fill out adult garments abandoned the juniors department and migrated to the women's section for more sophisticated clothing, which was fine with retailers. It didn't matter which department girls liked as long as they shopped, and *Seventeen* sent them flocking to stores.

Wanting to appear older has been a constant of teenage life — it's a big appeal of the prom. Preteens want to look like their high school sisters; high schoolers want to look like college women.[12] Prom is a prime opportunity for girls to fulfill womanly fantasies. *Seventeen*'s advertisers obliged them by linking the prom to weddings. One early piece of ad copy read

> It's the time of year, I guess, with Valentine's Day just around the corner, to get lyrical — to dream about a long, swooshy dress for Prom ... and having a date with the most wonderful boy! Starts a girl thinking. About the future. I could be wrong, but this little tune might wind up as the wedding march.[13]

As retailers caught on to the importance of the teen market, they adopted Valentine's "more is better" approach to selling, staging in-store contests and events. And who was the template for teen loveliness? None other than Cinderella, who popped up as a theme in many an in-store promotion.[14] Prom magazines reference Cinderella repeatedly. She's tied to prom season almost as much as Santa is linked to Christmas. An example from a 1995 *Seventeen* reads: "Got a date with a prince? Slip into a dress reminiscent of Cinderella." An ad for Payless shoes reads, "Let's not forget, Cinderella snagged a prince with the perfect shoe."[15] Femininity, conformity, marriageability and princess imagery — especially the transformative fairy dust of new clothes — have been linked to the prom for decades.

Women's magazines have been important marketing tools since the beginning of the twentieth century. *Collier's* and *Saturday Evening Post*, for example, were created specifically as advertising vehicles. Publishers saw their primary service as gatherers of "eyeballs" for advertisers.[16] *Seventeen*, which Valentine envisioned as a paper-and-ink version of a teen girl's older sister, eventually fell in line with conventional commercial concerns. Annenberg pushed Valentine out before the magazine's sixth birthday for her high-minded attention to editorial content rather than advertising revenues.[17] The magazine has had a string of editors since then, but the mission has stayed the same: selling products to high school girls. To that end, the Cinderella story became one of the magazine's mainstays:

> Together [*Seventeen* and advertisers] composed a narrative that echoed the age-old fairy tale in which the princess begins her journey armed with beauty, finds her prince, marries him, and lives happily ever after in his castle on the hill. *Seventeen* ... offered the reader strategies for achieving its happy ending. They advised her not just on the products of body wear, body care, and domestic work, but also on romance and homemaking — how to capture the prince and run the castle.[18]

According to *Seventeen,* heterosexual attachment is the proper goal of the normal American girl, and the route to its achievement is through body improvement via their advertisers' products.[19] As critic Kimberly Phillips writes, "For a magazine aimed at teenage girls, *Seventeen* does a lot of reporting about men.... Far from encouraging independence, *Seventeen* only reinforces the cultural expectations that an adolescent woman should be more concerned with her appearance ... and her ability to win approval from men than with her own ideas or her expectations of herself."[20] To persuade a girl that she needs improvement, she must first be convinced that she is flawed. The advertising industry, which understood that dynamic from the outset, was all too happy to engender teen anxiety. Body odors and excretions were fertile ground for ads:

> Copy-heavy, poorly designed cautionary advertisements (that resembled political manifestos) encouraged consumers to revile everything rotten smelling, from head to crotch to toe. A 1950 ad with a silly line drawing of a non-descript fellow underscored the damning point with the line, "Let's be frank.... Is your breath on the agreeable side? Don't run risks. Before every date use Listerine Antiseptic. It sweetens breath instantly."[21]

Feminist writer Naomi Wolf is particularly critical of the magazine industry's willingness to exploit young women's insecurity. Describing magazine content as "beauty pornography," Wolf asserts that "good" and "bad" girl used to mean nonsexual and sexual. Now it means beautiful and ugly.[22] Many writers have weighed in on the hypocrisy of teen magazines. As columnist Sheila Gibbons notes:

> If the screaming pink and orange cover lines on mass-circulation teen magazines don't get to you, the mixed messages inside will. Has there ever before been a flood of such contradictory, confusing high-pressure "advice" directed at teen girls that serves their interests less? The magazines envision teen-age girls' lives as endless popularity contests in which the assumption is that the reader invariably has defects

What makes a
prom great:

PROM REPORT U.S.A.

Make yours the greatest!

We interviewed prom chairmen, questioned prom-goers, priced decorations and snooped behind the scenes of 167 proms to find out: what makes a prom great? What are the best refreshments, the most popular themes? What's new in fun and fanfare? Some Friday or Saturday night next month or in June—when most proms happen—you may be going to (or giving!) your own prom. To help you, we have pages and pages of gossipy details, tips, recipes and decorating how-to's for the most wonderful prom in the world. Yours. Where will it take place? Most, like ours at right, took place at school but many were held at country clubs, hotels or community centers. In Phoenix, Arizona, one high school took over part of a resort and held its prom in candlelit cabanas around a pool floating with orchids flown from Hawaii (all paid for by money from Junior class sales).

Bob Kelly

that need to be fixed. School is the main stage for efforts to attain popularity and snag a boyfriend (you can't have one without the other, it seems), but mostly, school is merely that — an environment for socializing. These magazines have little to say about the value of academic achievement, civic engagement or intellectual challenges. It's fair to say the brain is not the "hot" organ at the center of magazine content.[23]

Moral and ethical issues aside, self-doubt makes cash registers ring, especially at prom time. This copy from *Seventeen* clearly implies that every reader is in need of physical improvement: "There's nothing like the start of a beautiful friendship to start a girl on a buying spree ... to start her thinking of the cosmetics and toiletries that will improve her looks."[24] Improvement, according to *Seventeen* and other magazines, begins with reading advertisements and articles that just happen to mention certain products. Wolf observes that magazines use the pretext of the "credible source," the authoritative voice that pretends to be interested in the reader's welfare but is actually concerned with selling stuff. As Sharon Mazzarella notes in her article, "The Superbowl of All Dates," "Prom-oriented magazines are no different, except that the guides are on how to do one's hair and makeup especially for the prom.... These articles ... make conspicuous references to product brand names so that the reader doesn't inadvertently purchase the wrong brand of hair spray, for example. One can't use just any brand ... to get that 'prom-perfect hair.'"[25]

Before discussing the modern prom magazine further, let's take a look at *Seventeen*'s relationship to the prom and how it has developed through the years. Prom was popular in the 1950s but was decidedly passé in the 1960s, and the publication reflects that. Furthermore, high school students weren't nearly as worldly back then. The April 1961 issue of *Seventeen* has an article about prom themes that lists Alice in Wonderland and Lollipop Hop as two possible mise-en-scènes. (The key to transforming the gym is crepe paper, and lots of it.) There is one prom article in the 1962 issues and none the following year. The April 1964 issue (which cost fifty cents) mentions prom on the cover: "Newest looks in prom, party, graduation dresses," with layouts long on photographs and short on copy. The dresses are puffy, pastel, spaghetti strapped, and very chaste. The only prom article is about themes yet again, this time suggesting the Broadway shows *Carousel, Camelot, Can-Can, Brigadoon* and *Showboat*— an upgrade from the lollipop idea of yore.[26]

The magazine ran no prom articles from 1965 to 1973, coinciding with prom's low point in high school culture. During those years, high school students were painfully aware of the world outside their school walls. Many young men feared the grasp of the Selective Service and the possibility of a stint in

Opposite: "Prom Report" asks "What makes a prom great? What are the best refreshments, the most popular theme?" April 1962 *Seventeen*. Bob Kelly, illustrator (Hearst).

Vietnam directly after graduation. No lollipops for those students, but a dose of harsh reality — the April 1972 cover lists an article titled, "A New Way to Combat V.D."[27]

By the mid–1970s, prom was making a comeback of sorts. The cover of the April 1974 issue reads: "The right dress, the prettiest makeup for prom night," an early reference to the "right" things to purchase, namely, the dresses advertised within. The article "Pastels for Prom Night" is a five-page photo spread with white and African American models.[28] *Seventeen*, which for years had avoided any ethnicity other than white, had finally acknowledged the existence of people of color. (Publisher Walter Annenberg, a Jew, forbade Helen Valentine, also Jewish, from mentioning Chanukah in the magazine. The magazine's photographs currently underrepresent Latinas by about 8 percent, but its ratio of African American to white models is more or less correct.[29]) In the same issue, an article, "Look What We Found, a potpourri of special prom night looks," features flower-printed granny dresses that cover a girl from collar bone to ankle. The gowns are accessorized with shawls, platform shoes and ribbons, and described with several iterations of the word *funky*.[30]

In 1975, the cover copy included "The prettiest prom dresses at a price you'll like" (featuring checkered dresses with eyelets), and the articles include a column by First Daughter Susan Ford, whose senior prom was held that year at the White House. The April 1976 issue says almost nothing about proms. There's one small column advertising a contest for the best prom ideas, with the winner to be announced in the spring of 1977. The contest was apparently a bust; there's no mention of it again. Perhaps the $100 prize was an insufficient incentive. Between 1977 and 1981, there are no prom articles in *Seventeen*, aside from a 1980 opinion piece, "Long Live the Prom: Mocked in the sixties, ignored in the early seventies, the prom is back — bursting with old sentiment and new style." That's the author's contention, but the lack of prom advertising suggests otherwise.[31] The 1982 issue has a photo spread for dresses with a brief introduction that employs the princess theme: "In spring, fancies turn to love — and to prom night, the magical evening when fairy tale gowns and tuxedos change young women into princesses and their escorts into princes."[32] The 1983 issue has a small article about making your own evening purse and a one-page feature about prom dresses ("with star quality"), but the real focus on prom is a two-page ad for dresses from a company called Dance Allure. Between 1984 and 1989, prom disappeared from the magazine, resurfacing in March 1991 in a "Prom Special" issue. The cover of the May 1991 issue fairly screams, "Sex and the Prom — What Really Happens on the Big Night?" which turns out to be a cautionary article about the hazards of jumping into the sack with your prom date.

The breakout year for *Seventeen* and prom advertising was 1992. The May issue's cover article is "Best Prom Ever," and the book is loaded with ads for formal wear, a big change from previous years. So what happened in 1992? There may not be a definitive answer, but here's a theory. Two years prior, Primedia publishing launched *Your Prom* magazine. The publishers of *Seventeen* were determined to be *the* magazine for teen girls; recognizing that they had competition, they set out to meet it head on. By the spring of 1992, prom was a conspicuous theme in *Seventeen*, and its publishers had the advertisers to justify the shift in focus. Hearst publications bought *Your Prom* in 1999 and merged it with *Cosmo Girl*. Hearst folded *Cosmo Girl* in 2008 and bought *Seventeen*. Other

March 1991 *Seventeen* (Hearst).

teen magazines sprouted and died along the way: Hachette produced and then killed *Elle Girl*. Time discontinued *Teen People*. Condé Nast launched *Teen Vogue* in 2001, and it's currently *Seventeen*'s biggest competition. With more than twice *Teen Vogue*'s circulation, however, *Seventeen* is clearly the winner in the teen girl market, perhaps because it's been around the longest and has the most experience covering the prom and teen life.[33] In addition, *Seventeen* appeals to a wider demographic than *Teen Vogue*'s up-market readership. Many of the products featured in *Teen Vogue* are priced out of reach of the average consumer, making it more of an aspirational publication. *Seventeen* features affordable products for a middle-class consumer.

Since 1992, the spring prom issue has been a big draw for *Seventeen*'s advertisers. Once *Seventeen* got into the prom business, there were no holds barred on prom hype. Instead of running ads for prom frocks in April, the magazine started advertising products in March. Many proms don't take place until early June; *Seventeen* made prom shopping a three- to four-month season.

Teen Prom, *Seventeen* and *Teen Vogue*.

March articles (which were really photo spreads) featured Cinderella references: "A dress that would upstage Cinderella herself,"[34] and "Fairy Tale Prom."[35] As the magazine and its advertisers received bigger returns from selling prom items, the look they touted became more elaborate and adult, if not exactly sophisticated. Encouraging girls to look like a cross between a showgirl and a walking chandelier, the magazine promoted "Head to Toe Prom Makeovers," with corresponding advertisements (March 1994). The following years featured "Prom Countdown" (March 1995) and "Amazing dresses, glam hair, perfect makeup!" (March 1996). By 1994, the magazine's editorial content had shrunk considerably, and the book resembled a product catalog. The emphasis on purchasing clothes and items for body enhancement was so bald that by 1996, the March prom issue ran a contest with the come-on, "Meet a *Seventeen* merchandising editor!"[36] The March 1997 issue's cover story is "The Ultimate Prom, the hottest dress, sexiest hair, coolest date!" Note that the boy is last on the list. The book contains some fifty ads for dresses and other products, featuring an eighteen-page ad spread in the middle. There are ten articles total, if they can be called that. The magazine contains almost no text.

Hearst now publishes one spring issue per year of *Teen Prom* and *Seventeen Prom* as marketing companions to *Seventeen*. The 2011 issue of *Teen Prom* is not really a magazine at all but a catalog. There are 500 words of nonadvertising text in the 334-page book, mostly about Lucy Hale, an actress featured on the cover. *Seventeen Prom* has a proper table of contents listing thirty-three articles, which are almost devoid of words and are indistinguishable from the ads. "Ripped from the Runway," for example, is a photo layout of accessories that can be purchased online. The models all look as if they're at least ten years out of high school, which plays to girls' desire to look older. Many of the dresses would seem appropriate on a hooker working a Vegas casino, but not on a girl at a school dance. The editors of *Teen Vogue* agree. Their March 30, 2010, online edition has an article about "slutty chic," asking "Are ultra-revealing dresses sexy or skanky?"

> The new trend has many young girls purchasing dresses that, well, are leaving them practically bare with up-to-there leg slits, plunging necklines and provocative cut-outs — sometimes all in one dress! ... If you're searching for a way to stand out at prom without revealing too much, check out our ultimate prom guide with this season's top dress trends, hairstyles and accessories guaranteed to get you lots and lots of attention — the good kind![37]

That's a good example of how magazines have it both ways. The object of using *Teen Vogue*'s "prom guide," as they call their advertisements, is to get the "good" kind of attention, whatever that means. They conveniently neglect to define its unnamed opposite, bad attention, which could mean anything from obnoxious comments to sexual battery and simply let the reader's imagination run riot. If good attention means that boys look at attractive girls, then what's the point of making a skanky or nonskanky distinction if the eye is drawn to the wearer in either case? It's okay to be sexy, but not too sexy — but who draws the line? Apparently, it's *Teen Vogue,* who claims as its territory not just propriety but taste. Promoting very pricy clothes, *Teen Vogue* "solidifies feelings of economic and taste inadequacy in girls," according to *Branded* author Alissa Quart. "By introducing very young teens to female celebrity and the dressmakers who help create it, these magazines underline that girls are not complete or competitive if they don't wear label dresses at their junior high school dances."[38] Point taken, and it's not just magazines but all manner of media that have familiarized teens with celebrity. Girls feel pressure to look as polished as professional models. Whether skanky or demure, the important thing, if these publications are to be believed, is not behavior but appearance.

Seventeen makes a stab at mitigating their body improvement mandate with an online Body Peace Project that's supposed to support girls with body-related issues. It's essentially a list of awkward self-help mantras, such as "Quiet that negative little voice in my head when it starts to say mean things about my body that I'd never tolerate anyone else saying about me," and "Realize that the mirror can reflect only what's on the surface of me, not who I am inside." Readers can "sign" the page and make vows not to beat themselves up for carrying a few extra pounds or for scarfing down the occasional pizza.[39] The web page is not so much a project as a passing thought. *Seventeen* has also partnered with the makers of Dove soap, linking their site to the Dove Self-Esteem site that encourages girls to "embrace their unique beauty." The site advertises skin care products for girls ages eight to twelve and thirteen to eighteen because it's evidently never too soon to boost self-esteem with items made for one's own demographic segment.[40] Self-esteem messages are a drop in the proverbial bucket compared to the number of ways that *Seventeen* sells an idealized, often unattainable image of young womanhood. As one researcher discovered,

> In the 11 issues of *Seventeen* analyzed, sexuality was visually yoked to particular body dimensions: that of the slender, long-legged, full-breasted girl. While occasional fashion features offered advice on finding clothes to flatter various body types, the linguistic anchors of "sexy" or "hot" were never connected to those possibilities. Instead, "sexiness" was the province of the conventionally slim yet voluptuous.[41]

It should be noted that while *Seventeen*, *Teen Vogue* and other teen-oriented publications are now in digital form, teen girls still buy print. A trade ad put it succinctly with the line, "We surf the Internet. We swim in magazines." As of 2009, teen magazine readers numbered 13 million per month, and *Seventeen* in particular is still going strong.[42] Mindful that teens like their information on a number of platforms, print and online media are now constructed as complimentary sides of the same marketing coin.[43] The 2011 online *Seventeen Prom Guide* merges information and advertising in "advertorials," such as a video clip with a fashion expert who selects dresses for a pair of girls and tells them to be sure to use Venus razors (with a quick cut to a close-up of the product) because this year's dresses are "all about legs." After dressing the girls in extremely tight, short, glittery dresses, she quips, "All you need now is a date," as the girls giggle nervously.[44]

Seventeen's web site gives the viewer an interactive experience. Its *Seventeen Magazine Project* contains a blog by Jamie Keiles, who attended her prom in 2010. Reporting that the prom was her "most intensive and expensive beauty process" so far, Keiles set about preparing herself according to *Seventeen*'s guidelines. In spite of her plea, "Please make me look conventionally attractive," Keiles's salon piled on makeup and hair products. She spent roughly five hours getting ready between salon and home treatments and spent $461.50. (She spent $500 the previous year on her junior prom dress alone.) Her report of the prom is surprisingly honest considering the conventional stance of her web host:

We did all the prom poses with appropriate teenage awkwardness. Prom was at a surprisingly nice country club. When we arrived, everyone was herded up a grand staircase to walk past security so that drunk kids could be weeded out and their lives could be subsequently ruined. Luckily, nobody at the prom got busted. Lots of girls wore looks straight out of *Seventeen Prom*. Tans were orange, makeup was overdone, dresses were skimpy, and boobs were overly prominent. The majority of people looked great, though. Nothing made me feel closer to my peers than grinding to "ABC" by the Jackson 5. Ninety percent of getting ready for prom is for the pictures. Once you actually get to the prom, it turns out that it's a dark, sweaty room where everyone looks less good within 15 minutes of dancing. The room was a sauna of adolescent awkwardness, and we were really sweaty by the end of the evening. Afterward, we headed to a party at Dominique's boyfriend's house, where we swam, talked, and stayed up until 5 A.M. In short, prom was awesome, but one prom per lifetime is probably enough for me. If you are younger than me and you are reading this, I definitely recommend that you go to your prom, but just keep it in perspective.[45]

The people at *Seventeen Prom* were probably happy to hear that they influenced the purchases of Keiles's classmates. But the homogeneous appearance of the prom-goers is in direct opposition to "standing out," one of the most oft-repeated exhortations of the magazine. And as Keiles notes, all the preparation in the world won't keep a girl from wilting once she's on the dance floor.

In addition to *Seventeen Prom, Teen Prom, Seventeen* and its companion web site, *Seventeen.com*, Hearst also publishes a hardcover book, *Seventeen's Guide to Your Perfect Prom: A Planner and Scrapbook*. The spiral-bound tome is a workbook containing lined pages for notes and snapshots. It has several calendars for appointments and prom countdowns. The planning guide is so meticulous it would rival the organizational skills of a NASA mission commander. The book contains advice by experts in fashion, hair, makeup, fitness, skin, flowers, diet and love, the last from a young, good-looking male singer/songwriter. It also has places to swipe samples of foundation, blush, eye shadow, eyeliner, mascara and lipstick so that one's "prom colors" can be revisited at a later date. The message is clear: prom shouldn't be merely remembered — it should be enshrined. Replete with descriptors such as *magical, amazing, exciting,* and *perfect,* the book is distinctly jejune.[46]

Speaking of childishness, anthropologist Margaret Finders discovered that teen magazine reading begins with tween girls, who, sequestered in a friend's bedroom, peruse the pages as a social event. Junior high girls use the delivery of a magazine as an excuse for a sleepover, paging through the book and making comparisons between the models and each other. Asking questions like "Do you think I look like her?" and "Do you think those jeans would look good on me?" girls see the glossies as prototypes of correctness. "See," says one girl, "It shows you what's cool."[47] Appropriating the language in the magazines, girls describe each other as "having luxurious hair" or "skin you

show off your prom style!

There are a million dresses out there, but only one that's
your perfect match. Check out this style guide, and get ready to fall in love.

flirty & fun

STYLE TIP: Play around with color! A super-bright dress is even cuter with contrasting shoes.

cool cinderella

STYLE TIP: Live your fairy-tale fantasies with a frothy, floaty dress. Dainty shoes and jewelry finish the look.

'80s princess

STYLE TIP: Channel your inner Material Girl with black lace and layers. Sexy booties will keep it modern.

dress Sizes 0–30, Xcite, $308, xciteprom.com. **earrings** BCBGeneration, $42, Macy's. **gemstone bracelet** Grayce by Molly Sims, $95, graycebymollysims .com. **pearl bracelet** Lenora Dame, $105, lenoradame .com. **clutch** Coloriffics, $50, coloriffics.com. **heels** Sizes 5–10, AMI Clubwear, $28, amiclubwear.com.

dress Sizes 3–13, Morgan, $130, Sears. **necklace** A.V. Max, $63, avmaxaccessories.com. **earrings** Lulu's, $12, lulus.com. **ring** Fantasy Jewelry Box, $44, fantasyjewelrybox.com. **heels** Sizes 5–11, Pierre Dumas, $48, shoestation.com.

dress Sizes 2–12, Jessica McClintock, $238, jessicamcclintock.com. **earrings** Urbanog, $8, urbanog.com. **cameo necklace** Forever 21, $13, Forever 21 stores. **chain necklace** AMI Clubwear, $20, amiclubwear.com. **bracelet** Urbanog, $12, urbanog.com. **clutch** Coloriffics, $48, coloriffics .com. **booties** Sizes 5½–10, Make Me Chic, $19, makemechic.com.

STILL LIFES: JESUS AYALA/STUDIO D. STILL LIFES STYLIST: CLAIRE TEDALDI FOR HALLEY RESOURCES.

An "advertorial" using buzz words "princess" and "Cinderella" simplifies prom shopping with purchasing information for fully accessorized outfits, March 2011 *Seventeen* (Hearst).

could die for." They even ascribe the editorial copy to the models pictured in the articles. At that age, girls are unable to perceive the invisible adult hand behind the message. Furthermore, tweens can't tell the difference between editorial content and advertising.

> I asked Tiffany to explain about the advertisements in the magazine. She insisted, "There aren't any ads." And she proceeded to prove it to me. Pulling the latest issue of *Sassy* from her notebook, turning from ads to articles through full- and half-page ads, she argued, "This tells you about fingernail polish. This shows you about makeup. This is about zits and stuff. See?" ... While some parents may label teen magazines "fluff," they are neither benign nor neutral. They transport a powerful economic ideology into the lives of early adolescents.... Just as Tiffany's mother described this kind of reading as reading in which "you don't have to think," the girls demonstrate little ability to render such an ideology conscious. When one observes how readily these girls appropriate the words, experiences, and images as their own, one can hardly deny the impact of these texts upon the social construction of self.[48]

In other words, by the time girls reach prom time, they've been thoroughly indoctrinated into a culture that values the external and uses marketing images as a yardstick.

Magazines that promote prom spending depend on two trains of thought. The first is that the prom should be perfect. Unrestrained use of exclamation points and frequent repetition of words such as *glam, celeb, dream, gorgeous, ultimate, amazing*, most of all, *perfect* underscore the necessity of approaching the prom as if it were either a girl's wedding day or a movie premiere. *Seventeen Prom* (2011) exhorts the reader to "Have the Time of Your Life!" and "Be His Dream Date!" Having issued marching orders, the magazine offers a dizzying array of products to accomplish the assigned task. There are, as the cover notes, "896 Ways to Look Pretty!" It's hard to imagine anyone considering more than 1 or 2, but there they are, all 896 of them, in their Photoshopped glory, complete with listings of retail outlets and pricing. As Mazzarella notes, "The rhetorical strategy of these magazines is to build the prom up to be 'the most wonderful night of your life!' All this can be accomplished by using the 'right' hair care products."[49]

The second line of attack is creating insecurity, because without the guiding hand of the magazine, one is liable to commit "Prom Beauty Blunders!"[50] A girl should not even presume to select the proper underwear without the magazine's advice, as "What You Wear Under Your Dress Really Counts!" attests. Furthermore, if the prom isn't perfect, it can only be one other thing: a disaster. There is no middle ground, and articles like "Trauma Proma" make the case.[51] But never fear. Wayward breasts, torn gowns, acne breakouts and other prom disasters can be avoided with careful planning and purchasing, as *Teen Vogue*'s "Prom Countdown" advises — never mind what actual prom-goers like Keiles have to say. In thirty days ("A New Tip Every Day!") one can ward off any mishap.[52] If only it were true. Prom publications sell a promise of perfection that assumes an absolute control of one's body and environment that neither a dictator nor a wizard could pull off.

The girl is even responsible for her date. If he isn't enthralled by her enchanting appearance, if he's uncomfortable in formal wear and awkward posing for pictures, that's her fault. Yet again, the magazines provide the solutions, which tend to run to common sense and basic decency: Don't ditch your date for someone else; if he's from another school, introduce him to your friends; talk to him; don't freak out if something goes wrong.[53]

Prom magazines pivot easily to the other side of the argument:

> "You're so obsessed with making your prom perfect that you've been in a total planning frenzy," the reader is told. She is then advised to "remember the prom doesn't have to be perfect to be fun. Besides, no matter how much you plan, something's bound to go wrong." This is an interesting tactic, since on the next page is a sidebar titled "Prom Trauma Survival Guide" which begins: "It's supposed to be perfect."[54]

Not all girls succumb to the message of enforced perfection, however. Sociologist Nicole Zlatunich studied how teen girls relate to prom magazines. She confirms what others have said: Prom magazines promote an image of perfection that can only be achieved through heterosexual romance and the right products. No girl is ready for the prom until she engages in serious shopping and body improvement. As one girl in her study remarked, "It's like you must be really ugly if you can't get a date for prom."[55] Like Finders, Zlatunich discovered that girls who are younger than the target market read the publications uncritically. High school readers, however, use "strategic selectivity" as they process the meaning of magazine content. Many of the high school girls she interviewed were critical of the magazines' emphasis on romance: "They have all these articles, how to find a perfect date, how to get a date, how to have a romantic time.... I mean what if you just want to go and not have this romantic time? I don't understand that."[56] African American girls were the most discerning readers and were highly skeptical of the notion of a romantic high school dance. These girls took their cues on beauty and relationships from their mothers and grandmothers, not magazines. They were not at all idealistic about boys and did not count on them for romance and intimacy. Zlatunich concludes that high school seniors do not take every word of prom magazines as gospel, but they absorb the messages in varying degrees. Prom magazines don't reflect the reality of proms, but they do provide a frame of reference. Without that, prom would exist in a cultural vacuum. As one girl says, "[Prom] has to look like something we've seen before, you know. Or it wouldn't be, like prom."[57] Magazines aren't the only media that provide a roadmap for prom-goers. In the next chapter, we'll see how other cultural influences prime very young shoppers for prom night.

9. Pint-size Princesses
Prep for Prom

"The plain fact of the matter is that businesses have only two major sources of new customers. Either they are switched from competitors, or they are developed from childhood."

— James U. McNeal, marketing expert

A mere $54.95 will buy a "Crown Package" in a certain salon, which includes "hairstyling, shimmering makeup and nails." An additional $135 will get you the "Castle Package," containing all the above plus several professional photographs in a princess-themed holder, a party dress and choice of accessories. The young lady who avails herself of the salon's "perfect pampering" would be all set for prom, except for one thing: she needs to finish preschool and then continue all the way to her final semester of twelfth grade. The salon in question is the Bibbidi Bobbidi Boutique at the Walt Disney World Resort, where girls as young as three years old can be "magically transformed into princesses," at a variety of prices, plus tax.

Where Disney dares to tread, its competitors rush in. Beauty spas abound for girls who can count their age on one hand. Some salons sponsor birthday parties so the birthday girl and her pals can enjoy celebratory "mani-pedis" en masse.[1] The Texas-based salon franchise Sweet and Sassy will pick up its customers in a pink limo for a "Diva for a Day" or "Party Princess" package.[2] As *Newsweek* writer Jessica Bennett reports:

This is the new normal: a generation that primps and dyes and pulls and shapes, younger and with more vigor. Girls today are salon vets before they enter elementary school.... According to market research firm Experian, 43 percent of 6- to 9-year-olds are already using lipstick or lip gloss; 38 percent use hairstyling products; and 12 percent use other cosmetics.... Today's girls are getting caught up in the beauty maintenance game at ages when they should be learning how to read — and long before their beauty needs enhancing. Why are this generation's standards different? To start, this is a group that's grown up on pop culture that screams, again and again, that everything, *everything*, is a candidate for upgrading.... Forty-two percent of first- to third-grade girls want to be thinner, while 81 percent of 10-year-olds are afraid of getting fat.[3]

Whether Disney leads the culture or follows it is hard to say. It's probably a bit of both, but the "diva-ization" of childhood, as Bennett suggests, is now pervasive. If elementary school girls can be convinced they need cosmetics, high school girls are easy pickings. Teen girls are conditioned to spend at prom time owing to one primary factor: years of exposure to intensive marketing that promotes a narrowly defined feminine ideal. That basic concept can be broken down into its component parts: belief in the necessity of consumer products, female competition, a culture of narcissism and market segmentation.

Girls who want to look like princesses at prom time don't come up with the image all by themselves. They have been raised on all things pink and princess, which is exactly the way retailers want it. By the time girls reach their senior year in high school, they have been sold to every day of their young lives by Disney, Disney wanna-bes, and a million other businesses that recognize a lucrative market. The images of young womanhood that play out at

Dresses for princesses on a budget by Cherokee, the in-house brand at discount retailer Target, 2012.

**Infant T-shirt with Minnie Mouse and slogan, "I'm a total fashionista. I ♥ shopping,"
2012.**

prom time are the result of specific product lines and ad campaigns that have
been researched and tested by the best marketing minds in the business.

No corporation is better at marketing to girls than Disney. Little girls
have proven to be such good customers that the company goes after them (via
their mothers, of course) on day one. Elizabeth Carter, who gave birth in January 2011, was presented with a Disney Cuddly Bodysuit for her daughter
while they were still in the hospital. "It surprised me that Disney was in there
promoting something right as the baby was born," says Carter, "but we figured
as new parents we weren't in a position to turn things down. And I have to
say, Olivia looked fabulous."[4] Carter sums up a familiar ambivalence about
Disney's ubiquity in children's lives. Parents sense something not altogether
benign in the company's aggressive marketing, but are often won over by the
products. Say what you will about the way Disney does business, the bottom
line proves that consumers like what the company sells. Little girls start asking
for specific Disney items at around age three. Disney wants them right from
the cradle, so the company goes to work on mommy before the ink is dry on

Tiny tutu with Cinderella and other Disney Princesses, 2012.

the hospital bill. Disney is developing a full line of baby products such as infant formula that moms currently procure elsewhere, but not for long if the company has its way. Employing a military metaphor, Andy Mooney, chairman of Disney Consumer Products says, "Apparel is only a beachhead."[5]

There is so much potential business in dressing girls up from the get-go that even cottage industries (housewives on Facebook and eBay) find plenty of customers in the wake of Disney's marketing juggernaut. Princess Couture Designs,[6] for example, sells fabric flowers to bedeck the female infant head. No hair? No worries. The bejeweled and beaded blossoms are attached to a colored elastic band for strapping onto a cute, bald pate. The look is reminiscent of the Disney line for infants and toddlers, meaning it's long on shiny satin and shades of pink. The site is one of dozens on Facebook alone with the word *princess* in the company name that sells bling and flash for the preambulatory, preverbal set. Psychology professor Jean Twenge discovered that roughly a fourth of the clothing available for her two-year-old daughter had "Little Princess" on it. Nordstrom carries a tank top retailing at $44 that identifies the wearer as a "Juicy Couture Princess," or as writer Megan Basham notes, "someone whose parents can afford to buy designer shirts that will end up stained with ketchup or jelly."[7] Shoppers who prefer to shop down-market can find a full array of affordable princess clothes at Target, with no extra charge for irony.[8]

If some mothers and their girl offspring go with the princess program all the way from pram to prom, Disney is principally to blame (or thank, depending on your proclivities). Disney's most successful marketing coup in recent years is their princess line of products for girls age three and up. Mooney attended an ice show in 2000 and was fascinated to see girls in homemade princess costumes. The Disney marketing executive did not overlook the obvious gap in the company's product line and went to work immediately on an array of princess items. Mooney commodified Disney's animated female leads (Cinderella, Snow White, Sleeping Beauty, Little Mermaid, et al.) by printing the characters' images on everything from sweatshirts to sippy cups. Those with the funds can transform their kids into princesses by virtue of the 26,000 Disney products emblazoned with the royal title.[9] Very young girls are able to identify the look of each princess (Cinderella is blonde, Snow White is a brunette), but they don't necessarily know the stories. What they do know is that princesses are ultra-feminine (meaning they wear pink and don't make noise or run around), they're special, and they're in charge. In other words, today's tyke in a Little Mermaid tutu is tomorrow's promzilla in a chiffon princess dress.[10] Peggy Orenstein, author of *Cinderella Ate My Daughter*, reports about her daughter, Daisy:

> As if by osmosis she had learned the names and gown colors of every Disney Princess — I didn't even know what a Disney Princess was. She gazed longingly into the tulle-draped windows of the local toy stores and for her third birthday begged for "a real princess dress" with matching plastic high heels. Meanwhile, one of her classmates, the one with Two Mommies, showed up to school every single day dressed in a Cinderella gown. With a bridal veil.[11]

Disney has saturated the market so thoroughly that "princess culture" is part of the collective parlance, as Orenstein soon learned. Dressing up and make-believe are nothing new. What troubles many social critics is that Disney princesses don't actually *do* anything. They're not even especially nice. Writer Mary Finucane noticed that her three-year-old daughter stopped running and jumping when she started wearing the princess get-ups. When she saw her daughter sulking on the steps of their house "waiting for her prince to come," that was the last straw. Fincucane's blog, "Disney Princess Recovery: Bringing

A Disney Princess display at Target in Beaverton, Oregon, 2012.

Sexy Back for a Full Refund," is her attempt to break the hold that Cinderella and her fictional sisters have on little girls.[12] She's up against a lot. Disney is putting its considerable marketing muscle behind a new princess. Sofia the First is the protagonist of a new TV series aimed at children ages 2 to 7, whose real purpose is the spawning of a fresh line of consumer products.[13]

Today's store-bought princesses need only be passive and pretty in pink, a social construct that prom-goers and mothers like Finucane know all too well.[14] The version of "Beauty and the Beast" in Disney's book *12 Princess Stories*, puts a finer point on the options available to potential princesses. The Beast tells the female protagonist, Belle, that she "can go anywhere you like [in the castle] except the west wing,"[15] perhaps a sly reference to the portion of the White House in which the executive branch conducts its business. Whether coded or not, the message in all the Disney princess stories is the same: life begins and ends with a wedding.

Disney purports to give little girls what they want, but critics disagree. As one writer says, "Disney has always viewed children as an enormously productive market to fuel company profits.... Old Walt Disney clearly understood the appeal to innocence as a useful alibi while mining the realm of childhood fantasies in a 'relentless quest for new images to sell.'"[16] Disney's childhood

Young shoppers examine Disney Princess items on a Target store "end cap," Beaverton, Oregon, 2012.

fantasies work their magic on grown-ups, too. The modern bride can have her fairytale wedding, complete with a gown in the style of a Disney princess.[17] If you want the whole monty, you can have your wedding at Walt Disney World or Disneyland with all the princess services (pumpkin coach, anyone?) and "merch" the company is happy to provide.[18] The Cinderella prom dress is merely the halfway point between toddler dress-up and a very real ceremony with serious adult implications.

Disney isn't the only company that jumped on the princess bandwagon. Christian retailers such as A Different Direction carry a line of God's Girlz dolls dressed in spandex and sparkly tiaras. Church-going girls proudly wear T-shirts emblazoned with slogans like "Yes, I am a princess." In an attempt to differentiate the line from secular competitors, the small print reads, "I'm the daughter of the King."[19] Encouraging self-esteem is one thing, but sowing the seeds of narcissism is quite another. A princess item here or there is no problem, but experts have observed that girls who are immersed in princess culture soon demand the privileges of rank. Research has shown that these girls have difficulty later in adjusting to the requirements of teachers, employers and mates who didn't sign on to be adoring subjects.[20] The effect at prom time is predictable: girls with modest means break the bank to dress like their favorite celebrity. Basham writes, "Today, even as the economic crisis continues, many middle-class parents aspire to give their daughters the best of everything, 'the best' meaning the most expensive."[21] As another reporter notes,

Forget keeping up with the Jones'. This year, prom season is all about keeping up with the Kardashians. It's no longer good enough to have a dress that looks like the one Taylor Swift wore at an awards show, teens girls want the same dress, even if it means spending $1,000 or more on their prom fashion.[22]

Girls who find princesses too passive can play with Bratz dolls, which are back on the market after a legal dispute over ownership and provenance. The Bratz characters (Yasmin, Cloe, Sasha, Jade, Dana and Meygan), are edgy little girl/women with a "passion for fashion."[23] The dolls embody a child's view of grown-up success and personhood. By turns athletic, entrepreneurial, artistic, and above all pushy, Bratz dolls are tiny plastic role models for future promzillas. Sasha, for example, is "not afraid of confrontation — she knows who she is, what she wants, and how to get it!" Jade is "always on the cutting edge of cool — the ultimate fashionista!"[24] Marketers of Bratz dolls employ the word *sassy* a lot, which, as Orenstein notes, is kid code for "sexy."[25]

The TLC reality series *Toddlers and Tiaras*, which shows the world of child beauty pageants, lets viewers draw their own conclusions about heavily made-up, sassy little girls. Parents who think their child could win the pageant in a walk can watch with satisfaction and/or envy, and others undoubtedly recoil in horror, certain that they would never tart up *their* daughter for the sake of a trophy. As Orenstein complains, "We're talking about emphasizing beauty and play sexiness to girls two, three and four years old. I don't think you want your four-year-old thinking about sexiness on any level."[26]

The problem with inculcating artifice and superficiality is that there never seems to be a ceiling (or a floor) on it. No look is over the top, no child is too young. There are more and more ways to indulge the juvenile whim every year. Lavish, expensive parties for children are common. Twenge, author of *The Narcissism Epidemic*, cites "the Bat Mitzvah where 'N Sync was the band. In Houston, it's a catered $20,000 pink-themed party for 50 seven-year-old girls who all wore mink coats, like their moms."[27] Some bat mitzvahs, quinceañeras, and sweet sixteen parties are so extravagant that prom night is almost a let-down. After all, the girl is the star of the show in the former occasions, but she has to share the stage with her classmates on prom night. The only way to win the prom night competition is to out-bling the other girls.

My Super Sweet Sixteen, an MTV reality program, showcases the trend of teen narcissism and female competitiveness. The show "features rich teens planning their lavish 16th birthday parties. Each episode features almost every facet of narcissism: materialism, overcompetitiveness, appearance obsession, the quest for fame, manipulativeness."[28] One girl's sense of entitlement was so overblown that she commanded her friends to change clothes, hair and nail polish to suit her fancy. She had final approval on her friends' dates, too. Only the extremely photogenic need apply. As one commentator says, "Their blingy flings are not celebrations of accomplishment; they're celebrations of self.... Each guest of honor is really after one thing: 'I feel famous.' ... Far from joining polite society like the debutantes of the past, the kids gleefully rip through social graces, alienating friends and sacrificing tact."[29] What's worse is that teen viewers don't see the problem. They are not appalled by extreme extravagance and bad manners; they're envious. When one girl's parents give her a car worth $100,000, her friends' response is "I want that car." There is no mention at all of how much college tuition or groceries a hundred grand could buy. Even worse, the parents on the show make the whole spectacle possible. As one mother says of her daughter's demand to cordon off an Atlanta street that provides access to a hospital emergency room as well as the party venue, "If Allison wants it, make it happen."[30] Teen viewers make comparisons between their own lives and media images, often to the detriment of their self-perception. As researcher Debbie Naigle concludes, "adolescents, because they haven't reached the cognitive level to critically analyze and determine reasonable levels of realistic goals, are more vulnerable to media images. They are more likely to take at face value all images and scenarios portrayed in the media."[31]

If girls as young as three see themselves as princesses and if teen girls behave like despots, market segmentation — the practice of identifying and selling to smaller and smaller slices of the population — is partly the cause. Marketer researchers have their business quite literally down to a science.

They have studied the Millennial generation like organisms in a Petri dish and know the differences between what children of all ages will buy and how to make them want what's on offer. In the teen girl market, targeting alpha females is the key. The social leaders in a given high school set the styles.[32] That's just one aspect of the full teen profile that market researchers continually refine. A report from Mediamark Research, for example, breaks down the kid market by age, ethnicity, location, education, income, spending habits and influence on adult purchases.[33] Marketing expert Jason Rivera knows more about what motivates young people than they do: "There are tweens, 8- to 12-year-olds, then you have 13- to 15-year-olds vs. 16- to 18- or 19-year-olds and up. Age 16 is a magic year for a lot of teenagers. They're starting to come more into their own and are looking forward to being older. When looking to motivate the teen to do anything, it all comes down to what are you or the brand going to do for them?"[34] Rivera knows exactly which brands each teen segment finds attractive and can see the next trend on the horizon.

Peter Zollo's book, *Wise Up to Teens: Insights into Marketing and Advertising to Teenagers*, also demonstrates that there's little about adolescents that marketers don't know. He slices the teen market into four types: Conformers, Passives, Edge and Influencers.[35] These categories are merely a jumping-off point for further demographic dissection. The field of market research that Eugene Gilbert pioneered in the 1940s is a full-blown industry that exists to help retailers separate teens from their money. There's nothing inherently wrong with any of that; it's just that the culture as a whole has become fixated on enhanced appearance through consumer products. One mother said of the $6,000 price tag on her daughter's prom dress, "I didn't have the opportunity to wear this type of dress when I was younger," as if spending big were a prize in itself.[36] *Branded* author Alyssa Quart says, "Of course, all of this intrusive marketing would be fine — just the way the shilling game is played at this late date — if it didn't deeply affect teens themselves. The personae, self-images, ambitions, and values of young people in the United States have been seriously distorted by the commercial frenzy surrounding them."[37] As one teen remarked, "The pressure to look amazing on prom night is huge. We want to be like that celebrity [Kim Kardashian] for one day."[38]

Prom marketing begins to take effect during the tween years, 8 to 12. Tweens want to be older. According to Zollo's research, 12- and 13-year-olds want to be 17, those who are 14 to 16 want to be 18, and the 17-and-up crowd just want to get on with it and be adults. "The more you talk to teens and analyze their behavior and attitudes," Zollo says, "the more you begin to understand that they live a step or two ahead of where they really are. They are constantly thinking about their immediate future — usually from a social perspective. Because they are surrounded by older teens, they see the benefit of being older."[39]

Having been bombarded for years with images of what a proper prom-goer should look like, a teen shopper has been conditioned to spend well in advance of the big night, economic status notwithstanding. As a matter of fact, a low economic level is no barrier to excessive spending. Conspicuous consumption is greater in poor neighborhoods than in affluent ones. When it comes to keeping up with the Joneses, a show of relatively pricy, small stuff can compensate for a dearth of big-ticket items. In other words, depending on one's neighborhood, it can be more important to look well-off than to be well-off, which is why buying an expensive prom dress can seem like the natural thing to do.[40]

Teens themselves make it easy for marketers. Ignored during the economically stressed 1970s and '80s, teens grabbed marketers' attention again in the 1990s with the advent of the Millennial cohort. One important event was the release of *Titanic* in 1997, a movie that drew teen girls to malls and theaters in droves. Marketers woke up to the presence of an unprecedented number of young spenders. "Characterized as 'America's most free-spending consumers,' numerous articles in the mainstream and trade presses were quick to reference an increasing amount of statistical information detailing teen spending."[41] Millennials like to shop. It's not as if marketers need to twist any arms. Trends and brands are particularly important to this generation, which benefits retailers. As expert Pamela Danziger explains,

> There are any number of reasons the teen and tween market is appealing to retailers and apparel marketers. Their bodies are growing and changing, thus creating a dependable repeat business as kids outgrow their old clothes. Their tastes and styles are also changing at a split-second pace, which predisposes this market to be continually on the prowl for the next trend look. The teen market is expected to grow 37 percent faster than the total U.S. population through 2008, thus based on sheer numbers alone they are an attractive niche market to target the future.[42]

If corporations, market researchers and media don't make the prom dress sale, a final push from schools does the trick. High school administrations are now partners in the prom marketing game, soliciting corporate sponsorship and using class time to sell clothing. Some high schools offer elective courses in fashion marketing and merchandising, and the final project is a prom fashion show. New Trier High School in Winnetka, Illinois, teaches an apparel marketing course that's as popular with boys as girls. The course is designed to teach "business and marketing aspects of merchandising, specifically how the production, distribution, and promotion of the goods and services in fashion and retail are developed and delivered."[43] The culmination of the course is a prom dress fashion show and charity event to supply prom dresses to low-income Chicago students. The course syllabus contains material from *Ad Age*. Savvy Millennial teens learn how to sell clothes while getting an inside peek at the industry that courts them as customers.

Local retailers are only too happy to help high schools stage fashion shows. It's a sure-fire way to present their products to potential customers. Enlisting popular girls to model the garments adds an extra helping of fashion-forwardness to the items on view. Fashion show production is promoted as a learning experience, which is fair — a successful, well-run show is a feat of planning and organization. One blogger suggests that representatives from limo companies, hair salons, florists and accessory shops be included to make short presentations.[44] Fenton High in Fenton, Michigan, has a full prom expo. Promoted as a "one-stop shop" for prom, the expo showcases dress and tux retailers, photographers, beauty salons, limo services, florists, tent and table rental companies and souvenir suppliers. In a nod to academics, the event is billed as a fundraiser for the school newspaper.[45]

When high schools are strapped for prom funds, they go to businesses for sponsorship. Corporate logos in public schools are nothing new; they appear on vending machines and sports fields. The Los Angeles Unified School District, to name one, is planning to plaster logos all over its schools in exchange for desperately needed cash.[46] A corporate presence at the prom is merely an extension of a practice that's already well established. Jersey Village High in Houston offers levels of prom sponsorship. The Gold level will set a business back $2,500, and allow the sponsor to display banners, flyers and coupons at the dance. For $500, you can be a White sponsor and have your business mentioned in all prom correspondence. The Cypress Falls Prom Project (also in Houston) offers T-shirts with your company's logo for distribution to all prom attendees for a Golden Eagle sponsorship of $1,500.

Prom marketing is inescapable. Like it or not, high school kids are going to know what's hot and what's not for prom. Prom becomes more like a wedding rehearsal every year. (The 2012 special prom issue of *Seventeen* refers to invitations as "proposals."[47]) The lure of a grown-up, dress-up evening has become irresistible to many teens. While teens enjoy the preview of adult life, some adults are taking a nostalgic look back. A recent trend in nuptials is — wait for it — the prom-style wedding.[48]

10. Prom and Profits

"Between tickets, attire, shoes, accessories, flowers, limousines, photographers and after-parties, the average family with a high school student attending the prom spent a whopping $807 this year, according to a recent survey by Visa."

— CNNMoney.com, June 16, 2011

High hopes are in the air at prom time, but who knows how the winds of fortune will blow? The night could be a smashing success or a humiliating disaster — for the service providers and retailers, that is, who rely on prom night for revenue. Prom is not kid stuff for businesses that make as much as 20 percent of their annual income during the season. Limo companies, photographers, makeup artists and service people of all sorts are linked in a web of consumer and business-to-business prom night commerce.

Clothing is the most obvious must-have consumer item. A Google search for "prom dress" turns up more websites than rhinestones on a tiara. The number and variety of garments that are available with a mouse click is overwhelming. Whether tight, short, flouncy, elegant, plain or fancy, demure or scandalous, there's a web page with dresses for every size, shape, taste and pocketbook. There are dozens of dress makers in the prom business, and many online retailers feature the same manufacturers. Terani, Clarisse, Jovani, Tony Bowls, Faviana, Mori Lee and Jasz are a few of the well-established brand names. Terani packs advertising buzzwords into their pitch: "Red carpet glam meets chic affordability with the lavish styling of Terani prom gowns. Celebrated for their unique spin on elegant evening wear, a Terani Prom Dress is the ultimate fashion-forward standout for the fashion-forward teen."[1] Some sites' inventories contain everything for the well-prepared girl, and then some. Promdressshop.com, for example, sells double-stick tape to keep a strapless bodice from migrating southward. If that doesn't provide enough protection against a wardrobe malfunction (a phrase now used without a trace of irony), there's a glue that adheres fabric to skin. ("It stays!") The under-developed teen can correct Mother Nature with silicone self-adhesive bras (formerly known as "falsies"). The site also offers slips and evening gloves, both "scrunchy" and straight. The vendor does other retailers a favor by insisting that the properly attired prom girl purchases the following items in addition to a dress ("Make sure you have it all!"):

- Shoes
- Undergarments
- Earrings
- Necklace
- Bracelet
- Temporary Tattoo
- Shades
- Handbag
- Body glitter
- Eye jewels
- Tiara
- Toe ring
- Garter
- Shawl
- Gloves
- Diamond lip sparklettes
- Dual eye shadow
- Belly jewel
- Belly chain[2]

A shopper could easily forgo all of it except the dress, shoes and underwear, but retailers are not in the business of encouraging simplicity.

The savviest retailers are connecting to teens where they live — on their smart phones. National retailers such as David's Bridal have been in the prom business for years and have become adept at marketing to teens. The company runs print ads in February telling girls to text them with PROM, which gives them "content" (ads) on their cell phones about the firm's offerings. Ad recipients are encouraged to connect to a special mobile-ready website, which lets them vote on their favorite dress out of five displayed onscreen. Creating active consumer involvement is always good, and the voting results give the company a crucial, timely look at which styles will move off the racks. "David's Bridal was able to gain access to insight that would not otherwise have been available until they were in the middle of the season," says David Geipel, CEO of Qwasi, the company that designed the mobile marketing campaign for David's Bridal. "They very successfully polled the tastes of their customers going into the season. That gives them the ability to react and confirm their

Cocktail-length dresses, the popular style for spring, 2011.

marketing mix."[3] Geipel designed the mobile campaign to accommodate cell phones with a variety of capacities and functions. One important component is the store locator, which works off a user's ZIP code. Girls who voted on their favorite dress were texted a thank-you note that included the location of the nearest store.

David's Bridal is on their game, but other retailers lag behind consumer interest. Bill Tancer, an expert in online marketing, thinks that many retailers are missing the boat:

> When we stumbled upon the pattern for prom dress searches, one of the first things we did was to talk to a number of our department store clients. A good portion of them said they plan their marketing for prom dresses in March, April and May. They don't do anything in January. Our data highlighted that consumer searches spiked in January, yet all of the brands weren't doing advertising until later.[4]

That said, there are plenty of department stores that offer party dresses on their sites year-round. Walmart.com has several dresses for under $20. Neiman Marcus can put you into a frock for $360 and higher for homecoming, a winter formal, prom or any other dress-up occasion.

Prom dresses at Davidsbridal.com, 2012.

Tuxedo sales and rental outlets have traditionally been mom-and-pop businesses, but national firms have made big inroads into the market in recent years.[5] In 2001, the Gingiss Formalwear Company, which opened in Chicago in 1936, bought Gary's Tux, a California firm that started in 1933. Operating a total of 439 stores in 34 states, the Gingiss Group was sold to After Hours[6] in 2003 and sold again a few years later to Men's Wearhouse.[7] Mitchell's Formalwear is another company with national aspirations. After Mr. and Mrs. D.Q. Mitchell's homegrown Atlanta business was taken over by majority shareholders in the mid–1990s, the new management set about expanding. Well established on the Eastern Seaboard, the company is looking at loca-

Dress shoes for rent at a Los Angeles–area Men's Wearhouse, 2011 (J. Malone).

tions west of the Mississippi. Dick Weir, vice president of marketing, says, "It's time. This is one of the most fragmented industries in the world."[8]

The big retailers are growing, but small tux outfitters are keeping pace by providing extra customer service.[9] Richard Turner is a small business owner in Jacksonville, Arkansas. His TuxDeluxe store is the only place in town for tux rentals, but he's not taking any chances. To ensure that the local boys come to him at prom time, he showcases his clothing at the high school fashion shows. Balky prom dates don't even have to visit his store. Turner makes house calls.[10]

TuxTown in Carson City, Nevada, has a tux mobile, which is a rolling sales room, dressing room and photography studio. As their website states,

Let our No Stress Tuxedo Express come to you! We want your experience to be as hassle-free as possible, which is why we offer our mobile tuxedo service. Tuxedo Hotline's No Stress Tuxedo Express is fully self-contained and equipped to handle on-the-spot fittings and alterations if needed.[11]

Tuxedos and "formal" high-top, vinyl sneakers at a Los Angeles–area retailer, 2011 (J. Malone).

Peer-to-peer sales pitches are the most effective of all, so TuxTown offers $10 off the rental fee for every referral. Steer enough customers their way, and your tux is free. There are many such mobile tux services around the country, providing not only suits but shirts, ties, vests and even kilts.

Retailers find out what manufacturers are producing by attending trade shows. The National Prom Market, held yearly in Chicago, is an enormous showcase for dozens of exhibitors and is strictly for the trade. (The expo management requires three pieces of identification certifying retail bona fides.) Held at the downtown Merchandise Mart, the expo gives buyers a timely look at dress lines by Jovani, Alyce Designs, Terani and dozens of others. Trade shows are highly competitive, and exhibitors go all out. The expo is a three-day event featuring "the latest styles from the industry's top names in prom, pageant, quinceañera, special occasion and accessory resources."[12]

The National Prom Market is a closely guarded business-to-business event, but there are plenty of expos for retail customers. Prom and Pageant Expositions is touted as "the largest and only nationally touring expo in the U.S. aimed at teens." The show promises to "immerse" teens in the clothing, cosmetics and financial services (budgeting advice) they need for prom. The expo, which in 2007 appeared in San Francisco, Los Angeles, Houston, Chicago, Atlanta and New York, included celebrity guests, musical performances from "national recording artists," fashion shows, contests, prizes, shopping sprees

Charlotte's, a small retailer in Portland, Oregon, advertises its 2012 prom dresses.

and workshops on hair and makeup. The promoters note that "Our online newsletters and blogs will be written by teens for teens. The event is in large part by teens for teens. Our overall goal is to empower, engage and entertain teens everywhere."[13] That's a lot of responsibility to put on the backs of prom shoppers, but that kind of hype is par for the course.

There are smaller expos, often organized by an enterprising retailer on a local level. The Dream Prom and Social Occasion shop in Easton, Massachusetts, is a dress outlet and couturier (dresses custom designed and sewn) that sponsors fashion shows and expos. Owner Fallon Branco pulls in a few other local business owners to stage the event at a nearby mall. A lucky attendee wins a "Prom Prize Pack" that includes tux rental, gift certificates and a photo portrait session.[14] As previously mentioned, some prom expos are homemade affairs. Rancho Bernardo High in southern California held an expo in 2011 in the school gym that drew over 1,000 visitors. Students modeled clothing from participating retailers and some 50 vendors pitched in, offering discounts on limo service, flowers, hair and makeup.[15]

If a traditional prom dress doesn't suit, a girl can always use her home improvement skills. Duck brand duct tape may seem like an unlikely prom sponsor, but the maker of this handy, fix-all tape hands out scholarships each year in their Stuck at Prom contest for the most creative dresses and tuxes made

Prom dresses featuring metallic fabric, flounces and ruffles. Portland, Oregon, 2012.

from their product. The first place winner receives $5,000. Not bad for a product that costs less than $10 per roll.[16] Featuring colors like electric blue and chrome, a contestant can be as festive as she likes. Sarah Lyons, a teenage seamstress in Wyoming, Michigan, entered the contest to earn money for college. "I learned [sewing] from my mom and grandmom when I was like 10, and I just gradually got better," she says. "I thought about my dad and grandpa because they tried to fix everything with Duck Tape. It was complicated trying to figure out how to make [the dress] but once I figured it out, it was easy." Sarah's creations, a matching gown and tuxedo with black, green, white and red tape, made the 2011 contest's top ten, netting her a $500 cash prize.[17]

Before anyone buys a prom ticket or hires a vendor, they have to know the particulars of the event and which businesses serve their area. That's where printers come in, who garner their annual share of high school and business-to-business trade. Proms.net, one of many similar sites, is an online vendor that supplies printed material for proms. High school committees can go online and order "Prom Invitations in many styles with a full range of imprint colors, a great selection of imprint fonts, and an all new selection of prom artwork." Offering an emailed proof and downloadable PDF, the site promises that "This system will virtually eliminate the disappointment of misspelled names or other errors." The site also offers posters, napkins and laser printed signs. They supply "memory books" (photo/scrapbooks) directly to prom committees and prom photographers.[18] Printers also make business cards that feature the prom services of photographers, makeup artists and limo companies.

A big online prom vendor is Stumpsparty.com, whose inventory includes table skirts, confetti, vases, lights, centerpieces, banners, backdrops, napkins and catering supplies — everything for dressing up a venue for a formal dinner dance. Prom photographers also make use of this vendor and others for portable photographic backgrounds. Americanprom.com carries all of the above plus curtains, chandeliers, arches, columns, borders and set pieces in a variety of themes. In a bit of a stretch, they suggest that the prom committee "Honor Democracy with an Egyptian Themed Prom." Concocted during the "Arab spring" of 2011, the copy reads, "Plan a unique prom that is relevant to current world events! An Egyptian prom theme can be real history in the making for your school!"[19]

Stumps, American Prom and similar companies sell prom favors. Apparently no modern prom is complete without souvenirs. Picture frames, key chains, photo albums, clocks, cell phone straps, candles and embossed candy boxes are some of the keepsakes that go home with prom attendees. It would seem that nothing is controversy-free in today's high schools, and that goes for prom favors, too. Glassware is a common item provided by party favor vendors, and some schools have taken heat for handing out engraved champagne flutes, wine and shot glasses. "I don't think it's the brightest thing," says Police Chief Norbert Micklos of Ohio Township, who makes presentations every year at prom time about the hazards of drunk driving. "It sends the wrong message." The students at Avonworth Senior High respectfully disagreed and ordered shot glasses for the boys and champagne flutes for the girls imprinted with the date of the dance.[20] A principal in Pennsylvania was surprised when the purchase order he signed reading "prom souvenirs" turned out to be shot glasses. Souvenir suppliers do work-arounds by filling glassware with votive candles and calling the items candle holders.

The tradition of prom dates exchanging corsages and boutonnieres is still in place, and florists don't wait for prom time to start marketing their goods. The trade publication *Florists' Review* urges shop owners to stay in touch with potential customers all year long.

> Get involved with school clubs and activities. Sponsor a team or a club. Place ads in school papers and yearbooks. Present in-school floral demonstrations. Distribute

coupons. Get on the prom committee. Two or three weeks before the proms take place, arrange with school officials to set up booths to show examples of your prom creations.[21]

Shirley's Flowers and Gifts in Rogers, Arkansas, draws customers to the store with a fun pre-prom event. Filling the store with pizza, cookies, beverages, candlelight and music, owner Jo Buttram encourages teens try on corsage samples while advising them on choices and taking orders. Her average sale is $50, compared to the $15 to $20 price point charged by other florists. "It's all about show and sell," Buttram says. She also offers a wide variety of bracelets, and her staff of fifteen "very naturally" ups the order by suggesting the addition of "rhinestones, pearls or something custom made." Buttram often attracts more than 100 teens to the store with her enthusiastic promotions. To keep up sales momentum, Buttram sponsors an after-prom photo contest on Facebook, where the prom-goer with the most "likes" receives four movie tickets.[22]

Heather McVay, owner of Bellevue Florist in Nashville, cleverly uses teens' online behavior to spread the word about her shop. "Tag me," is the magic phrase that exposes her wares to thousands of high school students. Prom-goers take their own photographs during the evening and post them online. A tag connects viewers of a given page to McVay's Facebook page. She uses prom photographs as her profile picture, changing the image daily and thanking those who post on her wall. Her sales increased by 40 percent the year she caught on to the power of tagging a Facebook photograph.[23]

Jim and Elaine Mills capitalize on prom season by using the millennial group's penchant for customizing. They offer "design consultation" appointments at their store, The Basket Tree Florist. Teens girls book with Elaine early and often to ensure that their prom flowers complement their dresses and are one of a kind. "I just love to talk with the girls and have them describe what they want," Mills says. "It stirs my creative energies and I work very hard to make sure they have something that is very special for their prom night."[24]

Makeup artists and hair stylists get their piece of the prom action by featuring prom night on their web pages. Rouge, a Boston cosmetic store, says on its website, "Let a Rouge artist have you looking even more glam for your big night out! We can create any look you want from super natural to prom diva, it's your choice. We do lashes, too, and have lots of styles to choose from."[25] False eyelashes have made a comeback recently after their height of popularity in the 1950s and '60s. Online tutorials abound for those who have difficulty applying the springy little critters. As makeup artist Kandee says, "If you're ever going to wear fake lashes, prom is the time to slap a pair of false lashes on!"[26]

A big part of prom fun is the trip to the venue, and whether clients are flush or flat broke, a proper prom includes a limo ride, according to limousine companies. The rationale for spending as much as $100 per passenger can be summed up in two words: drunk driving.[27] No parent wants their child involved in a car accident, and the fear of drunkenness on the highway is the main driver (pardon the pun) of prom limo bookings. Better to pay a sober professional than risk a tragedy. Prom-goers have had bad experiences with limo bookings on occasion. One hears nightmarish stories about dirty, banged-up vehicles and nasty drivers, but all in all, limo companies comport themselves expertly. The limo industry encourages parents and students to do their homework by asking lots of questions: Does the driver have a chauffeur's license and is the company fully insured? How old is the vehicle, and can they see it before they book? Will there be a written contract, and what are the required deposits and fees? What is the customary tip, and what is the hourly charge for extra stops? A thorough discussion before booking protects the clients and the limo company, which is why the industry welcomes close scrutiny.[28] Houston Limo Service tells prospective customers to shop around with at least four companies.

Car services routinely encounter a number of occupational hazards and problems, but ferrying a passel of giddy teens carries its own set of headaches. For every prom booking, limo companies have to sell themselves twice, first to the teens and then to their parents. "You are now selling to the 16- to 19-year-old age range," advises *LCT* (Limousine Charter and Tour) magazine. "At the same time, you are also selling your services to the parents of the 16- to 19-year-olds. The students still want excitement, lights, loud sound, new, fancy, unique, and cool chauffeurs. However, the parents are looking for safety, reputation, reliability, rules and a fair price."[29] Some of the usual problems that arise are disputes about hourly minimums and whether the tip is included in the fee. Excited prom-goers often miscalculate their ability to pay for a limo and cancel at the last minute.[30] The biggest problem by far, however, is youthful misbehavior. Driver Andrew Doyle says that most kids are just having good, clean fun, but some girls who are subdued in front of their folks go a little wild as soon as the car is out of sight of the house. That's why he and many other drivers insist that the driver/passenger partition stay open. One thing he absolutely will not tolerate is boys being disrespectful to their dates. If he hears misogynistic name-calling, he pulls over, takes the offenders out of the car and gives them a fatherly talking to. The embarrassed boys always return to the back seat with an apology on their lips.[31] If a driver finds drugs, alcohol, tobacco or weapons, he'll phone the parents and end the party right then and there. That's why "Prom Promise" agreements are standard in the industry. In addition to specifying prohibited items and behaviors, the contracts mandate hefty fees for clean-ups (for sick passengers, usually) or any rips or stains on upholstery.[32] "[Students] are told they will be treated like young adults if they act like young adults," says Craig Mehlsack, owner of Top of the World Limo in Suffolk County, New York. "Last year I had only one problem. Those customers were taken home within five minutes. Everything is in our contract."[33]

Most limo companies make it through prom season with little difficulty because they are experienced and professional. In a competitive market, they have to be. However, anecdotal evidence suggests that the limo business may be recession-proof. "May. Wow. What a month," limo operator Brad Gregory said of the 2010 season. "I never in my wildest dreams would have believed how well prom season [went]. If we're still in a recession, I sure can't tell."[34] On the other hand, James Romero of In the Scene Limousine in Tempe, Arizona, says, "Families are tighter on what they want to spend for the kids for prom." Another owner mentions that although many customers are shopping around for the lowest price, his bottom line has increased because more people want to book.[35]

For many companies, the economy is less of a problem than scheduling is. When all the high schools in a locale hold their proms on the same night, limo companies are hard pressed to accommodate. "Years ago, you had proms on Thursdays, Fridays, and even Wednesdays in the month of May and June," says Jim Powers, owner of Allstar Limousines in Farmingdale, New York. "The business was well-diversified over the months. But now it comes down to one weekend [in] June."[36] The upside to the scheduling crunch is that more prom-goers are booking far in advance to ensure they have their ride of choice. Powers also sees the need to diversify his fleet. The eight- to ten-passenger limo is becoming obsolete. "Everyone these days wants either an SUV or a bus," he says. "These vehicles run from 18 to 22 passengers in size. It's as if the whole prom class wants to go in one vehicle. Much of it has to do with celebrities using SUVs and everyone wanting to follow that trend."[37] Companies that can handle large parties capitalize on the millennial preference for doing things in groups and are able to offer a reasonable per-person rate.

Perhaps the biggest trend in prom limo service is the party bus. A $1400 a night charge may not sound cheap, but the buses hold up to 34 people and provide a rolling party venue. Rip City Party Bus and Portland Party Bus are two companies serving the Portland, Oregon, metro area that promote themselves as the most fun, safe way to travel. In a conveyance featuring flat-screen TVs, laser lights, high-end audio systems and dance floors, teens can start the prom before they arrive. That's the come-on for the kids. For the parents, the issue is safety, and Portland Party Bus has this to say:

Passenger Safety is the Highest Priority — And parents have no fear. Should you have any reservations about sending your children to their prom and fearing what might happen on a party bus, don't worry. Portland Party Bus has everything under control.

We offer an on board security system insuring [*sic*] that everyone will remain safe and sober. We are also fully insured and meet all safety standards throughout the industry.

We value the safety of our passengers. Everyone at Portland Party Bus is committed to providing safe transportation so that parents can feel at ease about their teens being in the hands of our trained professional chauffeurs.[38]

The company requires its teen passengers to sign the usual good behavior pledge, in this case, the "I Promise Teen Limousine Contract." Each passenger and a parent has to sign a log and list a cell phone number for emergency contact. It's tricky business being the party bus and the safety bus company at the same time.

Once the kids arrive at the prom, the first stop is the photographer. Experienced prom photographers know how to set up an efficient, assembly line operation to move the kids through the process and wrap up the job. The set-up is all important. Forrest and Pat Davisson are a husband-and-wife team who have shot prom photos for years. They rent backdrops that they hang on portable poles, steam at the venue and tape to the floor to eliminate wrinkles.[39] Establishing one lighting set up is crucial. It would take far too long to change the lighting for each couple.[40] Pat collects the money and fills out order envelopes. She goes down the line, straightening ties and tucking in bra straps. She also helps couples choose a pose from a chart so that there's no dithering in front of the camera. Pat always enjoys prom bookings. The clothes are fun to see and the kids' enthusiasm is infectious.[41] There are many husband-and-wife teams in the event photography business. Photographers who don't work with their spouse usually have an assistant. Some photographers used to retouch prints and send them out several days after the event. Now, with digital photography and portable printers, pictures can be delivered on the spot. Reorders can be handled through websites and downloadable files, and most photographers offer a variety of packages and prices.

Teens with money to burn and high-maintenance egos can hire their own paparazzi. Companies such as Celeb-4-A-Day and Paparazzi for Hire will provide any combination of photographers, videographers and faux bodyguards you care to employ. Fees range from $300 to $3000 for a fake "celebrity stalking." The "paps" will follow you to the door of the prom venue while calling your name, asking "who" you're wearing and snapping your picture. Impressing one's classmates while blinding them with high-powered flashes is just the thing for making a grand entrance.[42]

No person is as crucial to the success of the actual dance than the DJ.

Apart from showing off one's outfit and socializing, the point of the prom is dancing. Whether the crowd wants to get on the dance floor and stay there depends on how well the DJ controls the collective mood and energy level. The first job is securing the booking. DJ Brian O'Connor sends out postcards to schools in his area and meets with prom committees. He plays song samples on his laptop computer, which is loaded with selections. If the committee wants to know if he has a particular tune, the answer is "Sure." He also presents testimonials and dresses nicely to impress school administrators.[43]

Drawing from contemporary and oldie Top 40 lists, DJs shape an evening according to the BPM, or beats per minute, of each song. The arc of an evening's program is generally slower to faster, with some variations along the way to keep things interesting. The DJ may dedicate certain songs to personalize the event, or to get everyone on the floor for a slow dance. Experienced DJs have a play list in mind, then adjust the order of songs according to the feel and flow of the evening. Well-known songs are recommended. As DJ Jason Weldon says, "If your crowd has to stop and try and recognize your next song, find the beat and start dancing again, you have failed." He recommends taking notes about which songs work best for future reference. "Every time I start a party, I watch people," he says. "I watch to see who is tapping their fingers, their feet. I know they're doing this subconsciously, because they're enjoying what they're hearing. This is my first great clue to what I'll be playing that evening — in fact, I have a good idea of how I'm going to start my set."[44] Weldon starts and ends each set with a slow song, something in the 90–100 BPM range. From there he builds the tempo to the 135–140 range. "I want them to start excited, but I want them to finish wild," he says. "Every good DJ should know what makes his crowd move. The worst feeling in the world for a DJ is playing a song and feeling the energy leave the room ... you can almost feel the negative word-of-mouth you're generating."[45] A successful DJ, according to Weldon, is one who keeps the party-goers on the dance floor.

Some DJs hand out request cards before the prom to ensure that they have the tunes a particular group wants to hear. This also prevents scrambling to accommodate on-the-spot requests. Catering to the girls' taste is important. They are the ones who really want to dance and get the party going. Boys mostly want to stand around and look cool. DJs are often responsible for presenting the prom queen and king and playing whatever theme song the committee has chosen. The biggest pitfall is playing songs with inappropriate lyrics, hence the invention of the national Do Not Play list, compiled by long time DJ Ric Hansen, who says,

Over the past several years, dances have become a challenge for school administrators. Lyrical content in hit dance music has become increasingly raunchy. Teen dance trends have thrown up red flags and administrators have become frustrated with how to deal with it. At the same time, school personnel have had even less time to devote to the dance program. One of the catchiest, most danceable song of the year (2011) has probably one of the worst messages for pre-teens and teens. [The kids] are singing it, you know. Maybe not in front of you. But the song was heard at least every 90 minutes on radio most of the summer, and I guarantee every kid in America knows and can sing every word.[46]

Hansen is talking about a sexually explicit song that references whips and chains, but he could be talking about any number of contemporary songs. His Do Not Play list (on the website for School Dance Network) is a generous gesture to his competition, to ensure that no DJ loses a repeat booking by playing a suggestive or profanity-laden song. He has a chart that lists the exact problem with each offending song and suggests clean, edited versions when available. This description of one song is unequivocal: "Known nasty rap guy is the featured artist. Makes sense that this song is like most of the rest of the Gangsta rap stuff he's known for. Laced with most nasty words you can think of. Avoid this garbage at schools." He says about another song, "Search out the clean version with no guns, no bullets and no violence, and this one is safe to play."[47] Hansen also sells paraphernalia for chaperones, including T-shirts and buttons emblazoned with "Freak Patrol — Violators Will Be Removed."

Assuming that prom-goers make it through the formal festivities problem-free, the next stop is the after party. Some schools plan their own event in conjunction with parents and community sponsors. The object is to keep kids substance-free and off the street on a late night out. It's not as easy as it sounds. Everything costs money, and a successful after party isn't cheap. Few schools have the budget for such a party, so first a committee must be formed to plan the event and find sponsors for funding. There are liability issues, so it's prudent to consult an attorney and an insurance agent. Perhaps medical waivers should be signed by all attending students and their parents. The venue may need security. The parking lot may require a patrol. The event should be chaperoned; the chaperones should have a background check. There's registration, payment and dress codes to consider. Then there's food, decorations, music, games and activities. After parties often feature video booths, psychics, hypnotists, casinos, bands and laser tag. Raffle tickets are a big draw, especially if the prizes are iPads, Playstations and concert tickets. It all costs money. An after party can be more complicated than the prom itself.[48]

Just like the prom, the after party has to have a theme. Companies such as Americanprom.com sell full sets of decorations for after parties as well as the prom. There seems to be no end of themes with accompanying set pieces, center pieces, banners and drapes: western, featuring cowboy boot mugs and a brown and yellow color palette; 1950s theme with soda shop backdrops; Hawaiian luau with leis and floral banners. The list goes on.[49]

The after party is such an entrenched tradition that it's spawned a number of businesses that provide the full experience. After Prom in New York City is one such company. Basically a night club for minors, After Prom hosts dances for a younger crowd that wants to feel older and connected to the world of celebrities:

> Whatever happens After Prom this year, it has to be good. If you're looking to have one of the best nightlife experiences on one of the most important nights of your life, you'll be excited to know that Playhouse is hosting After Prom Parties in New York City.
>
> Prom only comes around once in a lifetime, and while the majority of the focus revolves around your activities after the big dance, Playhouse will be one of the most anticipated events of the year. Just picture yourself rolling up to the velvet rope in a stretch limo with your closest friends for a grand entrance. When it comes to an all-out party experience, you can't get any better than this! Special VIP packages and Ultra VIP Tables will be available to up the ante on your night.
>
> Want to know what it's like when Diddy comes to Playhouse? This will give you the authentic feel as official Promtime DJ's will be serving up the best in Hip-Hop, house, Top 40 and more. No matter what musical stylings you're into, rest assured that you'll be dancing from beginning to end. There's nothing like creating endless memories that'll last a lifetime, and this year Playhouse is ready to be your ultimate After Prom party solution.[50]

Promtix.com is another company that provides a late-night club experience for teens. To reassure parents, they post this on their website:

> We do not mix teenager's [sic] with the general public. We work extremely hard to provide safe and secure environments for prom-goers who otherwise would be driving around NYC with nowhere to go. Please assist us and your children by directing them to only the most professionally organized events in NYC.[51]

Whether helping kids get dressed, groomed or delivered safely to the event and home again, there's money to be made from prom night. It's not even necessary to sell a product or a service. Just ask Patty the Prom Pro, who bills herself as a "prom consultant." Her website and blog provide space for prom advertisers, but she doesn't actually sell anything to site visitors.[52] Whether actual, virtual or theoretical, the big high school dance is an easy math equation: Prom equals profit.

11. Fantasy Prom

"Senior year. Second semester. Six weeks until graduation. Six weeks until the end of high school. Three weeks until Prom. For Nova Prescott, the counting down had started a long time ago — back in freshman year, on the very first day of school."

— Ellie O'Ryan, *Prom*[1]

Proms are so emblematic of the teenage experience that almost every story set in a high school has a scene at the big dance. If you're writing about adolescent awkwardness, sexual awakening and social competition, prom has it all. At the prom, every clique is represented. Every social struggle is acted out and won or lost in a scene of high drama. The quest for the perfect fairy tale ending is resolved in triumph or tears.

The literary category known as young adult (YA) fiction is full of prom stories. The genre is becoming more popular all the time — sales have grown by 25 percent since 1999.[2] YA fiction tells stories tailored to the teen demographic and portrays situations that are both familiar and strange. Everything from an ordinary school day to an historical event to an imagined future are fodder for the teen reading market. YA books allow teens to examine issues that concern them: their role in life, whether they can make a difference, coping with hardship and setbacks and, of course, relationships. The genre can be dark, edgy, funny and profane. Writing partners Katie Crouch and Grady Hendrix note that "Writing YA as an adult is a chance to rewrite being a teenager. It's an opportunity to relive high school in a more perfect manner. Who doesn't want to be 16 and living in a mansion? And hooking up with the hot guy?"[3] Crouch and Hendrix often add mystical touches to their stories — a Southern debutante has supernatural powers, for example. According to literary agent Miriam Kriss, the paranormal craze in YA fiction has been going on for about a decade and shows no sign of slowing. Publishers are buying all things angelic, dystopic, fanged and furry, and all of these elements are showing up at fictional proms.[4]

YA book covers are often illustrated in this graphic style.

YA and proms are a natural fit. Many novels with a prom have conventional story lines with no supernatural elements, but virtually all of them have an overlay of fantasy: the homely, awkward girl who gets the ideal guy in the final scene (Cinderella, in other words); the antisocial girl who is swept up in a wave of sudden, unexpected popularity; the lonely, insecure girl who discovers that her biological father is a movie star. These things don't usually happen in real life, but that's the charm of the prom. It's a big, broad canvas that can accommodate any girl's projection of the perfect high school moment. Because proms have become so identified with girls, prom fiction invariably centers on a female protagonist. Basically, every prom tale is a fantasy. The reality of proms is usually too mundane to make for good storytelling. In real life, girls get dressed, they attend, they go home, and life goes on. Fictional proms end in a transformation. The girl matures into a woman in the space of the evening, or she finds her path in life, or she finds her permanent prom date, say, a hunky vampire who will never grow nose hairs or a pot belly — and, more to the point, who pledges his undying devotion.

Creating subdivisions of prom tales is a somewhat arbitrary exercise, but for the sake of discussion, I'll create two categories: the usual Cinderella fantasy — unlikely girl gets the great guy (or its converse, the alpha female sees a disreputable boy in a new light) — and paranormal fantasy, which includes vampires, werewolves, demons, telekinesis and time travel. In the next chapter, we visit the dark side. Here, we'll look at the usual fantasy prom as portrayed in print, television and film.

Writers of YA fiction, television and film scripts aren't trying to break new ground when it comes to portraying the prom. No matter how fantastic they make the set-up or resolution of the plot, writers rely on prom stereotypes to make the story relatable for young readers and viewers. Prom is a framework for further romanticizing an event that has already taken on mythic proportions. Prom stories are heightened portrayals of real life in the way that operatic singing is a theatrically heightened way of expressing dialog. The paradox is that prom is considered to be a quintessential high school experience, yet it's completely outside the parameters of a normal high school day. In some respects, the prom is an anti–high school experience, a dress rehearsal for adulthood without the burden of adult commitments. In most cases, there's no babysitter to pay and ferry home at a reasonable hour. Teens at the dance *are* the babysitters, and this is their chance to act like the grown-ups they'll become some day. In other ways, the prom is a distillation of high school. The big dance is the last opportunity to raise one's social standing, even a score, revise one's persona or hang out with a long-standing peer group now on the verge of dissolution. Those are the story lines that arise in many a prom story.

In actuality, the high school routine is often quite dull. To hold the reader's attention, fictional proms have to be more exciting than the real thing. That requires two elements: a protagonist with a compelling outward struggle and an equally compelling inner struggle. YA writers understand this and use the world of their protagonists to fill out the rather spare dramatic question of "Will she find an acceptable date?" Prom stories often deal with life outside of school. The themes of loneliness, aimlessness, insecurity, absent parents, eating disorders, financial pressure and impending adulthood pop up with regularity. The real drama is the emotional arc of the protagonist because it's a foregone conclusion she'll find the right guy by the last page. A comparison of prom stories reveals some striking similarities. Here's a look at a few representative novels, films and TV shows with an eye toward their common and disparate elements.

Alyson Noel's novel *Art Geeks and Prom Queens*[5] contains a number of familiar components, starting with a protagonist named Rio. (Writers of prom fiction tend to go for quirky names.) Her story is that of the outsider, a familiar archetype in YA fiction. Rio is struggling. She misses the friends she left behind at her old school. She feels physically awkward and resents having to remake herself to fit in with the cool kids at her new school. An aspiring photographer (apparently the career goal of choice for YA heroines), she thinks of herself as an "art geek." Her mother doesn't understand her reluctance to fit in and wants her to be popular. Pretty much any teenager who has ever changed schools can relate to Rio's problems.

Noel takes this well-known set of adolescent difficulties and magnifies them. Rio's mom isn't just fixated on appearances. She's a former "almost super-model." Her father isn't just a successful defense attorney, he's famous.

> I'm sixteen but almost seventeen, named after a Duran Duran song.... My mom dated one of the members for three weeks back when she was a model, but she's very vague about which one. Still, sometimes I fantasize it was the really cute one and that he's actually my real dad, and that any day now he'll come claim me and take me away from this crazy house. My real dad is "very busy making money for my mom and me" ... but he probably travels more than a rock star, and sometimes I think Larry King and the camera crew at CNN get to talk to him more than I do.[6]

Rio isn't just tall, she's model material herself:

> I pull my zipper all the way up, making sure my chest is completely covered, since in the last year it's gone from nonexistent to Jessica Simpson proportions, and I'm not entirely happy about it. Not to mention the five-inch growth spurt that has me clocking in at just under five feet ten, and my new shiny straight teeth no longer covered in metal braces. I mean, this is what it must feel like for those *Extreme Makeover* contestants. Only I didn't ask for any of this. And it might sound crazy, but I was actually way happier as a short, chubby, acne-splattered, flat-chested dork.[7]

Noel lets the reader pity and envy the narrator on a number of counts: Rio has a dad who cares about her, but whom she rarely sees. She has a mom who looks great superficially but who abandons her emotionally. She misses her old school, but her new California school is in a location as close to a fantasy as an American high school can get. Rio is dissatisfied with her body, but she's clearly a gorgeous specimen. The reader can identify with her self-identification as a geek and make a favorable comparison to her physical gifts at the same time. Apparently being tall, blonde, big-busted and even-toothed is not all it's cracked up to be. The reader, who is more likely to be "a short, chubby, acne-splattered, flat-chested dork" — an average teen girl, in other words — can enjoy a bit of schadenfreude while still identifying with the smart, artistic, self-aware protagonist. The story is largely about the travails of beauty and unexpected popularity, problems that most teen readers would be happy to tackle. To the protagonist's credit, she struggles with the significance of her good looks and artistic tendencies. "And then it hits me: My dad's a brainiac geek, but who did he marry? Another brainiac? No! He married the prom queen!!!!!!"[8]

A big party stands in for the prom in this story, but the concept of *prom queen* runs throughout. Is it better to be smart or pretty? The answer, according to this story, is that it's best to be both, but pretty certainly doesn't hurt, especially in high school. Rio confronts a number of other problems along the way to self-acceptance: drug use, sexual pressure, phony friends, bulimia and, most of all, parental neglect. Even the villain of the piece isn't really bad, she just lacks adult guidance. These are issues with which most teen girls have a passing familiarity.

In *Will Work for Prom Dress,*[9] author Aimee Ferris mines some of the same territory. In the story, the first-person narrator with the whimsical name is Quigley, who also wants to be a photographer. Her friend has the glamorous mom, in this case, a well-known fashion designer. In YA fiction, modeling, designing, show business and celebrity are often merged into one vaguely outlined career track.

The absent dad is also the best friend's, and the big revelation in the story is that he's a movie star. Glamorous moms and missing dads with new, younger wives crop up with regularity in prom stories, the former playing to the adolescent need for fantasy and the latter referencing a situation in which many teen girls find themselves (minus the movie star component). Writers of YA fiction address the real problems of their teen readers, and with a divorce rate of 50 percent in the United States, living with a single parent definitely makes the list of teen concerns. Statistics show that two out of three marriages ending in divorce have minor children in the home.[10] The YA character who struggles with an absent father is often a surrogate for the reader.

Quigley is as self-aware as Rio, if not as open-hearted. Her triumph over her classmates, according to the custom of the genre, is dating a young man who is well out of high school. Quigley is the character that many teen girls are in their own minds: too cool for school. She plans an "anti-prom party" at her house but attends her school dance anyway because her talented boyfriend makes her a great dress. She and the rest of her prom night foursome view the scene with detached amusement:

> The hall looked more like a wedding than a prom, with white twinkly lights covering the walls and dripping like icicles down from the ceiling and chandeliers. A long aisle, surrounded by round candlelit tables with red rose centerpieces, led up to a dance floor in front of a stage. We posed for a group shot beneath the cheesy rose heart trellis backdrop and headed in to snag a table.[11]

At the end of the story, Quigley wins a full scholarship to the Rhode Island School of Design. The prom, as it turns out, is a footnote in Quigley's life. For the character, the real action has nothing to do with high school. As in the real world, life is up the road in the unwritten future.

Nicolette is the heroine of *Top Ten Uses for an Unworn Prom Dress,*[12] another story featuring father/daughter estrangement. As in Ferris's story, the dad has a new wife and child, and Nicolette feels unwanted and abandoned. Her dad's departure caused severe financial hardship for her and her mother, so Nicolette purchases her prom dress from a vintage store. Her date cancels, hence the unworn dress of the title. The dress itself is a character in the story, and like many actual high school girls, Nicolette fetishizes the garment, trying it on repeatedly in the solitude of her room:

> The Dress was pink organza, called "cotton candy" by the owner of the vintage clothing store where I found it. Strapless, the top almost looked heart-shaped from the way it was tapered in at the waist, and the fabric was embroidered with tiny roses that covered miles and miles of crinoline.... Now, think what you will, but the word "magic" did come to mind. What it did for my curveless, shapeless figure was otherworldly.... Without hesitation, I'd forked over every last cent of the money my grandmother had left me. And for what? So The Dress would hang behind my door like last year's backpack? ... Or for moments like this, when I zipped myself inside the pink perfection and gazed into the mirror in secret admiration.... Why was I torturing myself this way? That prom was ancient history.[13]

Nicolette is cute but not beautiful — just good-looking enough to be a YA narrator with whom the reader can identify. In addition to a hostile relationship with her father, she's in a continual verbal sparring match with an older boy, her best friend's brother, who turns out to be (no surprise) her ideal prom date. On her way to the conclusion, the author explores the themes of envy, popularity, revenge and competition.

In Abby McDonald's *The Anti-Prom*,[14] yet another character is estranged from her father. Jolene is the outsider character who attends prom without a date but with a boatload of attitude. Her divorced dad has a new wife and a set of twin babies that always come before Jolene and her needs. She's a lot like Quigley: a seventeen-year-old girl whose self-aware, snarky attitude is a bit too knowing to be credible. She's one of three narrators. Bliss is the popular girl whose date hooks up with another girl. His perfidy elicits the lament known to many actual prom-goers: "It was supposed to be freaking perfect."[15] Meg is the unpopular sad sack whose mother died and left her emotionally adrift. This story is structured in the reverse of most prom books, starting at the prom and leaving it behind after the first twenty-five pages. It's really an up-all-night tale in which each character attempts to even a score and in the end realizes that there was no score in the first place. The popular girl concludes prom night happily single, the outsider makes her peace with the world, and the sad girl winds up with the usual fictional first prize, a college boy.

The Anti-Prom is an examination of high school stereotypes. All of the stories are about rejecting the high school value system of superficial popularity, sexiness and scoring boyfriends while avoiding a reputation for sluttiness. True romance inevitably triumphs, which means rejecting the noisy jock for the quiet, soulful boy. It's the reticent, artistic one who invariably sees what's underneath the heroine's surface, although her surface qualities are in play for most of the story. Skillful authors pull off a neat trick by creating

narrators who are often too articulate and analytical for their age but who resonate with young readers. Every girl wants to be witty and hip in her own
mind while fitting in with her classmates. Identifying with the narrator allows
the reader to indulge in a bit of no-one-understands-me adolescent angst along
the route to a well-dressed happy ending.

Not all prom stories have a protagonist with a big problem, but the ones
without this component tend to lack dramatic tension. *Prom Crashers* is one
such story that starts with the usual conundrum: "Prom was in less than a
month, and Emily Bronson still didn't have a date."[16] Traveling the well-worn
narrative path of girl finds boy, girl loses boy, girl finds boy again, Emily goes
to every prom in town in search of the boy whose phone number she lost.
She finds him eventually and forges a bond of true love, an obvious turn of
events, but readers may not find the effort worth it.

Ashley, the narrator in *Prom* by Laurie Halse Anderson,[17] refers to herself
as "normal" throughout the story. That's a fair description if "normal" means
aimless, more conversant with detention than homework and prone to risky
behavior such as getting drunk late at night with strangers on a playground.
The story starts with the theft of the prom fund by the math teacher, which
puts the event in jeopardy. Ashley doesn't much care, which makes it hard for
the reader to care. Her studied detachment represents a certain facet of the
teen psyche, but the lack of a driving motivation for the character enervates
the story. All prom stories are ultimately the same: The girl has to make it to
the dance and have a really great time or a bad enough time to ignite emotional
growth. For the story to work, the prom has to matter.

Prom Anonymous,[18] by Blake Nelson, is another story with three protagonists. Told in the third person, the characters are more fully developed than
in the books described so far. The plot is very simple: Three girls decide to
triple date for the prom. The beautiful one is sexually active — the detailed
description of quick, unsatisfying backseat sex is believable and unusual for
YA fiction. Her horn-dog boyfriend makes out with another girl at the dance,
which sparks her realization that prom is about celebrating high school with
her entire class, not just the big man on campus. The Latina character is beset
by prejudice and a longing for the school tennis star, who has problems of
his own: He suffers from mental illness, a very real but unusual subject for a
prom story. The geeky girl is more or less coerced into attending. Her blind
date turns out to be (again, no surprise) her soulmate. In YA fiction, Cinderella
is the girl with no social skills or fashion sense who winds up with a prince
of a fellow.

One prom heroine deserves a special mention: Margarita is the title character of *Fat Hoochie Prom Queen*,[19] a rollicking, funny story by Nico Medina.
Margarita, a former child actress, cuts a social swath through her Orlando high

Art Geeks and Prom Queens, Prom (based on the Disney movie) and ***Fat Hoochie Prom Queen.***

school. She has a copious capacity for booze, food and partying. At five foot ten, 200 pounds and counting, she swears like a longshoreman. Medina goes to the outer, more mature edge of YA fiction with Margarita, who has two bouts of blackout drinking and in one scene wakes up on a football field in her grass-stained party dress next to an empty Krispy Kreme donut box. The fantasy elements are a fabulous high-rise condo owned by her gay best friend's wealthy mom, as well as the mom herself, a permissive socialite who hosts a big senior class party.

Fat Hoochie Prom Queen is a revenge tale. Margarita used to be a Disney actress, but she lost a career-making role to her rival, Bridget, who also wants to be prom queen. In a satisfying twist, neither of them is crowned, and Margarita eventually realizes that Bridget's life as a teen star is no picnic. It's a rare prom story that talks about the reality of show business instead of the supermarket tabloid version.

Speaking of show business, Disney has a repertoire of prom stories all its own. *Prom,*[20] a 2011 Disney feature film, is another examination of high school stereotypes, listed in the opening voice-over by the protagonist, Nova: "High school. It happens to everyone: athletes, overachievers, drama queens, misfits, jokers." The movie takes us through the ups and downs of representatives of those groups and ends at the dance, as traditional prom stories do. The movie and the book (a scene-for-scene novelization of the screenplay) make much of the big "ask," or romantic invitation. Nova, who belongs squarely in the overachiever camp, meets cute and is paired with the school bad boy,

Prom Crashers and Laurie Halse Anderson's ***Prom.***

who is neither actually bad nor a poor choice for prom date. Disney, which makes its money by staying in the middle of the road, culturally speaking, is not about to break the mold here. Nor does it hurt that the actor playing the role has cheekbones that could hold up a building. In fact, the fantasy element of *Prom* (the movie) is its cast of conventionally pretty actors. Firm of body (although some look to be well into their third decade) and symmetrically featured, these young actors look as if they stepped out of an Abercrombie and Fitch catalog. The movie ends with the two leads locked in a clinch on the dance floor. The culmination of the story is their first kiss, to which every prior frame of the movie has led. That's the "happily ever after" of teen fiction — not the "I do" of adult romantic comedies but the chaste lip lock that signifies every teen girl's wish: popularity, sexual attractiveness, emotional and sexual safety, emotional fulfillment and that *je ne sais quoi* that exists in the realm of teenage romantic fantasy. Although the movie has all the requisite elements of a conventional prom story, it did poorly at the box office, grossing $10 million against an $8 million production budget, a weak result for a studio used to much bigger profits.[21] Perhaps the straightforward story was too simplistic for today's young movie-goers. However, the film did have one particularly memorable line, spoken by the class wit: "Prom is the Olympics of high school. Three people have a good time, and the rest of us have to live on with shattered dreams."

High School Musical 3: Senior Year[22] is another Disney film that features a prom. It could be slotted in the supernatural fantasy group, but musicals are so much a part of American popular culture that no one is surprised when characters break into song. One of the big production numbers, "A Night to Remember," cleverly portrays high school boys' resistance to dressing up, girls' insistence on dressing up and the fun that ultimately ensues. The film made a respectable $42 million on its opening weekend, proving the value of high-energy storytelling with superb movement and music.[23]

The Suite Life on Deck is a Disney Channel TV series (2008–2011) about twin boys who receive their high school education while living on a cruise ship. The prom episode[24] gave the director an opportunity to move the characters around the set in a more creative way than usual and add a little extra energy to a weekly formula.

Saved by the Bell[25] is another kids' show set in high school. Portraying familiar types such as the straight–A student, the fashionista, the jock and so on, the show had a couple of prom episodes in its four-year run (1989–1993). The senior prom show, which was aired toward the end of the series, romantically matches the characters appropriately and concludes with some long-awaited kisses for the girls in the audience who had crushes on its cute male stars. The episode is notable for its western hoe-down theme, which includes two valuable components for its writers and producers: Jeans and plaid shirts are far less budget-draining than formal wear, and square dancing allows for some humorous moments as the lead girl is whirled away from the lead boy every time he tries to talk to her.[26]

Another example in the high school TV show subgenre is the prom episode of *Glee*.[27] Dramatizing all the usual sturm und drang about who shall attend with whom and the ruthless jockeying for prom queen, the fictional high school class crowns a gay male character as queen, causing momentary consternation followed by thunderous applause. A couple of lines of dialog sum up the traditional prom philosophy:

> You can get married as many times as you want. There's only one junior prom.
>
> I just wanted to be Cinderella, just for one night. Isn't that what prom is supposed to be about?[28]

The episode highlights how the prom can either solidify one's social standing or provide an opportunity to change it. All the pre-prom anxiety of selecting the right clothes, corsage and so on is realistically shown, bursting into song notwithstanding. The prom scene itself is an excellent portrayal of an actual dance with both slow and up-tempo numbers.

Episodic television makes frequent use of the prom. *Dawson's Creek*[29] had three prom episodes in its six-year run (1998 to 2003). In the episode "The

Anti-Prom," a character has "the prom sex talk" with her date prior to the evening, in which she solemnly informs him that he will not be getting laid on
prom night, at least not with her. She then berates him after the dance for
not attempting to get jiggy with her, the male writer's concept of a fickle teen
female's mindset. The episode features couples talking in hushed tones about
"our relationship" as they confer in two-shots, tight photographic framings
of two actors, often from the neck up. The actors speak their lines earnestly
and then walk away in sadness or outrage to argue again later. One episode
contains the line that's spoken verbatim or paraphrased almost every romantic
dramedy ever made: "Go get her. You'll regret it if you don't."[30] The show
was a prime time soap opera for young people. Its prom episodes were chances
to make the interactions of the characters a little more intense than usual and
allowed the costumer to adorn the uniformly good-looking cast in gorgeous
clothes.

One Tree Hill[31] is another nighttime soap aimed at younger viewers. Its
story lines are melodramatic. In the episode "You Call It Madness, But I Call
It Love,"[32] a character answers the door in her prom gown, expecting to see
her date, and is instead punched in the face by her maniac stalker. He proceeds
to inject her with a sedative and tie her to a chair in the shadowy basement,
where he continues to torment her. Help arrives in the form of a female classmate, who manages to stab him with an enormous kitchen knife. In a sub-
sequent scene, the girls arrive at the prom, apparently having refreshed their
hair-dos and makeup, just in time for the victim to be crowned prom queen.
The series had three prom episodes before its characters graduated and moved
on to story lines about post–high school life.

In the "Losing My Religion" episode of *Grey's Anatomy*,[33] the characters
are coerced into attending a prom held in the hospital (the show's setting) on
behalf of a well-connected patient. The prom itself figures very little in the
story, but once again, the attractive actors look more polished and done up
than ever in their well-tailored formal wear. In a scene reminiscent of *La Bohème*,
one character cuddles her recently deceased lover's body while wearing a stun-
ning, floor-length mauve gown.

There are many more books, TV shows and movies about proms, but
we'll end this discussion with two that are clearly in the Cinderella mold: The
film *Pretty in Pink*[34] is a story in which the lead character, Andie, is her own
fairy godmother: She sews the titular pink chiffon prom dress that's featured
in the final scene. She's a poor kid from the wrong side of the tracks, and
suffice it to say that the snobby Prince Charming of the piece sees her true
worth in the end. The ending kiss takes place in a parking lot, a small injection
of reality in a light, romantic confection.

Never Been Kissed,[35] a 1999 movie starring Drew Barrymore, takes the oft-told tale and gives it a few original twists. Barrymore's character is the awkward ugly duckling who goes undercover to report on the doings of the modern high school. At first repeating the fashion and friendship mistakes of her own high school experience, the character gets a makeover from her brother (standing in for the fairy godmother) and falls for the prince, or in this case, the high school English teacher. Bonding over a love of literature, they have an emotional scene at the ball (senior prom). It's the prince who flees in this telling, but Barrymore gets her man, declaring, "Find out who you are, and try not to be afraid of it," whatever that means. Not that it matters. The final kiss ensues, and that's what the Cinderella/prom story is all about.

In the straightforward prom fantasy, all endings are happy. The obstacles along the way tend to be recalcitrant adults, balky boys, lack of funds or self-esteem. But what if Prince Charming is undead? What if Cinderella is dead and doesn't know it? As we see in the next chapter, not even the Grim Reaper can defeat a determined girl on prom night.

12. Surreal, So Real

"You guys are going to have a prom if I have to kill every single person on the face of the Earth to do it."
—*Buffy the Vampire Slayer*, season 3, episode 20, "The Prom"

Prom night has finally arrived. The decorative lights are twinkling, the fountain is gushing, the bucket of pig blood is in the rafters and the vampire hunter has a sharp wooden stake tucked into her garter. It's just another senior dance at Horror High in the land of paranormal proms. If there are two things that go together like teenagers and proms, it's teenagers and horror stories.

From Stephen King's *Carrie* to the *Prom Night* movies, the usual princess types are turned into wallflowers and the queen of the dance is the spawn of Satan. Vampires and demons can be darkly romantic — just the ticket for teen girls — whereas bloody violence is often a draw for boys. If you combine gore and romance, you've got a winner. There are no limits on what can happen in an author's imagination, and the prom is fertile ground for teen fright night. No one knows that better than YA writers such as Stephenie Meyer and Kim Harrison, who have been combining stake-outs with make-out sessions to critical acclaim and enormous sales figures. The short story collection, *Prom Nights from Hell*,[1] for example, demonstrates that the evil perpetrated by prom-goers is good fun and good business.

In "The Exterminator's Daughter,"[2] Mary doesn't want to go to the prom, but she has to. Her best friend is attending with a dishy vampire named Sebastian Drake, who happens to be the son of Dracula. Mary's mom, an exterminator of evil creatures, was turned into a vampire by Dracula (he lives!), and the only way to turn her back into a human is to kill the count himself. Dispatching Drake, Mary reasons, will draw Dracula out of hiding. That's the plot. The *story* is Adam's attraction to Mary. She's like no other girl in his posh Manhattan prep school, and he's been intrigued every since he saw her in history class. The combination of the heroic and quotidian is what makes this story an engaging read.

The Saint Elegius Prep prom committee really outdid themselves this year. Securing the four-story grand ballroom at the Waldorf Astoria was a feat all its own, but transforming it into such a sparkling romantic wonderland? Miraculous. I just hope all the rosettes and streamers are fire-proof. I'd hate to see them go up in the flames that are bound to appear when Drake's corpse begins to self-conflagrate after I stab him in the chest.[3]

Not even the threat of having her throat torn out can dim Mary's attraction to Adam. After she dispatches Drake, she and Adam decide that Dracula (and her mom) can wait until the dance is over. Prom only comes once.

"The Corsage"[4] is a retelling of the horror classic, "The Monkey's Paw."[5] A faded corsage stands in for primate digits in this story, in which our protagonist makes an ill-fated wish: "I wish for the boy I love to ask me to the prom."[6] He does so, painting "Frankie, will you go to the prom with me?" on the town water tower. Then he falls to his death — the classic horror twist on the adage, "Be careful what you ask for."

In "Madison Avery and the Dim Reaper,"[7] the title character wants a ride home from the dance. Who knew her soul has been listed for culling by the handsome stranger who lures her into his car and flips it over an embankment? Madison wakes up in the morgue in her torn and bloodied prom dress, not quite dead but definitely not alive. There's life after high school, but not for Madison.

Miranda, the protagonist of "Kiss and Tell," wouldn't mind going to the prom, but she's having an awful time managing her superpowers, which emerged in middle school.

She still remembered the exact moment she realized that not everyone heard the things she heard, that she wasn't normal. She'd already spent the first half of her seventh-grade year at Saint Bartolomeo School — the part after the screening of the *Your Body is Changing: Womanhood* video — puzzled by all the changes they didn't list, like uncontrolled bursts of speed and randomly crushing objects you were just trying to pick up and hitting your head on the ceiling of the gym when you were doing jumping jacks.[8]

It doesn't help that Miranda has to spend prom night guarding an ancient being who inhabits the body of a boy-crazy girl, or that the only thing she has to wear is her red, white and blue roller derby costume. She represents every teen girl who can't get it together socially but knows how special she really is.

In "Hell on Earth,"[9] a demon disguised as a high school girl wreaks havoc on the prom, causing break-ups and arguments wherever she goes. Fortunately for the prom-goers, Gabe, a half-angel, is also at the dance. His presence drains the evil right out of the girl, proving that there's nothing as compelling as a cute boy with dreamy blue eyes and angelic parentage.

The stories in the collection run from whimsical to scary, and the one common thread is the prom. Each author has an entirely different approach to the prom story assignment, which demonstrates the versatility of the prom as a narrative backdrop.

For sheer staying power, no prom story of the dark variety beats *Carrie*. First published in 1974, Stephen King's novel is still in print, the latest edition coming out in 2011.[10] The 1976 movie,[11] starring Sissy Spacek in the title role, is a classic of teen horror flicks. The Broadway musical based on the film (1988) is notable for being one of the biggest flops to ever stink up the Great White Way, a true horror story for its investors. You can't keep a good creep show down, though, and the musical was reworked and revived in March 2012, receiving a lukewarm review in *The New York Times*.[12] *Carrie* is Cinderella for sadists — the story of a downtrodden girl who gets a shot at a happy ending only to suffer a horrible humiliation that triggers a disaster.

Carrie is a lonely girl who lives with her religious fanatic mother. She is the school scapegoat with telekinetic powers, who makes objects explode when she's angry or upset. She's invited to the senior dance out of pity and is crowned prom queen, only to be doused with pig blood in her brief moment of glory. Ever put-upon, even Carrie has limits. Covered in blood, she telekinetically destroys her school, her town, most of her classmates, her mother and herself.

King developed the character based on two of his real-life classmates. In a new introduction for the 1999 paperback edition, King writes,

> Tina was pudgy and quiet, so backroad you could cry. There is a goat in every class, the kid who is always left without a chair in musical chairs, the one who always winds up wearing the KICK ME HARD sign. This was Tina.... Sandra lived about a mile and half from the little house where I grew up.... I was struck by the crucifix hanging in the living room.... Until I saw that hideous, dominating Cristo — the impaled figure on the cross running blood in freshets from hands and feet and side, eyes upturned in a grisly combination of agony and compassion — I never understood how religious [the Irvings were] or how strange. That religion was part of what kept kids away from Sandy. As with Tina, there was something else as well. Something that broadcast STRANGE! NOT LIKE US! KEEP AWAY! on a wavelength only other kids can pick up.[13]

Is there a place at the prom for the odd girl out? The answer according to King is a definitive "no." Prom is a night for fitting in, not for letting your freak flag fly, especially if that flag has warned people off ever since the first grade. King gets at something fundamental about the social dynamic of high school. The pressure to conform runs headlong into the urge to establish a distinct self-identity. Teenagers, especially in the Millennial age, strive to be unique, but if you're too different, woe betide you. King (and others) don't

view childhood as a time of innocence. It's a kid-eat-kid world in which cru-
elty runs rampant, but be careful who you persecute. That strange-looking
girl in the ill-fitting clothes may be more than capable of retaliating. Messing
with her at the prom might be a capital offense.

The novel's title character is an unlovely creature, sweat-stained, bovine
and clumsy. King makes it easy to pity Carrie but not to like her. Her telekinetic ability is fascinating but not attractive, and there's no love lost for the
character when she meets her demise. The Carrie of the motion picture is an
altogether different person. Spacek was a luminous young actress who had
not yet achieved stardom when she played the role, but a big career was clearly
in her future. Photographed to appear almost translucent, Spacek, whom the
camera "loves," in the parlance of the industry, brings an otherworldly quality
to the character. It's her psychological strangeness that alienates her classmates,
not her striking good looks. Spacek's inchoate animal terror at the sight of
her own blood sets the tone for the rest of the movie. The film opens with a
scene about a girl who doesn't know what menstruation is and a group of mean
girls who have fun at her expense, and it's the scariest part of the film. The
special effects at the end (doors slamming, flames bursting, knives flying) are
almost laughable in comparison. It's Spacek's commitment to the material that
saves the movie from risibility. The opening shower scene and the pig blood
drenching at the end bookend the story, lending a whole new meaning to "the
curse," and underlining how humiliating bodily functions can be for adolescents. Not for nothing do the fear and promise of sex trigger her latent powers.
Her mother, played to a fare-thee-well by the redoubtable Piper Laurie, rails
against the prom as a sinkhole of evil, and she's right. By the time Carrie is
through, the school is a hellscape. If the story has a moral, it's "Be careful who
you pick on."

Stephenie Meyer's *Twilight* series is another story that's had big success
in print and onscreen. The prom scene in *Twilight* is a relatively small part
of the saga, but it sets up the next installment and has all the requisite ingre-
dients for a teen female fantasy. Bella, the heroine, is yet another outsider.
Transplanted from sunny Phoenix, she starts anew in drizzly Forks, Washington, where she meets her handsome classmate Edward, who happens to be a
vampire. Romance and adventure ensue. Bella's something of a pain, but
Edward understands her. At the end of *Twilight*, the first book in Meyer's series,
Bella finds herself at the prom.

> "I brought you to the prom," he said slowly, finally answering my question,
> "because I don't want you to miss anything. I don't want my presence to take any-
> thing away from you, if I can help it. I want you to be *human*. I want your life to
> continue as it would have if I'd died in nineteen-eighteen like I should have."
> I shuddered at his words, and then shook my head angrily. "In what strange par-

Carrie, Twilight, Prom Nights from Hell.

allel dimension would I *ever* have gone to prom of my own free will? If you weren't a thousand times stronger than me, I would never have let you get away with this."[14]

Poor Bella doesn't want to spend time at a boring high school dance. She wants Edward to turn her into a vampire. Edward saves the evening with a romantic declaration, and Robert Pattinson, the actor who plays the role in the movie, smolders appropriately, especially for a guy whose body is supposed to be room temperature.

"Bella." His fingers lightly traced the shape of my lips. "I *will* stay with you — isn't that enough?"

I smiled under his fingertips. "Enough for now."

He frowned at my tenacity. No one was going to surrender tonight. He exhaled, and the sound was practically a growl.

I touched his face. "Look," I said. "I love you more than everything else in the world combined. Isn't that enough?"

"Yes, it is enough," he answered smiling. "Enough for forever."

And he leaned down to press his cold lips once more to my throat.[15]

Fans of the book had high expectations for the movie. As one reporter notes, "Not since Harry Potter has a book-to-film journey inspired so much enthusiasm — or so much anxiety."[16] Fortunately for the filmmakers, they seem to have adapted the book satisfactorily and cast the right actors. The movie opened in the number one position on its first, crucial weekend, netting 36.1 percent of the total domestic box-office take.[17]

Ordinary, good-looking high school boys don't stand a chance anymore. A beating heart is no help at all in the competition to date the prettiest girl in class. Buffy the Vampire Slayer kills "vamps," and like Bella, her boyfriend is undead, too. Writer/director Joss Whedon created the character for his 1992 movie,[18] but Buffy really took off as a cultural phenomenon in the TV series that ran from 1997–2003. The prom episode was one of the series' most memorable.[19] Buffy attends alone, having been dumped by her handsome vampire boyfriend, Angel, earlier in the day. Buffy bucks up as vampire slayers tend to do, and dispatches the demon who threatens to ruin the prom. "I'm over the whole 'Buffy gets one perfect high school moment' thing. But I'm certainly not going to let one subhuman ruin it for the rest of the senior class." Her fellow seniors reward her with a "Class Protector" award, saying "We don't talk about it much, but it's no secret that Sunnydale is not like other high schools. A lot of weird stuff happens here." Weird, indeed. Buffy receives her due, and as a final fillip, Angel shows up in a tux just in time for a slow dance, and Buffy has her perfect high school moment after all.

The show was popular because it had something for everyone: snappy dialog, fight scenes, interesting relationships and romance. More than that, Whedon tapped into a universal truth: High school is hell. The good moments are to be treasured because there aren't very many of them.

The *Prom Night*[20] movie series borrows its structure from Agatha Christie's *And Then There Were None*,[21] in which a group of people in an enclosed setting get bumped off one by one. In the first of the film series, simply titled *Prom Night*, the story begins with a confusing and inexplicable prologue in which a little girl is killed in an abandoned school building. Cut to present day (1980), and Jamie Lee Curtis is one of the dead girl's classmates, all grown up and ready for prom.[22] The movie is interesting as a period piece in which disco rules and prom dresses look like flannel nightgowns. Prom is an oddly casual affair, the truest marker of its era. The day of the event is an ordinary school day, and no one is pictured getting ready or stressed out. The dance is in the gym, which has been festooned in a desultory fashion, a well-observed touch by the film's set decorator. (One female extra is costumed in jeans.) In an unsuccessful attempt to give Curtis a *Saturday Night Fever* moment, the movie features her in an extended disco pas de deux. The most entertaining moments are a close-up of the prom king's severed head on the gym floor and Curtis fending off the ax-wielding, ski-masked psycho murderer with a folding chair. After leaving an impressive body count, the killer is unmasked, revealing a heretofore minor male character whose face is slathered in women's makeup — a bagatelle of random, nonsensical weirdness.

Prom Night[23] was remade in 2008 with slicker production values. The students apparently attend the Academy for the Genetically Gifted, each young player more gorgeous than the next. In the updated version, the prom takes place in a hotel, giving the characters many more spaces in which to run around and shriek. The movie alternates between scenes of bloody stabbings and high school girls delivering cutting remarks: "Wow. Your dress. It's so simple." The filmmakers refer to themselves indirectly by giving their fictional prom a Hollywood/red carpet theme. If the movie has a point, it's "You think your prom was bad? A maniac murdered my date."

The second film in the original string of *Prom Night* movies is *Hello Mary Lou: Prom Night II*.[24] Like the first film, it starts with a prologue set in 1957 in which bad girl Mary Lou cheats on her prom date and meets a fiery death. Cut to present day (1987) and good girl Vicki needs a prom dress. In a nod to *Carrie*, the girl's stingy, rigidly religious mother refuses to spring for one. The usual high school types are on deck: bad girl, good girl, bohemian/arty type, mean girl. A bit light on gore (the second death comes 25 minutes into the film), the real action takes place in the movie's final prom scene in which Vicki, having been possessed by the spirit of havoc-wreaking Mary Lou, destroys the prom in Carrie-like fashion.

Prom Night III: The Last Kiss[25] uses all the conventions of the prom horror movie with a comic twist. Meant to be more funny than scary, the movie skewers itself with sly jokes heard over the school PA system. Mary Lou Maloney is back, having re-entered the world via an evil jukebox. This time the story is a Faustian tale in which Mary Lou grants her dream date supernatural athletic powers while dispatching everyone in the way of his success. Parents are goofy, teachers are clueless and cops are ineffectual. All the clichés are presented with tongue in cheek, and if there's anyone to root for, it's Mary Lou.

Prom Night IV: Deliver Us From Evil[26] takes itself very seriously. The villain in this case is a crazy Catholic priest who has a problem with teenage sex. Basically, he's against it, and to no one's surprise, he turns out to be the demented murderer. The story takes place after the prom in an isolated house in the woods where two couples have gathered to get drunk and have sex. All the usual teen horror elements are in place: nubile girls clad in their undies run around the empty house and surrounding woods while their dates are dispatched by the killer who no one seems to see lurking within arm's reach. Taken together, *Prom Night* and its sequels comprise an oeuvre all their own.

At the other end of the pop culture spectrum lie the nonfiction accounts of prom, and depending on one's point of view, some of these are scarier than the horror stories. *Prom Night in Mississippi*[27] (referenced in chapter 6) documents the first mixed race prom ever held in the small town of Charleston. Historically, neither the school nor the community would sponsor a dance for all students, so in 2008, actor Morgan Freeman offered to pick up the tab if the color line were broken for this one occasion. The school administration agreed, and the filmmakers let the viewers in on the process.

By and large, the students are in favor of the plan. Resistance comes primarily from parents and grandparents who, even in the twenty-first century, see fraternization of races as contrary to natural law. As Chasidy, a senior girl says, "It's 2008. Why are you still going back to an attitude you had 50 years ago?"[28] An impressively mature boy identified as "Billy Joe," says, "You can't change them. They've done lived their life. But they try to tell you how to live yours, and that's where the conflict comes in. But I love 'em and I accept the fact that they are racist."[29]

Freeman, who views the problem as fear of interracial sex says, "The bugaboo of sex has absolutely drowned out common sense."[30] The prom is held successfully, but the following year, without Freeman's sponsorship, the school once again holds separate dances for black and white students.

Hali Lee's documentary *Prom Night in Kansas City*[31] is the filmmaker's way of coming to terms with her personal prom obsession. She films girls as they photograph themselves shopping and getting made up. Lee documents a range of proms, from the nondancing Center Place Restoration School in Independence, Missouri, to the LGBT dance in Kansas City, where anything goes.[32] Lee also captures a range of attitudes:

> "I don't want to go to prom because it stands for everything that is evil and wrong about high school."
> "It's like Junior Wedding Day."
> "You could be class president, but to be prom king...."

Lee apparently succeeds in banishing her ghosts of proms past, but she notes that "Prom is still a really big deal here."[33]

The World's Best Prom[34] is about the annual city-wide shindig in Racine, Wisconsin. The town is small and close-knit. High school graduation is celebrated in high style, and the local Rotary Club has sponsored the prom afterparty since 1952. As one student says, "I like two things about Racine: the lakefront and the prom."[35] A red carpet and Klieg lights make for a Midwestern Hollywood experience for the entire population. Even if you don't know a student, the street along the red carpet is the place to be on prom night, where students arrive in everything from rowboats on wheels to tractors. "This is the highlight of your high school career," says one student, adding, "You're on TV!"[36]

Prom is also the focus of memoirs. In *Do-Over!*, author Robin Hemley relives some of his childhood experiences, including the senior dance. He strives to make peace with his inner teenager. "I've spent the better part of my adulthood trying to coax that cowardly, nail-biting, dishonest, sixteen-

Kings and Queens, The Time of My Life and ***Do-Over!***

year-old I was (longingly staring after the ne'er-do-wells and their dates) out of his untidy and grubby little fox hole."[37] Hemley's feelings about proms are no doubt shared by others:

> My idea of a prom conjured loneliness, alienation, and terror. Around the same time as my sad little school dance memory, Stephen King published *Carrie*, with its memorable prom scene. And the movie *Grease* came out not long after. These are the two poles of high school dance experiences, and even those of us who never got in the front door of a prom still have a prom experience, even if it's only known as longing. On the prom spectrum, more people I know tip toward the *Carrie* side of things, humiliated and isolated, than dancing up a storm with Olivia Newton-John and John Travolta.[38]

Hemley has his do-over with the object of his adolescent affection. Serendipitously, his old high school crush, now married, is head of alumni relations at the school and agrees to accompany him to the dance. Hemley's campaign to reinvent his teenage self is ultimately unsuccessful. It seems that once a geek, always a geek, and no amount of adult accomplishment can rehabilitate the past. Hemley, like most of us, fantasizes about experiencing high school armed with the knowledge and experience we gained after graduation. What smooth characters we would have been!

In the personal essay collection, *The Time of My Life*,[39] 17 writers recount their prom experiences. The stories are so varied and specific, that it's impossible to draw any conclusions other than there's the idea of prom, and then

Prom guides.

there's *your* prom. Most of the writers had a terrible time in high school. That may or may not be typical. It's possible that adolescent melancholy is standard for nascent writers, whose propensity for deep thinking and individuality isn't exactly the winning formula in high school. The most upbeat story is about a guy who escorts two Swedish exchange students to the dance and ends the evening with a threesome in the woods — a sexual fantasy right out of *Penthouse* magazine. The saddest tale is about a girl who lives with a foster family. Mistaking sexual attraction for intimacy, she blurts out her history to her date just as he's about to deliver the much-anticipated goodnight kiss. Instead of a smooch, he abandons her without a word and never speaks to her again. As another writer in the collection says, "There is humiliation and there is prom night."[40] Whatever occurs on this night of nights is magnified tenfold and frozen in memory like a bug in amber.

Prom night success is often measured by how well the evening stacks up with the pop culture ideal of heterosexual romance. Things are still dicey for gay students, who often pair up with an opposite-sex date to deflect unwanted attention. There are many such stories in *Kings and Queens: Queers at the Prom*.[41] As transgendered writer Jenny (née James) Boylan says, "People who think of their prom as this 'great night,' I think it's because their experience matched mythology. And mine didn't."[42]

Prom, as evidenced by the proliferation of etiquette guides, is a comedy (or tragedy) of manners. Success is not just a question of matching the romantic template, it's a measure of one's ability to navigate the rough seas of high school society. Offering advice on everything from proffering a proper invitation to recovering from rejection, books such as *Prom and Party Etiquette*[43] and *The Ultimate Prom Guide*[44] are published primarily for the edification of girls. Boys are known to toss out the script and behave however the mood strikes them, including, as one writer recalls, torturing the live goldfish misguidedly placed in centerpiece bowls for an "Under the Sea" theme.[45]

All the research and planning in the world can't guarantee an enjoyable evening. In fact, overplanning may be the leading cause of prom disappointment. Movies and novels are no help. Prom is what it is — for each person individually. It looms large for a time, and in hindsight it shrinks, becoming a little cameo of memory to be dusted off periodically and enjoyed or shoved back in its box, never to be spoken of again.

13. Last Dance

"It was nice to make things right, and I actually went to prom and had a good time in the TV world. The real world wasn't so much fun."
— Nicholas Brendon, actor, *Buffy the Vampire Slayer*

Prom night is one of the most evocative word pairings in the language — right up there with *tax audit, wedding day* and *jury duty*. Prom is not just an event, it's a concept, a meme. The phrase evokes not only a specific dance but an abstract concept. *Prom night* is shorthand for mismatched dance partners, social anxiety, ill-advised clothing and tricky peer group dynamics. *Prom queen* is not a neutral term, either. The prom queen is the girl you want to be, and if you don't have the crown, you have a free pass to hate the girl who does. A book called *Tripping the Prom Queen*[1] is about female rivalry, and the author knows that readers understand the meaning of her title. Tolstoy remarked that happy families are all alike; every unhappy family is unhappy in its own way. So it is with prom. A good prom is unremarkable, but a bad one yields some really great stories. That's why the negative associations with prom tend to stick in our collective frame of reference.

Nowadays, any annual gathering of formal-clad adults is a prom. The yearly White House Correspondents' Association Dinner, for example, is often called the journalists' prom, or in a less flattering version, the nerds' prom.[2] A "Senior" Prom is a cute way of referring to a social gathering of older folks. Adult or do-over proms are springing up all over the place. It seems that a second shot at a good prom has a powerful appeal. A recent event in Green Bay drew couples ranging in age from twenties to sixties. The ad for the dance read, "Prom the way you always wanted it. Where the punch is spiked, you don't have to hide the booze and the band plays loud." Randa Genke went all out for the event, buying a new dress, having her hair done and springing for a spray tan. "I've been thinking about it for weeks," she said. "I could hardly sleep last night I was so excited."[3] You can have another prom, but fair warning: It might be just as awkward as your first one. Jello shots and spiked

182

Homecoming queen Jillian Schmitz, whose unexpected win caused peer group envy, St. Louis Park High, Minnesota, 1999 (Jillian Schmitz).

punch can make the evening more tolerable, but they are no guarantee that your date will be attentive or that you'll have a good time. On the other hand, attending with your spouse eliminates the suspense about getting lucky at the end of the night.

The Mom Prom is a nationwide event for charity, and perhaps it's prom the way it should be: girls only and for a good cause.

> Mom Prom was created in Canton, MI in 2006 at St. Thomas a Becket Catholic Church. It is a ladies night out for charity in which women wear their old prom gowns, bridesmaids dresses, or wedding gowns. It is a real prom with a DJ, karaoke, a tackiest dress contest, and a game to crown the new queen. This is a wonderful, hilarious night in which women can dance the night away, have fun with friends, and help a worthy cause. We hope to have ladies groups from across the country create their own proms, raising money for charities that are close to their hearts. So look for that old gown in the back of your closet and get ready to dance, dance, dance while helping those in need.[4]

The title character in the 1986 film *Peggy Sue Got Married*[5] traveled back in time to her high school formal, a fantasy that many people entertain. We'll never have the chance to undo the moments we regret or relive the ones we cherish, but we can look back at our teen years with humor and affection. That was the appeal of *The Awesome 80s Prom*, an interactive theater piece

Zombie prom queen costumes at partycity.com and halloweenexpress.com, 2012.

that ran from 2007–2011 in Portland, Oregon, and skewered all the usual teen stereotypes:

> The *Awesome 80s Prom* is a brand new blast-from-the-past interactive show in the style of "Tony and Tina's Wedding" and "The Donkey Show" set at Wanaget High's Senior Prom ... in 1989! All your favorite characters from your favorite 80s movies

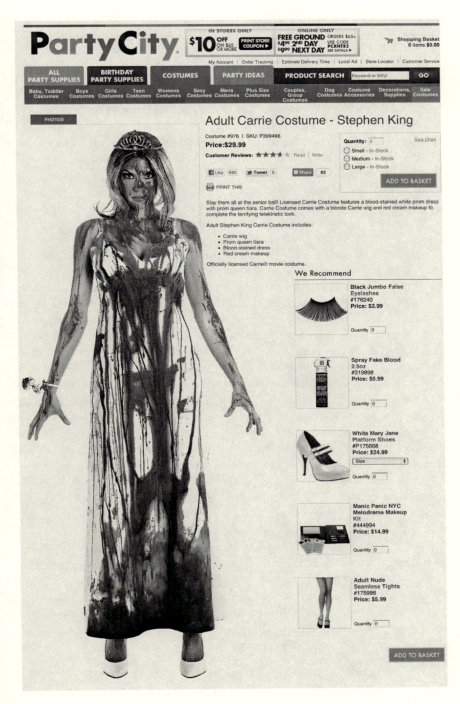

Adult "Carrie" costume, partycity.com.

are at the THE PROM, from the Captain of the Football Team to the Asian Exchange Student, from the Geek to the Hottie Head Cheerleader, and they're all competing for Prom King and Queen.[6]

The high school types referenced in prom spoofs are so familiar, they've become like stock characters in a commedia dell arte. The goth, bloodied zombie girl is the date from hell. She's so well known that both Halloween Express and Party City offer zombie prom queen costumes on their websites. If you really want to scare your date, get the Carrie costume, complete with a canister of fake blood. If you want to play it cute, buy the regular prom queen outfit, and don't forget the platinum blonde bouffant wig.[7] We're looking in the fun house mirror: Real prom outfits are like dressing up for Halloween, and Halloween costumes mimic the prom.

Prom is important to high school students, their parents, vendors and, by default, school administrators. Prom-goers comprise a fresh crop every year, but some adults are involved annually. In a way, prom is more entwined with the lives of adults than with the kids who attend and then move on. Prom generates a lot of anticipation and prep time for an event that lasts a few hours. It exists more in the build-up and recall of the evening than the event itself. Prom is not exactly important, but it creates a lot of drama. More paradoxical than a Zen koan, prom represents everything that's right and wrong with American teens. Depending on your point of view, prom is an occasion for wretched excess and undue sexual pressure, or it's an indicator that the kids are all right and due for some dancing.[8]

Some high schoolers attend prom and have a good time, some have a less than good time, and some don't go at all. If you have a prom night keepsake, say, a photograph, shot glass or dried corsage, chances are your prom was enjoyable. After all, who keeps a souvenir from a lousy evening? We go through life making memories. We wrap some in tissue paper and store them in the back of the closet. Some we take to the trash. Whether the stuff of your prom is in the closet or a landfill tells the story.

Prom is a teenage Rubicon. Once crossed, there's no going back. Prom attendance makes you different from the kid you used to be, but not because you're more experienced sexually (although that may be the case), and it's not because you wore some dress-up clothes. The divide is the marker between fantasy and reality. Prom is an early life lesson on the difference between the anticipation of a thing and the thing itself. Very few life events are as awful or as wonderful as one anticipates, and that's true for prom. If prom is a rite of passage, it's not from child to adult. It's from dreamer to realist.

As anyone who's been to one can tell you, there is no such thing as a perfect prom. There's also no profit in saying so, which is why *Seventeen* and all the other vendors of prom goods are going to keep on selling the dream.

Prom queen costume with platinum blonde wig.

And why not? The things of childhood are put away soon enough. If there are proms, it's because our society is flush with cash and healthy young people. If we can take the time to stage a school dance, we're probably not under attack, battling economic depression or in the midst of a natural disaster — or at least, taking a well-deserved break from that harsh reality. To employ one last analogy, prom is our canary in the coal mine. Long may she sing.

Chapter Notes

Chapter 1

1. Karal Ann Marling, *Debutante: Rites and Regalia of American Debdom* (University Press of Kansas, 2004), 63, 73, 176.

2. Jane Elizabeth Hegland, *The High School Prom: A Case Study of Expectations and Dress for an American Ritual* (Thesis: University of Minnesota, 1995), 51–2.

3. DeWitt C. Reddick, "It Was Only Fifty Years Ago," *The Alcade*, March 1975, 17.

4. Michael Perna, Jr., "Junior Prom—1929," *Shrewsbury Chronicle*, Sept. 22, 2009.

5. Marling, 175.

6. Joseph F. Kett, *Rites of Passage* (Basic Books, 1974), 12–16.

7. Thomas Hine, *The Rise and Fall of the American Teenager* (Harper Collins, 1999), 121–3.

8. Ibid., 123–32.

9. Kett, 21–8.

10. Ibid., 36.

11. "Keating-Owen Child Labor Act of 1916," www.ourdocuments.gov (National Archives). Accessed March 11, 2011.

12. Kett, 137.

13. Ibid., 127.

14. Ibid., 153, 183, 189, 216.

15. Ibid., 129.

16. Ibid., 235.

17. Ibid., 153–4.

18. Ibid., 126, 130.

19. Ibid., 245.

20. Hine, 139.

21. www.ourdocuments.gov

22. "State Compulsory Attendance Laws," http://www.infoplease.com/ipa/A0112617.html. Accessed March 11, 2011.

23. Kett, 127.

24. Hine, 139.

25. Hine, 172–3.

26. Kett, 41–2.

27. "Loretta Young Quotes," http://www. brainyquote.com/quotes/authors/l/loretta_young.html. Accessed March 3, 2011.

28. Beth L. Bailey, *From Front Porch to Back Seat: Courtship in Twentieth Century America.* (Johns-Hopkins University Press), 1988, 15–19.

29. Hine, 197.

30. Bailey, 22.

31. Ibid., 22–4.

32. Hine, 200.

33. Hine, 188.

34. Ibid., 194.

35. Bailey, 31–4, Hine, 200.

36. Grace Palladino, *Teenagers: An American History* (Basic Books, 1996), 8. Bailey, 26. Hine, 201–2.

37. Kett, 247. Jon Savage, *Teenage: The Creation of Youth Culture* (Viking, 2007), 320.

38. "Vince Lombardi Quotes," http://www.brainyquote.com/quotes/authors/v/vince_lombardi.html. Accessed March 3, 2011.

39. Hine, 164–5.

40. Young and Young, 26.

41. Savage, 279.

42. William H. Young and Nancy K. Young, "World of Youth," *American Popular Culture Through History: The 1930s* (Greenwood Press), 2002, 18.

43. Ibid., 19.

44. Young and Young, 19–20.

45. Hine, 197.

46. Ibid., 204.

47. Palladino, 52.

48. Hine, 225.

49. Savage, 446, 453.

50. Hine, 227

51. Howe, Neil and William Strauss. *Generations: The History of America's Future, 1584 to 2069.* (William Morrow and Company), 1991, 264.

52. Ralph G. Giordano, *Social Dancing in America, A History and Reference, vol. 2, Lindy Hop to Hip Hop, 1907–2000* (Greenwood Press), 2002, 87.

53. Ibid., 88–91.

54. Savage, 322. also Kai Fikentscher, *"You Better Work!" Underground Dance Music in New York City* (Wesleyan University Press), 2000, 23.

55. Lucy Rollin, *Twentieth Century Teen Culture by the Decades* (Greenwood Press, 1999), 136. also Hine, 226.

56. Ibid., 239. Hine describes the "zoot suit riots," which took place in Los Angeles in May and June of 1943. The riots are outside the purview of this book, but for further reading, see Hine and Palladino.

57. Palladino, 51.

58. Ibid.

59. Peterson.

60. Email interview, February 26, 2011.

61. Andrea Lavinthal and Jessica Rozler. *A Single Girl's Guide to Living It Up*. New York: Simon Spotlight Entertainment, 2005, 3.

62. Stuart Elliott. "MTV Strives to Keep Up with Young Viewers." *New York Times*. January 31, 2011, B5.

63. Jane Elizabeth Hegland. *The High School Prom: A Case Study of Expectations and Dress for an American Ritual*. Thesis, University of Minnesota, 1995, 106–7.

64. Felicity Hannah Paxton. *America at the Prom: Rite and Regeneration*. Dissertation in American civilization, University of Pennsylvania, 2000, 40.

65. Bari Nan Cohen. "Belle of the Bash." *Young and Modern Prom Special*. Spring, 1998, 64.

66. http://teranicouture.com/first_page.php. Accessed December 1, 2011.

67. http://www.promdressshop.com/Prom-Dresses.aspx. Accessed November 29, 2011.

Chapter 2

1. Rollin, 169.

2. Ibid., 178.

3. Bailey, 110–11.

4. Strauss and Howe, 285–6. (The term "Silent Generation" is their coinage — as useful a one as any.)

5. Stephanie Coontz, *The Way We Never Were* (Basic Books, 1992), 24, 171. African-Americans, Mexican-Americans, Puerto Ricans and other minorities did not share in the postwar glow. They suffered from all sorts of discrimination, and their poverty rates were high. (Coontz, 30.)

6. Ibid., 30.

7. Hine, 232–3.

8. E.G. Ingersoll, "Spare-Time Jobs for High School Kids," *The Kiplinger Magazine*, April, 1954, 39.

9. Oakley, 145.

10. Brett Harvey, "Fitting In for Fifties Women," *The 1950s* (Greenhaven Press, 2000), 156.

11. Hine, 234.

12. "Changing Times," *The Kiplinger Magazine*, June 1950, 33.

13. Gilbert, 34.

14. "Changing Times," *The Kiplinger Magazine*, June 1950, 33.

15. "Should Teenagers Have Steady Dates?" *Jet*, October 1, 1959, 25.

16. Bailey, 53.

17. Ibid., 62.

18. Ibid., 20.

19. Ibid., 144, 151.

20. Ann Landers, "Straight Talk on Sex and Growing Up," *Life*, Aug. 18, 1961, 74.

21. Croker, Richard. *The Boomer Century: 1946–2046*. New York: Springboard Press, 2007, 28–9.

22. "Life Goes to a Party," *Life*, May 31, 1937, 82.

23. Ellen Melinkoff, *What We Wore*, New York: Quill, 1984, 55.

24. I, like my classmates, wore panty girdles to school. They held up our hose and kept what little jiggle we had in check. They were torture.

25. Melinkoff, 20–1.

26. Ibid., 20–1.

27. Brett Harvey. "'Fitting In' for Fifties Women," Stuart, A. Kallen, ed. *America's Decades: The 1950s*. San Diego: Greenhaven Press, 2000, 153.

28. Ibid. 59–60.

29. Ralph Freas, *The Billboard*, 1957.

30. Ralph G. Giordano, *Social Dancing in America, vol. 2* (Greenwood Press, 2006), 137.

31. Ibid., 142.

32. Ibid., 139.

33. Jimmy Snow, "Let the Good Times Roll," http://www.youtube.com/watch?v=mT8dBFrVpLA. Accessed on April 22, 2011.

Also. quoted in Giordano, 142.

34. Douglas Martin, "Randy Wood, 94, Founder of Dot Records," *The New York Times*, April 15, 2011, A25.

35. Giordano, 136–144.

36. Palladino, 130.

37. Ann Dils and Ann Cooper Albright, *Moving History/Dancing Cultures: A Dance History Reader* (Wesleyan University Press, 2001), 407.

38. Palladino, 134–5.

39. Giordano, 146–51.

40. *The Billboard*, April 3, 1961, 6.

41. "Name Band Failings," *The Billboard*, April 21, 1951, 24. "Teenagers Give Out," *The Billboard*, April 3, 1961.

42. "GAC's Plan Brings Bands to Teens and Vice-Versa," *The Billboard*, May 19, 1958.

43. "Name Band Failings," *The Billboard*, April 21, 1951, 24. "Teenagers Give Out," *The Billboard*, April 3, 1961.

44. Marietta Abell and Agnes J. Anderson, *School Dances and Proms: Complete Practical Suggestions for Planning and Staging School Dances and Proms* (T.S. Denison & Co.), 1962,126.

45. Ibid., 123–5.

46. Ibid., 129, 167.

47. "Judith Martin, Miss Manners Quotations," http://nickelkid.net/quotes/manners. html. Accessed on April 22, 2011.

48. "Youth: Crestubilee," *Time*, June 1, 1953.

49. "Prom Parties, 'tis the Season," *The Rotarian*, June 1958.

50. Dorothy Barclay, "Prom Begins: Parents Start Nail-Nibbling," *The New York Times*, April 30, 1957, 47.

51. Richard H. Parle, "Party After Prom to Charter Train," *The New York Times*, June 5. 1958, 33. "Norwalk Denied Permit for Post-Prom Party," *The New York Times*, June 7, 1958.

52. "The Prom Went On and On," *Life*, June 9, 1958.

53. www.browniecamera.com. And "1961 Commercial: Kodak Film Projector," http://www.youtube.com/watch?v=TiIsLVqSauw. Accessed on March 27, 2011. Also "1958 Kodak Commercial," http://www.youtube.com/watch?v=pHc7-37inrs. Accessed March 27, 2011.

54. Palladino, 156–8 and Hine, 238, 241.

Chapter 3

1. Interviews via email, David Schwartz, "Bill H." November 11, 2010.

2. Annie Gottlieb. *Do You Believe in Magic?* New York: Times Books, 1987, 9.

3. Ibid.

4. Hine, 249.

5. Howe and Strauss, 301.

6. Croker, 10.

7. Ibid., 12.

8. Hine, 250.

9. I hounded my mother for Bunny Bread, a snowy-white, squishy mass of cellulose fiber disguised as food, because I had seen the product's very persuasive TV commercial.

10. Croker, 17.

11. Croker, 41.

12. Penelope Eckert. *Jocks and Burnouts*. New York: Teacher's College Press, 1984, 9.

13. Cusick, 66.

14. Ibid., 46.

15. Cusick, 68.

16. Lyn Tornabene. *I Passed As a Teenager*. New York: Lancer Books, 1967.

17. "Adult Spy Goes to High School." *Life*, May 5, 1967, 97.

18. Susan J. Douglas. *Where the Girls Are*. New York: Three Rivers Press, 1994, 125.

19. Rollin, 236.

20. Palladino, 235.

21. Bailey, 61.

22. "FAQs: Popular 20th Century American Foods," http://www.foodtimeline.org/fooddecades.html#1960s. Accessed May 13, 2011.

23. Rielly, 97.

24. Melinkoff, 127.

25. Palladino, 229.

26. Here's my theory: The Beatles' music was a blast to listen and dance to.

27. David P. Szatmary. *Rockin' in Time: A Social History of Rock-and-Roll*. Saddle River, NJ: Prentice-Hall, 1987, 61.

28. Ibid., 62.

29. Jan A. Lowery. "Dance Through the Ages." *Ebony Jr.*, Nov. 1978, 27.

30. *Ebony*, Aug. 1991, 48.

31. *Jet*, Sept. 16, 1991, 35.

32. Ann Dils and Ann Cooper Albright. *Moving History: A Dance History Reader*. Bloomington, IL: Wesleyan University Press, 2001, 408.

33. Lowery, 27 and "Balto Goes 'Waddle-Waddle.'" *Billboard*, Aug. 18, 1962.

34. Harold Evans. *The American Century*. New York: Alfred A. Knopf, 1998, 557.

35. Daniel Yankelovich. "The Search for Self-Fulfillment." *America's Decades: The 1970s*. Mark Ray Schmidt, ed. San Diego, Greenhaven Press, 2000, 231.

36. Ibid. Burton I. Kaufman. "The War of October 1973 and the Oil Embargo," 46–7.

37. Steve Gillon. Boomer Nation. New York: Free Press, 2004, 14.

38. Alex Poinsett. "The Dixie Schools Charade." *Ebony*, Aug. 1971, 144.

39. "High School Dropout Rates by Race/Ethnicity," last modified 2009, http://www.infoplease.com/us/education/high-school-dropouts-race.html. Accessed May 13, 2011.

40. Marcia Chambers. "High School Dropout Rate at 45%, Macchiarola Reports to City Board." *The New York Times*, October 17, 1979.

41. "Album-Oriented Rock," last modified June 29, 2011, http://en.wikipedia.org/wiki/Album-oriented_rock#Freeform_and_progressive. Accessed June 29, 2011. Also Pat Jacobs. "FM Radio," http://www.loti.com/radio/Top%2040%20FM%20Radio.htm. Accessed June 29, 2011.

42. Editors of Time-Life Books. *Our American Century: Time of Transition: The 70s*. Alexandria, VA: Time-Life Books, 1998, 111–21.

43. Giordano, 221–23.

44. Ibid. 269.

45. Ibid.

46. Kai Fikentscher. *"You Better Work!"* Underground Music in New York City. Bloomington: Wesleyan University Press, 2000, 29.

47. Giordano, 224–26, 268–69 and Fikentscher, 26–9.

48. Beverly Gordon. "Blue Jeans as Self-Expression." In Stuart Kallen, *America's Decades*, San Diego: Greenhaven Press, 2000, 218–20.

Chapter 4

1. The birth years for Gen X are usually listed as 1965–1981, but there are variations.

2. Neil Howe and Bill Strauss. *13th Gen*. New York: Vintage Books, 1993, 18 and 61.

3. Michael Shaller. "The Truth About the 1980s Economy." In James D. Torr, ed. *The 1980s*. San Diego: Greenhaven Press, 2000, 59.

4. Valerie Steele. *Fifty Years of Fashion: New Look to Now*. New Haven: Yale University Press, 1997, 111.

5. *Wall Street* (dir. Oliver Stone), Twentieth Century–Fox, 1987.

6. Stuart A. Kallen. *The 1980s*. San Diego: Lucent Books, 1999, 66, 71–72. One bright note of the decade was the dismantling of the Berlin Wall in 1989.

7. Steele, 118.

8. Rollin, 285.

9. Ibid., 118.

10. Steele, 132–33.

11. "Biography: Nancy Reagan," http://www.pbs.org/wgbh/americanexperience/features/biography/reagan-nancy/ Accessed June 7, 2011.

12. Clare Lomas. *20th Century Fashion: The 80s and 90s: Power Dressing to Sportswear*. Milwaukee: Gareth Stevens Publishing, 2000, 6.

13. Linda Watson. *Vogue: Twentieth Century Fashion*. London: Carlton Books, 1999, 70.

14. Steele, 121.

15. Ibid., 135, 143.

16. Ibid., 146.

17. Ibid., 140–41.

18. Bailey, 143.

19. Rona Jaffe. "Listening In on New York's Elite Teenagers." *New York Magazine*, May 12, 1972, 56, 63.

20. Marcel Danesi. *Cool: The Signs and Meanings of Adolescence*. Toronto: University of Toronto Press, 1994, 93, 133.

21. Rollin, 289.

22. Ibid., 288.

23. Ibid., 289.

24. Palladino, 251.

25. Nancy Gibbs. "How Should We Teach Our Kids about SEX?" *Time*, May 24, 1993.

26. Anita Manning. "Teens and Sex in the Age of AIDS." *USA Today*, Oct. 3, 1988.

27. Kim Painter. "Teenagers Ponder: Is Everyone Doing It?" *USA Today*, March 5, 1991.

28. Howe and Strauss, 149.

29. Ibid., 181.

30. Craig Unger. "Attitude." *New York Magazine*. July 26, 1982, 26.

31. Martin A. Marty. *Daily Life in the United States, 1960–1990*. Westport, CT: Greenwood Press, 1997, 278.

32. Szatmary, 275.

33. Ibid., 272–76.

34. Ibid., 268.

35. http://www.inthe80s.com/80sdance.shtml.

36. http://www.thepeoplehistory.com/80scars.html, and http://www.thepeoplehistory.com/80scars.html, accessed June 25, 2011.

37. Szatmary, 287.

38. Marty, 279–80.

39. Szatmary, 308, 331.

40. Rollin, 333.

41. http://www.bookrags.com/research/1990s-fashion-bbbb-05/, accessed June 19, 2011.

42. Rollin, 333–34.

43. Ibid., 337, and Dena Babbs and Crystal Zobrist, "Gen Xers Lead Piercing and Tattoo Fad," http://www.jour.unr.edu/outpost/specials/genx.tattool.html, accessed June 22, 2011. Also see Benn Stebleton, "Painted and Poked: The Tattooing and Piercing of Generations X and Y," *Nashville Feed*, http://www.nashvillefeed.com/culture/painted-and-poked-the-tattooing-and-piercing-of-generations-x-and-y/, accessed June 22, 2011.

44. Rollin, 323–24.

45. Janet L. Fix. "Teen Spending Power: Awesome!" *USA Today*, Dec. 10, 1992, B1.

Chapter 5

1. Neil Howe and William Strauss. *Millennials Rising*. New York: Vintage Books, 2000, 14–15.

2. "By 2011, Teen Market Shrinks, Spending Clout Soars to $200 Billion." http://www.marketingvox.com/by-2011-teen-market-shrinks-spending-clout-soars-to-200b-031001. Accessed July 21, 2011.

3. Chris Woodyard. "Generation Y: The Young and Boundless Are Taking Over Pop Culture." *USA Today*. October 6, 1998, 1A.

4. Toby Elkin. "Teens Now Spend More Time Online than Watching TV." *Advertising Age*. July 8, 2003.

5. Howe and Strauss, 7.

6. Ibid.

7. Bruce Tulgan. *Not Everyone Gets a Trophy*. San Francisco: Jossey-Bass, 2009, 5.

8. Ibid., 8, and Tammy Erickson. "Trophies for Everyone? Debunking Another Gen Y

Myth." *Harvard Business Review, HBR Blog Network.* http://blogs.hbr.org/Erickson/2008/06/trophies_for_everyone_debunkin.html. Accessed July 19, 2011.

9. Jayne O'Donnell. "Marketers Keep Pace with Tweens: Fashion-Minded Girls Prove Rich, but Fast-Moving Target." *USA Today.* April 11, 2007, B1.

10. "The Millennials: Confident. Connected. Open to Change." Pew Research Center Publications. February 24, 2010. http://pewresearch.org/pubs/1501/millennials-new-survey-generations. Accessed January 7, 2011.

11. Tulgan, 5–6.

12. "Key Characteristics of Today's Adolescents: The Millennial Generation (1980/83–Present)." www.catholicyouthministryofdallas.org. Accessed July 17, 2011.

13. Karen S. Peterson. "In High School, Dating Is a World unto Itself." *USA Today.* September 3, 1997, D1.

14. "A Portrait of Generation Next." January 9, 2007. http://people-press.org/report/300/a-portrait-of-generation-next. Accessed January 26, 2011. Scott Keeter and Paul Taylor. "The Millennials." Pew Research Center Publications. December 11, 2009. http://pewresearch.org/pubs/1437/millennials-profile. Accessed on June 24, 2011. Also, Howe and Strauss, 7.

15. Amanda Lenhart. "Teens, Cell Phones and Texting." *Pew Research Center Publications.* http://pewresearch.org/pubs/1572/teens-cell-phones-text-messages. April 20, 2010. Accessed July 21, 2011.

16. Thomas Kaplan. "Next on Cuomo's Agenda: Preparing His 16-Year-Olds for Their Driver's Licenses." *New York Times.* July 26, 2011, A16.

17. "Cell Phones Key to Teens' Social Lives, 47% Can Text with Eyes Closed." http://www.marketingcharts.com/interactive/cell-phones-key-to-teens. August 2008. Accessed July 21, 2011.

18. Donna St. George. "Study of Teen Cellphone Use Reinforces Impression That They're Always Using Them." *Washington Post.* April 20, 2010, B01.

19. Richard Sweeney. "Millennial Behaviors and Demographics." New Jersey Institute of Technology. December 22, 2006.

20. "Got a Date for Prom? Enough to Fill a Bus." *Seattle Times.* May 5, 2010.

21. Ally Schettino. "Prom: Dates vs. Friends: Prom Debate." *Hawk Eye* (school paper, Hanover High School, Mechanicsville, VA). November 11, 2010.

22. See "Cell Phones Key to Teens' Social Lives."

23. Jenny Koepnick. "New Rule Requires Prom Bus." *Paly Voice.* October 21, 2002.

24. Schettino.

25. Ibid.

26. Peterson.

27. Ibid.

28. Benoit Denizet-Lewis. *American Voyeur.* New York: Simon & Schuster, 2010, 43–44.

29. Erika Stalder. *The Date Book: A Teen Girl's Complete Guide to Going Out with Someone New.* San Francisco: Zest Books, 2007, 10–11.

30. Ibid.

31. Peterson.

32. Email interview, February 26, 2011.

33. Andrea Lavinthal and Jessica Rozler. *A Single Girl's Guide to Living It Up.* New York: Simon Spotlight Entertainment, 2005, 3.

34. Stuart Elliott. "MTV Strives to Keep Up with Young Viewers." *New York Times.* January 31, 2011, B5.

35. Jodi L. Cornell and Bonnie L. Halpern-Felsher. "Adolescents Tell Us Why Teens Have Oral Sex." *Journal of Adolescent Health* 38 (2006), 299.

36. Sharon Jayson. "Study Challenges Myths of Teen Sex." *USA Today.* May 20, 2008, D7.

37. Email interview.

38. Laura Vanderkam. "Sexually Active Girls Lament: Why Didn't I Wait?" *USA Today.* June 12, 2003, A15.

39. Laura Sessions Stepp. *Unhooked.* New York: Riverhead Books, 2007, 62.

40. Lynn Ponton. *The Sex Lives of Teenagers.* New York: Dutton, 2000, 13.

41. Karen S. Peterson. "Girls Stand Up to Boys; Studies Find, and Teens Agree, That Sexual Boundaries Are Being Set." *USA Today.* April 23, 2002, D8.

42. Diane Mapes. "Virginity's Making a Comeback, Report Says." http://www.msnbc.com/ Posted and accessed on March 3, 2011.

43. Rebecca Wind. "No Crystal Ball Needed: Teens Are Going in the Wrong Direction." http://guttmacher.org/media/nr/2009/06//18/index.html. June 18, 2009. Accessed February 3, 2011.

44. Arienne Thompson. "16, Pregnant — and Famous." *USA Today.* November 23, 2010, D1.

45. Patrick Welsh. "Prom View Skirts Key Message." *USA Today.* June 10, 2003, A12.

46. *Jet,* May 14, 1990, 36.

47. L. A. Galloway. *This Is Not Your Parents' Prom.* Wheaton, IL: Have Vision Publications, 2002.

48. "Teen's Prom Ban Reversed Amid Outcry." http://www.msnbc.com/id/43004197. Posted May 14, 2011. Accessed May 15, 2011.

49. "Flashy You Tube 'Prom-posals' Rival Marriage Proposals." ABC News. http://abcnews.com/Technology/youtube-prom-posals-rival-marriage-proposals. Accessed May 15, 2011.

50. Kathleen Moore. "71% of Online Adults Now Use Video-Sharing Sites." Pew Internet

Reports. http://pewinternet.org/Reports/2011/Video-sharing-sites.aspx. Posted and accessed July 26, 2011.

51. Mary Gail Hare. "Prom Invitations Are Elaborate at McDonogh School." *Baltimore Sun*, June 3, 2011.

52. Ibid.

53. Ibid.

54. "Mom's First Prom." *Jet*. August 10, 1998, 26.

55. "High School Senior in Alabama Shares Prom Night with His Mom." *Jet*. May 29, 2000.

56. Rich Kizer and Georgeanne Bender. "Marketing to Millennials." *Craftrends*. June 2005.

57. Kit Yarrow and Jayne O'Donnell. *Gen Buy*. San Francisco: Jossey-Bass, 2009, 64.

58. Ibid.

59. Ibid., 65–66, 103.

60. Marisa Meltzer. "The Prom Dress Moves into the Designer Leagues." *New York Times*. June 1, 2011.

61. Ibid.

62. Ibid.

63. Christine Haughney. "Florida to California, Prom Dresses Selling." *New York Times*. May 3, 2009.

64. Ibid.

65. Ibid.

66. "What Goes Around Comes Around." *Newsweek*. October 1, 2009.

67. Maria Puente. "Tech-Savvy Teens Primp for the Prom Online." *USA Today*. April 26, 2000, D10.

68. Kayona John, creator. "West Hills Prom Dresses." http://www.facebook.com/group Accessed July 30, 2011.

69. Douglas Quenqua. "Upload a Prom Dress Photo, and Hope." *New York Times*. May 12, 2010.

70. Mary Klaus. "Midstate Girl Scouts Get the Gold through Community Service." *Patriot-News*. June 25, 2011.

71. Karen S. Peterson. "Teens Try to Squeeze Flash, Fashion into School Rules." *USA Today*. August 30, 1999, D6.

72. Ibid.

73. Hayley Phelan. "Slutty Chic a Popular Prom Dress Trend at Your School?" *Teen Vogue*. March 30, 2010.

74. Ibid.

75. Jayne O'Donnell. "Economic Downturn May Be Pulling Necklines Up." *USA Today*. March 9, 2009, B1.

76. Ibid.

77. Kathleen Schuckel. "School Daze." *Indianapolis Monthly*. September 2002, 173.

78. "Style: A Night to Forget." *Newsweek*. May 12, 2003.

79. Ibid.

80. Allison Samuels. "Bye-Bye Bad Hair Days." *Newsweek*. June 20, 2005.

81. "Tips on Tattoos." Prom Dresses. http://www.promdressesdirectory.com/promdresses/?p=136. Posted October 26, 2009. Accessed January 7, 2011.

82. "Piercing Gains Popularity." *Body Jewelry and Piercing Blog*. http://blog.piercingmap.com/archives/141. Posted June 26, 2007. Accessed January 7, 2011.

83. "Fake Bake Debate." *Newsweek*. April 15, 2008.

84. Pat Wingert. "Teens, Tans and Truth." *Newsweek*. May 10, 2008.

85. See note 79.

86. Wingert.

87. Ibid.

88. Deborah M. Marko. "Senior Guys Primp for VHS Prom." *The Daily Journal*. June 3, 2011.

89. Olivia Barker. "Why Freak Dancing Freaks out Schools." *USA Today*. June 1, 2001.

90. Ibid.

91. Tom Hallman Jr. "Grinding Rubs Teachers Wrong Way." *Oregonian*. November 11, 2010, A4.

92. Cindy Kranz. "Adults Freak over Teens' Dancing." *Cincinnati Enquirer*. May 29, 2001.

93. Hallman.

94. Ibid.

95. Barker.

96. Ibid.

97. Gracie Bonds Staples. "Programs Target Alcohol, Drugs during Prom Season." *Atlanta Journal Constitution*. April 1, 2011.

98. Tammy La Gorce. "Confronting Prom Night Drinking." *New York Times*. June 1, 2008.

99. Wendy Koch. "High Schools Join Call to Action Against Student Drinking." *USA Today*. October 17, 2007.

100. La Gorce.

101. Ibid.

102. Staples.

103. Marco R. della Cava. "No Dancing Around It: Proms Are Getting Strict." *USA Today*. May 21, 2003, A1.

104. Winnie Hu. "Holding Prom on a School Night." *New York Times*. April 13, 2010.

105. Ibid.

106. Kate Stone Lombardi. "Planning and Policing Prom Night." *New York Times*. May 6, 2007.

Chapter 6

1. *"Brown v. Board of Education."* National Archives. http://www.ourdocuments.gov/doc.php?flash=true&doc=87. Accessed August 12, 2011.

2. Susan K. Cahn. *Sexual Reckonings*. Cambridge, MA: Harvard University Press, 2007, 242.

3. Ibid., 72.

4. "Crime." *Jet*. November 21, 1957, 45.

5. Carmen K. Sisson. "Southern School Holds First Prom for Blacks and Whites." *Christian Science Monitor*. April 25, 2007.

6. Anna Shapiro. "Separate But Equal?" *Spin*. May 2003, 96, 99.

7. Ibid., 99.

8. "The Black Teen Explosion." *Ebony*. April 2004, 72–73.

9. Sara Corbett. "A Prom Divided." *New York Times*. May 24, 2009.

10. Ibid.

11. Morgan Freeman, quoted in *Prom Night in Mississippi*, dir. Paul Saltzman. Return to Mississippi Productions, HBO Documentary Films, 2009.

12. Eugene Kane. "Proms Take Unfortunate Steps Backward." *Milwaukee Journal Sentinel*. May 14, 2003.

13. "Georgia High School Students Return to Segregated Prom." *Jet*. May 26, 2003, 18.

14. Nia Hightower. "Memories of a Prom — In Color." Http://phobos.ramapo.edu. May 13, 2003.

15. "Integrated High School Prom." *Jet*. April 30, 2007, 46.

16. "Homosexual Receives Approval to Take a Male Friend to Prom." *New York Times*. May 13, 1979

17. "Boy, 17, Seeks to Take Male Date to the Prom." *New York Times*. April 11, 1979. Also "Homosexual Denied Male Escort Plans to Picket Providence Prom." *New York Times*. April 22, 1979.

18. "The Date of His Choice." *New York Times*. April 15, 1979.

19. Erik Eckholm. "In Isolated Utah City, New Clubs for Gay Students." *New York Times*. January 1, 2011.

20. PFLAG is Parents, Families and Friends of Lesbians and Gays, and GLSEN is the Gay, Lesbian and Straight Education Network.

21. Bob Moser. "Still Raining on Prom Night." *Out*. June 2006, 110, 113.

22. Ibid., 114.

23. William Henderson. "A Prom for All." *Advocate*. June 20, 2006, 27.

24. Etelka Lehoczky. "Young, Gay and Okay." *Advocate*. February 1, 2005, 31.

25. Gabriel Rotelle. "Shall We Dance?" *Advocate*. July 3, 2001, 72.

26. David Abel. "She Can't Bring Same-Sex Date to Catholic School Prom." *Boston Globe*. April 27, 2007.

27. "Superintendent of Schools Office Statement on the Bishop Feehan High School Prom." http://www.fallriverdiocese.org/newsDisplay.asp?ID=430. Issued April 27, 2007. Accessed August 18, 2011.

28. Matthew Hays. "All Dressed Up, No Place to Go?" *Advocate*. May 14, 2002.

29. Paul Vitello. "Hold the Limo: The Prom's Canceled as Decadent." *New York Times*. December 10, 2005.

30. Ibid.

31. Suzi Parker. "Constance McMillan Case: Proms as Gay-Rights Battlegrounds." *Christian Science Monitor*. March 23, 2010.

32. Kate Harding. "How Lesbians Ruined the Prom." Salon.com/mwt/broadsheet/2010/03/11/prom_cancelled. March 11, 2010. Accessed on January 19, 2011.

33. Parker, "Constance McMillan Case."

34. Michael A. Jones. "Take Your Prom Date to Georgia." http://gayrights.change.org/blog/view/take_your_gay_prom_date_to_georgia. Posted March 23, 2010. Accessed November 12, 2010.

35. "Male Student Wearing Dress Denied Entrance to Prom." *Jet*. June 12, 2006, 10.

36. "New Jersey's Derrek Lutz Wore a Dress to Prom. And Was Crowned Prom King." *Queerty*. http://www.queerty.com/new-jerseys-derrek-lutz-wore-a-dress-to-prom-and-was-crowned-prom-king-20100503/. May 3, 2010. Accessed August 19, 2011.

37. Molly Koweek. "Hudson High School Makes History: Elects Two Men as Prom King and Queen." Timesunion.com. http://blog.timesunion.com/highschool/Hudson_high_school_makes_history. June 11, 2010. Accessed December 18, 2010.

38. Brian Gillie. "Florida School Selects the Nation's First Transgendered Prom Queen." Examiner.com. http://www.examiner.com/strange-news-in-national/florida-school-awards-the-nations-first-transgendered-prom-queen. June 1, 2011.

39. Justin Jouvenal. "Gay Male Student Named Prom Queen." *Washington Post*. June 1, 2011.

40. Julie Scelfo. "Out at the Prom." *Newsweek*. June 9, 2003.

41. "Sharp Tongue." *Advocate*. July 5, 2005, 29.

42. *Prom Night in Kansas City*, dir. Hali Lee. Golden Pig Productions, 2002.

43. Ibid.

44. Sara Olkon and Steve Schmadeke. "Mormon Prom a Modest Good Time." *Chicago Tribune*. April 30, 2007.

45. Ibid.

46. Janet Thomas. "A Night to Remember." *New Era*. February 2007, 31.

47. Ibid.

48. Christy Jepson. "Mormon Prom Deep in the Heart of Texas." *Mormon Times*. April 11, 2009.

49. Ibid.

50. "Christian School Tells Boy to Skip Prom." Associated Press. Posted on msnbc.msn.com May 8, 2009. Accessed August 15, 2011.

51. "Prom 'Rebel': It Was Worth It." *The Early Show.* Cbsnews.com.http://www.cbsnews.com/stories/2009/05/12/earlyshow/main5008061.shtml. Posted on May 12, 2009. Accessed August 21, 2011.

52. See Olkon and Schmadeke, "Mormon Prom a Modest Good Time."

53. Todd Clippard. "Should Christian Teens Attend the Prom?" http://faughnfamily.wordpress.com/2007/03/20/should-christian-teens-attend-the-prom-by-todd-clippard. Posted March 20, 2007. Accessed August 15, 2011.

54. "The Muslim, All-Girl High School Prom." *Education Wonks.* http://www.educationwonk.blogspot.com/2007/06/all-muslim-girl-high-school-prom. Posted June 11, 2007. Accessed November 11, 2010.

55. "The Prom Exposed: Seeing It for What It Really Is." SoundVision.com. http://www.soundvision.com/Info/prom/exposed.asp. Accessed November 11, 2010.

56. Leslie Scrivener. "A Happily Dateless Prom." *Toronto Star.* June 29, 2003.

57. Samana Siddiqui. "The Prom: Not Just One Night of Haram." SoundVision.com. http://www.soundvision.com/info/teens/teen.prom problems.asp. Posted November 5, 2010. Accessed November 11, 2010.

58. "Homeschool Prom." Successful Homeschooling. http://www.successful-homeschooling.com/homeschool-prom.html. Accessed August 23, 2011.

59. Sherri Drake Silence. "A Night to Treasure: Collierville Hosts Prom for Special Education Students." *Commercial Appeal.* http://www.thecommercialappeal.com/news/2009/apr/27/a-night-to-treasure. Posted April 27, 2009. Accessed November 11, 2010.

60. Heather Miller. "Almost 300 at Iberia Parish Special-Needs Prom." *Daily Iberian.* May 18, 2010.

61. Michelle L. Klampe. "Elsinore High School Special Education Prom Is a Celebration of Friendship." *Press-Enterprise.* May 10, 2010.

62. Denise Smith Amos. "Students Honor Special Needs Students at Prom." *Cincinnati Enquirer.* May 15, 2011. http://content.usatoday.net/dist/custom/gci/InsidePage.aspx?cId=cincinnati&sParam=47198902.story.

63. Mary Brophy Marcus. "For One Cancer Patient, It Was a Night to Remember." *USA Today.* February 22, 2010.

64. "Anti-Prom: Super Prom." http://www.nypl.org/events/programs/2011/06/03/anti-prom-super-prom. Accessed August 23, 2011.

65. Corey Kilgannon. "A Prom for Students Who Don't Want One." *New York Times,* June 6, 2011.

Chapter 7

1. Ayssa White. "Is Prom Really a One Night Wonder?" *Towne Crier.* June 8, 2011. http://my.hsj.org/Schools/Newspaper/tabid/100/view/frontpage/articleid/447232/newspaperid/2667/Is_Prom_Really_A_One_Night_Wonder.aspx. Accessed June 8, 2011.

2. Jane Elizabeth Hegland. *The High School Prom: A Case Study of Expectations and Dress for an American Ritual.* Thesis, University of Minnesota, 1995, 106–7.

3. Felicity Hannah Paxton. *America at the Prom: Rite and Regeneration.* Dissertation in American civilization, University of Pennsylvania, 2000, 40.

4. Bari Nan Cohen. "Belle of the Bash." *Young and Modern Prom Special.* Spring, 1998, 64.

5. Amy L. Best. *Prom Night: Youth Schools and Popular Culture.* New York: Routledge, 2000, 147.

6. Louise Carus Mahdi, ed. *Betwixt and Between: Patterns of Masculine and Feminine Initiation.* Peru, IL: Open Court Publishing, 1987, 3.

7. Victor Turner. "Betwixt and Between: The Liminal Period in Rites of Passage." In Mahdi, pp. 4–9.

8. Lisa Graham McMinn. *Sexuality and Holy Longing: Embracing Intimacy in a Broken World.* John Wiley and Sons, 2004, 13–14.

9. According to researcher Richard G. Calo, slightly under one third of male respondents and one quarter of female respondents planned to lose their virginity on prom night.

Richard. G. Calo, Ph.D. *American Prom.* Nashville: Cumberland House, 2006, 141.

10. Paxton, 105.

11. Best, 99.

12. Ibid., 109.

13. Paxton, 126–27.

14. When prom begins with a promenade in the high school gym, family members attend but are required to leave when that part of the evening is concluded.

15. Michael Riera. *Staying Connected to Your Teenager: How to Keep Them Talking to You and How to Hear What They're Really Saying.* Cambridge, MA: Da Capo Press, 2003, 251.

16. Laura Buddenberg and Kathy McGee. "Prom's Real Purpose." Parenting.org, 2011. http://www.parenting.org/article/proms-real-purpose. Accessed September 18, 2011.

17. Best, 147.

18. Paxton, 55.

19. Raymond Hernandez. "From the Suburbs to the Inner City, Proms Endure as a Rite of Passage." *New York Times*. June 14, 1993.

20. Patrick Welsh. "Proms Equalize High School Life — Briefly." *USA Today*. June 4, 2003, A-11.

21. Ibid.

22. Best, 4.

23. Walter Kirn. "Will Teenagers Disappear?" *Time*. February 21, 2000.

24. Ibid., 64.

25. Personal interview, January 2, 2011. According to *Your Prom*, the average prom shopper goes to eleven stores and tries on twenty-five dresses.

26. Fashionfoiegras. "Cindy Crawford." http://www.zimbio.com/Cindy+Crawford/arti cles/2hehHy3Dlqs/Cindy+Crawford+says+wish +looked+like+Cindy. July 24, 2010. Accessed September 16, 2011.

27. Murray Milner, Jr. *Freaks, Geeks and Cool Kids*. New York: Routledge, 2004, 8.

28. Katy Kelly. "Prom Dress Obsessed: Searching for that Special, Memory-making Gown." *USA Today*, May 14, 1997, 1-D.

29. Ibid.

30. "Arm Candy." *Teen Prom*. April 2011, 150.

31. "Dress Up Your Date!" *Seventeen Prom*. March 2011, 115.

32. Best, 64.

33. Ibid.

34. To be fair, there are prom-goers with down-to-earth expectations who were well-pleased with the event.

35. Hegland, 159.

36. Ibid., 160.

37. *The World's Best Prom*. Matson Films, 2005.

38. Hegland, 73; Paxton, 171.

39. Welsh, A-11.

40. Best, 69.

41. Milner, 25.

42. Aline Tugend. "Peeking at the Negative Side of High School Popularity." *New York Times*. June 18, 2010.

43. Ibid.

44. Paxton, 366.

45. Hegland, 175.

46. Ibid., 365.

47. Ibid., 187.

48. Ibid., 175.

49. Montana Miller. "Taking a New Spotlight to the Prom: Youth Culture and Its Emerging Video Archive." *Journal of Popular Culture*, 33:1, 2010.

50. "A Portrait of Generation Next." Pew Research Center for the People and the Press. http://people-press.org/2007/01/09/a-portrait-of-generation-next/. January 9, 2007. Accessed September 21, 2011.

51. Miller, 12.

52. *Prom Night in Kansas City*. Hali Lee, director. Golden Pig Productions, 2002.

53. Miller, 18.

54. Best, 29.

55. Ibid., 29–31.

56. Joan Jacobs Brumberg. *The Body Project*. New York: Vintage Books, 1997, 98, 123.

57. Karen S. Peterson. "Knowledgeable Teens Still Starve for Attention." *USA Today*. July 18, 1997, D-8.

58. Paxton, 165.

59. Cyntha Ogden and Margaret Carroll. "Prevalence of Obesity among Children and Adolescents: United States, Trends 1963–1965 through 2007–2008." Centers for Disease Control and Prevention. http://www.cdc.gov/nchs/data/hestat/obesity_child_07_08_obesity_child_07_08.pdf. Last updated June 4, 2010. Accessed January 28, 2011.

60. Prom survey respondent, Paxton, 168.

61. Ibid., 168–71.

Chapter 8

1. "Prom Report." *Seventeen*. April, 1962, 157.

2. "Practical Money Skills for Life: Prom Spending Survey 2011." Visa. http://www.prac ticalmoneyskills.com/resources/pdfs/PromSur vey_050411.pdf

3. Promgirl.com: The online superstore. http://www.promgirl.com/prom-guide. Accessed on January 27, 2011.

4. *Your Prom* magazine, which began publication in 1990, was subsumed into *Teen Vogue* in 2002. *Cosmo Girl* was absorbed by *Seventeen* in 2008.

5. Kelley Massoni. *Bringing Up Baby: The Birth and Early Development of Seventeen Magazine*. Dissertation, Graduate Department of Sociology, University of Kansas, 1999.

6. Jon Savage. *Teenage: The Creation of Youth Culture*. New York: Viking, 2007, 448.

7. Ibid., 450.

8. Palladino, 102.

9. Ibid., 103–7.

10. Eugene Gilbert. *Advertising and Marketing to Young People*. Pleasantville, NY: Printer's Ink Books, 1957, 11.

11. Savage, 450.

12. Daniel Thomas Cook. *The Commodification of Childhood*. Durham, NC: Duke University Press, 2004, 129.

13. Massoni, 132. Citing an International Sterling ad, *Seventeen*, April, 1950, 5.

14. Jan Whitaker. *Service and Style: How the American Department Store Fashioned the Middle Class*. New York: Macmillan, 2006, 288.

15. Sharon R. Mazzarella. "The 'Superbowl of All Dates': Teenage Girl Magazines and the Commodification of the Perfect Prom." In *Growing Up Girls: Popular Culture and the Construction of Identity*, ed. Sharon Mazzarella and Norma Odom Pecora. New York: Peter Lang Publishing, 1999, 105.

16. Ann Anderson, *Snake Oil, Hustlers and Hambones: The American Medicine Show.* Jefferson, NC: McFarland and Co. Publishers, 2000, 40.

17. Massoni, 176–77.

18. Ibid., 138.

19. Ibid., 63.

20. Kimberly Phillips. "How Seventeen Undermines Young Women." Media Awareness Network. Jan./Feb. 1993. http://www.media-awareness.ca/english/resources/articles/gender_portrayal/seventeen.cfm. Accessed October 3, 2011.

21. Steven Heller. "Hey, Stinky! You're Too Fat, and Your Breath's Bad, Too." *Imprint*, 2010. http://imprint.printmag.com/branding/hey-stinky-you're-too-fat-and-you're-skin's-bad-too/. Accessed October 17, 2011.

22. Naomi Wolf. *The Beauty Myth: How Images of Beauty Are Used against Women.* New York: Anchor Books, 1991, 163.

23. Sheila Gibbons. "Teen Magazines Send Girls All the Wrong Messages." *WeNews.* October 29, 2003. http://www.womensnews.org/story/uncovering-gender/031029/teen-magazines-send-girls-all-the-wrong-messages. Accessed October 3, 2011.

24. Massoni, 105.

25. Mazzarella, 101.

26. "Prom Notes." *Seventeen.* April 1964, 188.

27. *Seventeen*, April 1972.

28. "Pastels for Prom Night." *Seventeen*, April 1974, 132–37.

29. "Seventeen and Race." Seventeen Magazine Project. May 31, 2010. http://www.seventeenmagazineproject.com/2010/05/seventeen-and-race.html. Accessed October 3, 2011.

30. "Look What We Found," *Seventeen*, April 1974, 144.

31. Laurel Graeber. "Long Live the Prom." *Seventeen*, April 1980, 176.

32. Gerard Gentil. "Prom Dresses." *Seventeen.* March 1982, 134.

33. Nat Ives. "The Last Page." *Ad Age.* December 15, 2009. http://adage.com/article/mediaworks/a-guide-magazines-ceased-publication/132779/. Accessed October 21, 2011.

34. "Prom Passion." *Seventeen*, March 1993, 187.

35. "Fairy Tale Prom." *Seventeen*, March 1995, 201.

36. "Prom Style." *Seventeen*, March 1996, 76.

37. Hayley Phelan. "'Slutty Chic' a Popular Prom Dress Trend at Your School?" *Teen Vogue*, March 30, 2010. http://www.teenvogue.com/style/blogs/fashion/2010/03slutty-chic. Accessed December 15, 2010.

38. Alissa Quart. *Branded: The Buying and Selling of Teenagers.* Cambridge: Perseus Publishing, 2003, 5.

39. "Sign the Body Peace Treaty." Seventeen.com. http://www.seventeen.com/print-this/body-peace-pledge?page=all. Accessed October 3, 2011.

40. Dove Self-Esteem Took Kit. http://www.dove.us/social-mission/self-esteem-toolkit-and-resources/. Accessed October 27, 2011.

41. Meenakshi Gigi Durham. "Sex and Spectacle in Seventeen Magazine: A Feminist Myth Analysis." *Journalism and Mass Communications Publications*, University of Iowa. May 25, 2007.

42. Tony Case. "After 65 Years, Seventeen Still One of the Cool Kids." *MPA Reports*, June 23, 2009. http://www.magazine.org/news/mpa_reports/mpa-reports-2009-seventeen-solutions.aspx. Accessed October 26, 2011.

43. Anne D'innocenzio. "Magazines Drop Print for Web to Reach Teens." *USA Today*, August 29, 2006.

44. "Your Guide to Prom!" http://www.seventeen.com/parties/prom/prom_gallery?click=svn_more. Accessed October 26, 2011.

45. Jamie Keiles. "Senior Prom." *Seventeen Magazine Project.* June 6, 2010. http://www.seventeenmagazineproject.com/2010/06/senior-prom-part-2.html. Accessed October 26, 2011.

46. Joanna Saltz. *Seventeen's Guide to Your Perfect Prom.* New York: Hearst Communications, 2007.

47. Margaret Finders. "Queens and Teen Zines: Early Adolescent Females Reading Their Way toward Adulthood." *Anthropology and Education Quarterly*, vol. 27, no. 1 (Mar. 1996), 79.

48. Ibid., 78, 81–83.

49. Mazzarella, 98.

50. *Seventeen Prom*, 2011, 222.

51. Ibid., 8–9.

52. "Our Thirty-Day Checklist to Plan the Perfect Prom!" *Teen Vogue.* http://www.teenvogue.com/style/2009/03/prom-countdown. Accessed October 25, 2011.

53. Elisa Benson. "Be His Dream Date." *Seventeen Prom,* 2011, 262.

54. Mazzarella, 99.

55. Nicole Zlatunich. "Prom Dreams and Prom Reality: Girls Negotiating 'Perfection' at the High School Prom." *Sociological Inquiry*, vol. 79, no. 3 (August 2009), 363.

56. Ibid., 366.

57. Ibid., 369.

Chapter 9

1. http://www.funnewjersey.com/upload_user/fun_with_kids/BEAUTY_SALON_HAIR_DRESSING_PARTIES_NJ.HTM. Accessed September 24, 2011.

2. http://www.sweetandsassy.com/index.php. Accessed September 10, 2011.

3. Jessica Bennett. "Tales of a Modern Diva." *Newsweek.* April 6, 2009, 42–43.

4. Brook Barnes. "Disney Looking into Cradle for Customers." *New York Times*, February 6, 2011.

5. Ibid.

6. http://princesscouturedesigns.blogspot.com.

7. Megan Basham. "Bringing up Princess: Turning Girls into Narcissists." *Wall Street Journal*, June 12, 2009.

8. A quick search for "princess outfits girls" at the Target website (www.target.com) will turn up many options.

9. Anne Murphy Paul. "Is Pink Necessary?" *New York Times.* January 21, 2011.

10. Joanne Laucius. "Princess Culture Turning Girls into Overspending Narcissists." *Ottawa Citizen*, August 18, 2010.

11. Peggy Orenstein. *Cinderella Ate My Daughter.* New York: Harper Collins, 2011.

12. Stephanie Hanes. "Little Girls or Little Women? The Disney Princess Effect." *Christian Science Monitor*, September 24, 2011.

13. Brooks Barnes. "For Disney, a Younger Princess." *The New York Times.* December 12, 2011, B-9.

14. Cathy K. Donovan. "When a Princess Costume Becomes a Culture." *Rutgers Focus.* February 5, 2008. http://www.news.rutgers.edu/focus/issue.2008-02-05.0513554387/article. Accessed January 28, 2011.

15. *12 Princess Stories.* New York: Golden Books, 2006.

16. Henry A. Giroux and Grace Pollock. *The Mouse That Roared: Disney and the End of Innocence.* Lanham, MD: Rowman & Littlefield, 2010, 33.

17. http://www.disneybridal.com/bridal gowns.html.

18. http://disneyweddings.disney.go.com/.

19. Basham.

20. Ibid.

21. Ibid.

22. Rachel Schwartz. "Teens Spending Like Celebrities on Prom Fashion." 7 Live. http://www.7liveonline.com/Teens-spending-like-celebrities-on-prom-fashions/8069523.

23. There is also a male character, Eitan.

24. http://www.bratz.com/index.php.

25. Orenstein, 48.

26. Interview with Ann Curry, *Today Show*, NBC, January 24, 2011.

27. Jean M. Twenge and W. Keith Campbell, *The Narcissism Epidemic: Living in the Age of Entitlement.* New York: Simon and Shuster, 2009, 99.

28. Ibid.

29. Ibid., 100.

30. Ibid., 101.

31. Debbie Naigle, "Literature Review of Media Messages to Adolescent Females." *Educational Communications and Technology.* University of Saskatchewan, February 2005.

32. Peter Zollo. *Wise Up to Teens: Insights into Marketing and Advertising to Teenagers.* Ithaca, NY: New Strategist Publications, 1999, 136.

33. Mediamark Research, *High Resolution Research.* http://www.magazine.org/content/files/teenprofile04.pdf.

34. "An Interview With Jason Rivera." eMarketer. June 10, 2010.

35. Zollo, 138.

36. "Extreme Proms — How Much Would You Spend?" *Good Morning America*, ABC. April 26, 2011.

37. Alyssa Quart. *Branded: The Buying and Selling of Teenagers.* Cambridge, MA: Perseus Publishing, 2003, 13.

38. See note 35.

39. Ibid., 204.

40. Twenge, 69.

41. Valerie Wee. *Teen Media: Hollywood and the Youth Market in the Digital Age.* Jefferson, NC: McFarland and Company, 2010, 34–35.

42. Pamela Danziger. *Why People Buy Things They Don't Need: Understanding and Predicting Consumer Behavior.* New York: Kaplan, 2004, 135.

43. John P. Huston. "New Trier Unveils Reality Show-Inspired Fashion Marketing Class." *Trib Local*, October 28, 2010. http://www.trib local.com/wilmette-kenilworth/2010/10/28/new-trier-fashion-marketing-class. Accessed November 1, 2011.

44. http://cmerry.wordpress.com/2007/02/28/have-a-prom-fashion-show. Accessed September 12, 2011.

45. Dana deFever. "Fenton High School Hosts Prom, Graduation, Senior Picture Expo." *Flint Journal*, Nov. 3, 2011.

46. Lauren Kelley. "LA Will Plaster Schools with Corporate Logos to Make Some Cash." *Alternet.* Dec. 16, 2010. http://www.alternet.org/newsandviews/article/396962/la_will_plaster_schools_with_corporate_logos_to_make_some_cash/. Accessed September 25, 2011.

47. "Wackiest Proposals." *Seventeen*, Prom issue 2012, 238.

48. http://www.beau-coup.com/blog/planning-tips/vintage-prom-wedding-theme. Accessed September 25, 2011.

Chapter 10

1. http://teranicouture.com/first_page.php. Accessed December 1, 2011.

2. http://www.promdressshop.com/Prom-Dresses.aspx. Accessed November 29, 2011.

3. Brian Quinton. "David's Bridal Takes Prom Dreams Mobile." *Chief Marketer.* June 10, 2009. http://bigfatmarketingblog.com/2009/06/10/davids-bridal-takes-prom-dreams-mobile/. Accessed November 29, 2011.

4. Brian Deagon. "Searches Give View of Society; Prom Dress, Engagement Ring Marketing Had Been Too Early." *Investor's Business Daily.* September 5, 2008.

5. "Tuxedos got their name from Tuxedo Park, the first planned residential community in New York. Emily Post's father was the architect. One evening, Griswold Lorillard, son of the founder of Tuxedo Park, came up with idea to wear a short black jacket without tails. The new fashion was a hit. Men ... would ask their tailors to make them a jacket 'like the ones worn in Tuxedo.' Ironically, the tuxedo was originally considered an informal dinner jacket (because of its short tails), and yet now it is the most formal attire for men to wear." Cindy Post Senning, ed., and Peggy Post. *Prom and Party Etiquette* (New York: Collins, 2010), 60.

6. After Hours is a May Co. subsidiary. May Co. also owns David's Bridal.

7. http://www.raymondcostello.com/html/gingiss.html. Accessed November 30, 2011.

8. Brenda Lloyd. "Mitchell's Formalwear Set to Go National." *Daily News Record.* May 5, 2000, 10.

9. One notable failure is Wal-Mart's foray into the tux rental business in 1994. The company market-tested the idea in two of its Supercenters, but the idea did not take off. Nations-Mart, the company that Wal-Mart subcontracted for its tux business, went bankrupt in 2008.

10. Susy Phillips. "TuxDeluxe." *Arkansas Business,* March 20, 2000, 23.

11. http://www.tuxtown.com/mobile-tux.htm. Accessed November 30, 2011.

12. http://www.nationalprommarket.com/exhibitor. Accessed December 1, 2011.

13. *Internet Wire.* Prom & Pageant Expositions Launches Largest and Only Nationally Touring Expo in the U.S. Aimed at Teens. April 9, 2007.

14. Maureen McCarthy. "Prom Expo to Be Held Saturday in Easton." Enterprise News.com. February 5, 2010. http://www.enterprisenews.com/news/x785863553/Prom-Expo-to-be-held-Saturday-in-Easton. Accessed November 14, 2011.

15. Elizabeth Marie Himchak. "Prom Expo is Sunday at Rancho Bernardo High." *Pomerado News,* March 3, 2011.

16. http://duckbrand.com/promotions/stuck-at-prom/vote-now.aspx. Accessed December 1, 2011.

17. "Wyoming Teen's Duck Tape Creations Make Contest's Top Ten." WZZM13. June 17, 2011. http://wyoming.wzzm13.com/news/education/update-wyoming-teens-duct-tape-creations-make-contests-top-10/58506. Accessed December 3, 2011.

18. http://www.proms.net/invitations_proms.htm. Accessed November 21, 2011.

19. American Prom Blog. "Honor Democracy with an Egyptian Themed Prom." http://americanprom.wordpress.com/2011/02/17/honor-democracy-with-an-egyptian-themed-prom/. Posted February 17, 2011. Accessed November 26, 2011.

20. Democraticunderground.com. "Oops! High School Prom Keepsakes Include Shot Glasses & Champagne Flutes." http://www.democraticunderground.com/discuss/duboard.php?az=view_all& address=105x1224093. June 3, 2011. Accessed November 26, 2011.

21. Teresa P. Lanker. "Dancing for Dollars." *Florists' Review.* February 2011. http://www.floristsreview.com/main/February2011/Dancing/html. Accessed November 23, 2011.

22. Ibid.

23. K. Krause. "Prom Parties Make Florist Top of Mind with Teens." *Society of American Florists,* April 7, 2011. http://safcms.memberfuse.com/?q=node/913. Accessed November 16, 2011.

24. "Local Florist Recognized for Innovative Prom Marketing Program." PRLog.org. April 10, 2010. http://www.prlog.org/10619908-local-florist-recognized-for-innovative-prom-marketing.html. Accessed November 16, 2011.

25. http://www.rouge.com/services-rouge.html. Accessed on November 21, 2011.

26. http://www.kandeej.com/2011/04/prom-makeup.html. Accessed November 21, 2011.

27. These days, parents have another worry: driving and texting.

28. "A Model Guide for Selling Prom Runs." *LCT.* April 13, 2011. http://www.lctmag.com/Operations/news/13540/A-Model-Guide-For-Selling-Prom-Runs. Accessed November 16, 2011.

29. "Prom Season is Here — Are You Ready?" *LCT.* April 6, 2011. http://www.lctmag.com/Operations/news/13529/Prom-Season-is-Here-Are-You-Ready. Accessed November 16, 2011.

30. "Houston Limo Guide: How to Select a Great Limousine." *Limousine Digest.* August 5, 2011. http://www.riveroakslimo.com/blog/tag/prom-night. Accessed November 23, 2011.

31. Gale Horton Gay. "Confessions of a Prom Limo Driver." *Champion Newspaper.com.* April 4, 2011. http://www.championnewspaper.com/news/890confessions — of-a-prom-limo-driver-890.html. Accessed November 16, 2011.

32. Ibid.

33. Peter Hildebrandt. "Cancel the Prom, Cancel the Limo." *Limousine Digest*. March 6, 2011. http://limodigest.com/OnlineArticles/mar 06/cancelprom.html. Accessed November 23, 2011.

34. Brad Gregory. "Blockbuster Prom Season." *LCT*. June 3, 2010. http://blogs.lctmag. com/limorace/archive/2010/06/03/Brad-Upda te-2-Blockbuster-Prom-Season.aspx. Accessed November 16, 2011.

35. "Being Asked to the Proms? Some Operators Seeing More Action." *LCT*. April 28, 2010. http://www.lctmag.com/print/13134/being-asked-to-the-prom-some-operators-seeing-more-action. Accessed November 16, 2011.

36. Hildebrandt.

37. Ibid.

38. http://www.pdxpartybus.com/proms. htm. Accessed December 8, 2011.

39. There are several companies that rent photographic backdrops for formal occasions: Stumps.com, Dozens of Muslins, Prism and Backdrop Outlet, to name a few.

40. In the days before digital photography, labs did not want to make constant adjustments in processing to accommodate lighting changes.

41. Interview, Pat Davisson, November 29, 2011.

42. http://www.pmzpaparazzi.com/phila delphia-event-planning/philadelphia-prom-photographers.html. Accessed December 10, 2011.

43. Brian O'Connor. "International DJ Expo's Pearls of Wisdom." *DJ Times*, vol. 6, no. 12, December, 2003.

44. Jason Weldon. "Program Your Way to More Paydays." *DJ Times*, vol. 18, no. 6, June 2005.

45. Ibid.

46. Ric Hansen. "Nasty Song Packaged for Teens." http://www.schooldancenetwork.com/ about and http://www.schooldancenetwork. com/2011/09/21/nasty-song-packaged-for-teens. September 21, 2011. Accessed November 21, 2011.

47. Ric Hansen. "A School Dance Do Not Play!" *Mobile Beat*, November 8, 2011. www.mo bilebeat.com/a-school-dance-do-not-play/ Posted November 8, 2011. Accessed November 21, 2011.

48. Lori Heatherington. *After Prom Party Guide*. Sandy, UT: ECKO House Publishing, 2006, 6, 11–15, 69.

49. http://www.americanprom.wordpress. com/2011/03/14/fun-affordable-after-prom-ideas. Accessed December 10, 2011.

50. http://www.promtime.com/venues-play house.php. Accessed December 10, 2011.

51. http://www.promtix.com/limelight nightclub.aspx. Accessed December 10, 2011.

52. http://prom-night.com/index.php/pat tys-prom-blog. Accessed December 10, 2011.

Chapter 11

1. Ellie O'Ryan. *Prom*. New York: Disney Press, 2011. Adapted from a screenplay by Katie Wech.

2. Katie Crouch and Grady Hendrix. "Writing Young Adult Fiction." *Slate Magazine*, June 22, 2011.http://www.slate.com/articles/arts/cul turebox/2011/06/writing_youngadult_fiction. html. Accessed December 12, 2011.

3. Ibid.

4. Miriam Kriss. "What's Working in the Young Adult Market?" *Writer's Digest*, November 1, 2011. http://www.writersdigest.com/editor-blogs/guide-to-literary-agents/whats-working-in-the-young-adult-market. Accessed on December 12, 2011.

5. Alyson Noel. *Art Geeks and Prom Queens*. New York: St. Martin's Griffin, 2005.

6. Ibid., 3.

7. Ibid., 7.

8. Ibid., 60.

9. Aimee Ferris. *Will Work for Prom Dress*. New York: Egmont, 2011.

10. "Divorce Statistics in the U.S.A." http:// www.divorceguide.com/usa/divorce-informa tion/divorce-statistics-in-the-usa.html. Accessed January 8, 2012.

11. Ferris, 254.

12. Tina Ferraro. *Top Ten Uses for an Unworn Prom Dress*. New York: Delacorte Press, 2006.

13. Ibid., 18–19.

14. Abby McDonald. *The Anti-Prom*. Somerville, MA: Candlewick Press, 2011.

15. Ibid., 4.

16. Erin Downing, *Prom Crashers*. New York: Simon Pulse, 2007, 1.

17. Laurie Halse Anderson, *Prom*. New York: Speak, 2005.

18. Blake Nelson. *Prom Anonymous*. New York: Penguin Group, 2006.

19. Nico Medina. *Fat Hoochie Prom Queen*. New York: Simon Pulse, 2008. *Fat Hoochie Prom Queen* has the most colorful title, but another book is notable for its many changes of title: *Girl Gives Birth to Own Prom Date* by Todd Strasser, was published by Simon and Schuster Books for Young Readers in 1996. It was reissued that year as *Next to You!* by Simon Pulse, and reissued again as *How I Created My Perfect Prom Date*. In 1999, it was adapted as a screenplay for the Twentieth Century–Fox film *Drive Me Crazy*.

20. *Prom*. Joe Nussbaum, director. Screenplay by Katie Wech. Disney, 2011.

21. Pamela McClintock, "Friday Box Office." *The Hollywood Reporter*, April 29, 2011. http://

www.hollywoodreporter.com/news/friday-box-office-fast-five-183767. Accessed January 11, 2012.

22. *High School Musical 3: Senior Year*, Kenny Ortega, director, John Barsocchini, writer. Walt Disney Company, 2008.

23. John Cairns. "High School Musical 3 Rocks the Box Office with $42 Million." *Film School Rejects*, October 26, 2008. http://www.filmschoolrejects.com/news/high-school-musical-3-rocks-the-box-office-with-42-million.php. Accessed January 11, 2011.

24. "Prom Night," *The Suite Life on Deck*, season 3, episode 21. Disney Channel. Original air date March 18, 2011.

25. *Saved by the Bell*. Sam Bobrick, creator. NBC Productions, 1989–93. Season 4, episode 21, "The Senior Prom." Don Barnhart, director. Original air date, November 7, 1992.

26. Ibid.

27. "Prom Queen," *Glee*. Eric Stoltz, director, Ian Brennan, writer. Fox Television, original air date, May 10, 2011.

28. Ibid.

29. *Dawson's Creek*. Kevin Williamson, creator. WB, 1998–2003.

30. Ibid., season 3, episode 22, "The Anti-Prom." Original air date May 10, 2000.

31. *One Tree Hill*. Mark Schwahn, creator. CW, 2003–.

32. Ibid., season 4, episode 16. Thomas J. Wright, director. Original air date, May 2, 2007.

33. *Grey's Anatomy*, "Losing My Religion," Mark Tinker, director, Shonda Rhimes, writer. Original air date May 15, 2006.

34. *Pretty in Pink*. John Hughes, writer/director. Paramount Pictures, 1986.

35. *Never Been Kissed*. Raja Gosnell, director. Fox 2000 Pictures, 1999.

Chapter 12

1. Meg Cabot, et al. *Prom Nights from Hell*. New York: HarperTeen, 2007.

2. Ibid. pp. 1–52.

3. Ibid., 40.

4. Ibid. Lauren Myracle, pp. 53–93.

5. W.W. Jacobs. "The Monkey's Paw," *The Lady of the Barge*. London and New York: Harper & Brothers, Publishers, 1906.

6. Ibid., 76.

7. Ibid., Kim Harrison. pp. 97–169.

8. Ibid., Miranda Jaffe. "Kiss and Tell," 171.

9. Ibid., Stephenie Meyer. "Hell on Earth," 251–304.

10. Stephen King. *Carrie*. New York: Anchor, 2011.

11. *Carrie*. Brian dePalma, director. MGM, 1976.

12. Garth Johnston. "Carrie the Musical Will Ruin Prom Off-Broadway This January." *The Gothamist*. June 1, 2011. http://gothamist.com/2011/06/01/carrie_the_musical_to_ruin_prom_off.php. Accessed January 21, 2011. and Ben Brantley. "Prom Night, Bloody Prom Night," *The New York Times*, March 2, 2012, C1.

13. Stephen King. *Carrie*. New York: Pocket Books, 1999, xiii–xiv.

14. Stephenie Meyer. *Twilight*. New York: Little Brown and Company, 2005, 495.

15. Ibid., 498.

16. Nicole Sperling, "The 'Twilight' Saga." *Entertainment Weekly*. June 16, 2008. EW.com. http://www.ew.com/ew/article/0,,20308569_20211840,00.html. Accessed January 23, 2012.

17. Box Office Mojo. "Twilight." http://www.boxofficemojo.com/movies/?id=twilight08.htm. Accessed January 23, 2012.

18. *Buffy the Vampire Slayer*. Fran Rubel Kuzui, director. Joss Whedon, writer. Twentieth Century–Fox Film Corp., 1992.

19. *Buffy the Vampire Slayer*, "The Prom." WB. David Solomon, director, Joss Whedon and Marni Noxon, writers. Original air date, May 11, 1999.

20. *Prom Night*. Paul Lynch, director. AVCO Embassy Pictures, 1980.

21. Agatha Christie. *And Then There Were None*. London: Collins Crime Club, 1939.

22. The picture is a riot of careless filmmaking. Although the story is set in Ohio, one shot clearly shows a view of the Pacific Ocean from somewhere in Southern California where the movie was actually filmed.

23. *Prom Night*. Nelson McCormick, director. Sony Pictures, 2008.

24. *Hello Mary Lou: Prom Night II*. Bruce Pittman, director. Norstar Releasing, 1987.

25. *Prom Night III: The Last Kiss*. Ron Oliver, Peter R. Simpson, directors. Norstar Releasing, 1990.

26. *Prom Night IV: Deliver Us from Evil*. Clay Borris, director. Norstar Home Video, 1992.

27. *Prom Night in Mississippi*. Paul Saltzman, director. Return to Mississippi Productions and HBO Documentary Films, 2009.

28. Ibid.

29. Ibid.

30. Ibid.

31. *Prom Night in Kansas City*. Hali Lee, Peter von Ziegesar, directors. Golden Pig Productions, Zeitgeist Films (dist.), 2002.

32. Ibid.

33. Ibid.

34. *The World's Best Prom*. Chris Talbot, Ari Vena, directors. Matson Films, 2006.

35. Ibid.

36. Ibid.

37. Robin Hemley. *Do-Over!* New York: Little Brown and Company, 2009, 219.

38. Ibid., 178.

39. Rob Spillman, ed. *The Time of My Life.* New York: Broadway Books, 2008.

40. Ibid., 79.

41. David Boyer. *Kings & Queens: Queers at the Prom.* Brooklyn: Soft Skull Press, 2004.

42. Ibid., 3.

43. Cindy Post Senning and Peggy Post. *Prom and Party Etiquette.* New York: Collins, 2010.

44. Sheryl Berk. *The Ultimate Prom Guide.* New York: Harper Entertainment, 1999.

45. Heather Wilhelm. "Surviving Girl Land: Sex, Lies & Proms. realclearbooks.com. January 25, 2012. Accessed January 25, 2012.

Chapter 13

1. Susan Shapiro Barasch, *Tripping the Prom Queen.* New York: St. Martin's Griffin, 2006.

2. Dana Milbank. "How the Journalist Prom Got Out of Control." *Washington Post.* April 28, 2011.

3. Jennifer Medina. "A Second Shot to Have the Best Night of Their Lives." *New York Times.* May 11, 2011. http://www.nytimes.com/2011/05/12/us/12prom.html?pagewanted=all. Accessed February 1, 2012.

4. Mom Prom. http://www.momprom.org. Accessed February 10, 2012.

5. *Peggy Sue Got Married.* Dir. Francis Ford Coppola. Tristar Pictures, 1986.

6. "Ken Davenport Presents the Awesome 80s Prom." http://www.portlandspirit.com/awesome80sprom.php. Accessed February 1, 2012.

7. These costumes can be found at http://www.halloweenexpress.com, http://www.partycity.com and http://www.buycostumes.com. Accessed February 1, 2012.

8. For a recent diatribe about proms, see Caitlin Flanagan, *Girl Land.* New York: Reagan Arthur Books, 2012.

Bibliography

Books

Abell, Marietta and Agnes J. Anderson. *School Dances and Proms.* Minneapolis: T.S. Denison and Company, 1962.

Alvarez, Julia. *Once Upon a Quinceañera: Coming of Age in the U.S.A.* New York: Penguin Group, 2007.

Anderson, Laurie Halse. *Prom.* New York: Penguin, 2005.

Asante, M.K., Jr. *It's Bigger Than Hip Hop.* New York: St. Martin's Press, 2008.

Bailey, Beth L. *From Front Porch to Back Seat: Courtship in Twentieth Century America.* Baltimore: Johns Hopkins University Press, 1988.

Barash, Susan Shapiro. *Tripping the Prom Queen.* New York: St. Martin's Press, 2006.

Berk, Sheryl. *The Ultimate Prom Guide.* New York: Harper Entertainment, 1999.

Best, Amy L. *Prom Night.* London: Routledge, 2000.

Boyer, David. *Kings & Queens: Queers at the Prom.* Brooklyn, NY: Soft Skull Press, 2004.

Browne, Ray B., ed. *American Popular Culture Through History.* Westport, CT: Greenwood Press, 2002.

Brumberg, Joan Jacobs. *The Body Project.* New York: Vintage Books, 1997.

Cabot, Meg and Lauren Myracle, Kim Harrison, Michele Jaffe, Stephanie Meyer. *Prom Nights from Hell.* New York: Harper Teen, 2007.

Cahn, Susan K. *Sexual Reckonings.* Cambridge, Massachusetts: Harvard University Press, 2007.

Calo, Richard G. Ph.D. *American Prom.* Nashville, TN: Cumberland House, 2006.

Cook, Daniel Thomas. *The Commodification of Childhood.* Durham, NC: Duke University Press, 2004.

Coontz, Stephanie. *The Way We Never Were.* New York: Basic Books, 1992.

Croker, Richard. *The Boomer Century 1946–2046.* New York: Springboard Press, 2007.

Cusick, Philip A. *Inside High School.* New York: Holt, Rinehart and Winston, 1973.

Danesi, Marcel. *Cool: The Signs and Meanings of Adolescence.* Toronto: University of Toronto Press, 1994.

Danziger, Pamela. *Why People Buy Things They Don't Need: Understanding and Predicting Consumer Behavior.* New York: Kaplan Publishing, 2004.

Denizet-Lewis, Benoit. *American Voyeur.* New York: Simon and Shuster, 2010.

Dils, Ann and Ann Cooper Albright. *Moving History Through Cultures.* Wesleyan University Press, 2001.

Douglas, Susan J. *Where the Girls Are: Growing Up Female With the Mass Media.* New York: Three Rivers Press, 1994.

Downing, Erin. *Prom Crashers.* New York: Simon Pulse, 2006.

Eckert, Penelope. *Jocks and Burnouts.* New York: Teacher's College Press, 1984.

Evans, Harold. *The American Century.* New York: Alfred A. Knopf, 1998.

Ferraro, Tina. *Top Ten Uses for an Unworn Prom Dress.* New York: Delacorte, 2006.

Ferris, Aimee. *Will Work for Prom Dress.* New York: Egmont, 2011.

Fikentscher, Kai. "You Better Work!" *Underground Dance Music in New York City.* Wesleyan University Press, 2000.

Friedlander, Paul. *Rock & Roll: A Social History.* Boulder, CO: Westview Press, 2006.

Gilbert, Eugene. *Advertising and Marketing to Young People.* Pleasantville, NY: Printers' Ink Books, 1957.

Gillon, Steve. *Boomer Nation.* New York: Free Press, 2004.

Giordano, Ralph G. *Social Dancing in America, a History and a Reference, vol. 2.* Westport, CT: Greenwood Press, 2006.

Giroux, Henry A. and Grace Pollock. *The Mouse That Roared: Disney and the End of Innocence.* Lanham, MD: Rowman and Littlefield, 2010.

Gordon, Beverly, "Blue Jeans as Self-Expression." In Stuart Kallen, *America's Decades*, San Diego: Greenhaven Press, 2000, 218–20.

Gottlieb, Annie. *Do You Believe In Magic? The Second Coming of the Sixties Generation*. New York: Times Books, 1987.

Heatherington, Lori. *After Prom Party Guide*. Sandy, UT: ECKO House Publishing, 2006.

Hemley, Robin. *Do-Over!* New York: Little, Brown and Co., 2009.

Herald, Jacqueline. *Fashions of a Decade: The 1970s*. New York: Facts on File, 1992.

Hine, Thomas. *The Rise and Fall of the American Teenager*. New York: Harper Collins, 1999.

Howe, Neil and William Strauss. *Generations: The History of America's Future, 1584 to 2069*. New York: William Morrow and Company, 1991.

_____. *Millenials Rising: The Next Great Generation*. New York: Vintage Books, 2000.

_____. *13th Gen: Abort, Retry, Ignore, Fail?* New York: Vintage Books, 1993.

Kallen, Stuart A. *The 1980s*. San Diego: Lucent Books, 1999.

_____. *The 1950s*. San Diego: Greenhaven Press, 2000.

_____. *The History of Rock and Roll*. Farmington Hills, MI: Lucent Books, 2003.

Kett, Joseph F. *Rites of Passage*. New York: Basic Books, 1974.

King, Stephen. *Carrie*. New York: Pocket Books, 1999.

Krulik, Nancy. *Prom! The Complete Guide to a Truly Spectacular Night*. New York: Grosset and Dunlap, 2002.

Lavinthal, Andrea and Jessica Rozler. *The Hookup Handbook*. New York: Spotlight Entertainment, 2005.

Lloyd, Brenda. "Mitchell's Formalwear Set to Go National." *Daily News Record*. May 5, 2000, 10.

Lomas, Clare. *20th Century Fashion: The 80s and 90s: Power Dressing to Sportswear*. Milwaukee: Gareth Stevens Publishing, 2000.

Mahdi, Louise Carus, ed. *Betwixt and Between: Patterns of Masculine and Feminine Initiation*. Peru, IL: Open Court Publishing, 1987.

Marling, Karal Ann. *Debutante*. Lawrence, KS: University Press of Kansas, 2004.

Marty, Martin A. *Daily Life in the United States, 1960–1990*. Westport, CT: Greenwood Press, 1997.

Massoni, Kelley. *Fashioning Teenagers: A Cultural History of Seventeen Magazine*. Walnut Creek, CA: Left Coast Press, 2010.

Mazzarella, Sharon R. *Growing Up Girls: Popular Culture and the Construction of Identity*. New York: Peter Lang Publishing, 1999.

McDonald, Abby. *The Anti-Prom*. Somerville, MA: Candlewick Press, 2011.

McMinn, Lisa Graham. *Sexuality and Holy Longing: Embracing Intimacy in a Broken World*. John Wiley and Sons, Inc. 2004, 13–14.

Medina, Nico. *Fat Hoochie Prom Queen*. New York: Simon Pulse, 2008.

Melinkoff, Ellen. *What We Wore: An Offbeat Social History of Women's Clothing, 1950 to 1980*. New York: Quill, 1984.

Meyer, Stephanie. *Twilight*. New York: Little, Brown and Co., 2005.

Milner, Murray Jr. *Freaks, Geeks and Cool Kids*. New York: Routledge, 2004.

Nelson, Blake. *Prom Anonymous*. New York: Penguin, 2006.

Noel, Alyson. *Art Geeks and Prom Queens*. New York: St. Martin's Griffin, 2005.

Orenstein, Peggy. *Cinderella Ate My Daughter: Dispatches from the Front Lines of the New Girlie-Girl Culture*. New York: Harper, 2011.

Palladino, Grace. *Teenagers*. New York: Basic Books, 1996.

Ponton, Lynn. *The Sex Lives of Teenagers*. New York: Dutton, 2000.

Post, Emily. *Prom and Party Etiquette*. New York: Collins, 2010.

Pratt, Jane. *For Real: The Uncensored Truth About America's Teenagers*. New York: Hyperion, 1995.

Quart, Alissa. *Branded: The Buying and Selling of Teenagers*. Cambridge: Perseus Publishing, 2003.

Rielly, Edward J. *American Popular History Through Culture: The 1960s*. Westport, CT: Greenwood Press, 2003.

Riera, Michael. *Staying Connected to Your Teenager: How to Keep Them Talking to You and How to Hear What They're Really Saying*. Cambridge, MA: Da Capo Press, 2003.

Rollin, Lucy. *Twentieth Century Teen Culture by the Decades*. Westport, CT: Greenwood Press, 1999.

Saltz, Joanna. *Seventeen's Guide to Your Perfect Prom: A Planner and Scrapbook*. New York: Hearst Communications, 2007.

Savage, Jon. *Teenage: The Creation of Youth Culture*. New York: Viking, 2007.

Schmidt, Mark Ray, ed. *The 1970s*. San Diego: Greenhaven Press, 2000.

Sessions Stepp, Laura. *Unhooked*. New York: Riverhead Books, 2007.

Shaller, Michael. "The Truth About the 1980s Economy." James D. Torr, ed. *The 1980s*. San Diego: Greenhaven Press, 2000.

Simmons, Rachel. *Odd Girl Out*. New York: Harcourt, Inc., 2002.

Solcedo, Michele. *Quinceañera: The Essential Guide to Planning the Perfect Sweet Fifteen Celebration*. New York: Henry Holt and Co., Inc., 2007.

Spillman, Rob, ed. *The Time of My Life*. New York: Broadway Books, 2008.

Stalder, Erika. *The Date Book*. San Francisco: Zest Books, 2007.

Steele, Valerie. *Fifty Years of Fashion: New Look to Now*. New Haven: Yale University Press, 1997.

Strasser, Todd. *Girl Gives Birth to Own Prom Date*. New York: Simon and Schuster Books for Young Readers, 1996.

Szatmary, David P. *Rockin' In Time: A Social History of Rock-and-Roll*. Upper Saddle River, NJ, 2010.

Thompson, Michael and Catherine O'Neill Grace. *Best Friends, Worst Enemies*. New York: Ballantine, 2001.

Tulgan, Bruce. *Not Everyone Gets a Trophy*. San Francisco: Jossey-Bass, 2009.

Turner, Matthew, ed. *U.S.A. Sixties*. Danbury, CT: Grolier Educational, 2001.

Twenge, Jean M., Ph.D. and W. Keith Campbell, Ph.D. *The Narcissism Epidemic: Living in the Age of Entitlement*. New York: Simon and Shuster, 2009.

Watson, Linda. *Vogue: Twentieth Century Fashion*. London: Carlton Books Limited, 1999.

Wee, Valerie. *Teen Media: Hollywood and the Youth Market in the Digital Age*." Jefferson, NC: McFarland, 2010, 34–35.

Whitaker, Jan. *Service and Style: How the American Department Store Fashioned the Middle Class*. New York: Macmillan, 2006.

Wolf, Naomi. *The Beauty Myth*. New York: Anchor Books, 1991.

Yarrow, Kit, Ph.D. and Jayne O'Donnell. *Gen Buy*. San Francisco: Jossey-Bass, 2009.

Zollo, Peter. *Wise Up to Teens: Insights Into Marketing and Advertising to Teenagers*. Ithaca, NY: New Strategist Publications, 1999.

Dress for an American Ritual." Thesis: University of Minnesota, 1995.

Massoni, Kelley. *Bringing Up Baby: The Birth and Early Development of Seventeen Magazine*. Dissertation, Graduate Department of Sociology, University of Kansas, 1999.

Miller, Montana. "Taking a New Spotlight to the Prom: Youth Culture and Its Emerging Video Archive." *The Journal of American Culture* (2010): 33:1.

Naigle, Debbie. "Literature Review of Media Messages to Adolescent Females." *Educational Communications and Technology. University of Saskatchewan*, Feb., 2005.

Ogden, Cyntha, Ph.D. and Margaret Carroll, M.S.P.H. "Prevalence of Obesity Among Children and Adolescents: United States, Trends 1963–1965 Through 2007–2008." Centers for Disease Control and Prevention. http://www.cdc.gov/nchs/data/hestat/obesity_child_07_08/obesity_child_07_08.pdf. Last updated June 4, 2010. Accessed January 28, 2011.

Paxton, Felicity Hannah. "America at the Prom: Ritual and Regeneration." Dissertation in American Civilization, University of Pennsylvania, 2000.

Pew Research Center Publications. "The Millenials: Confident. Connected. Open to Change." Pewresearch.org, accessed on 1/7/11.

Sweeney, Richard, University Librarian. "Millennial Behaviors and Demographics." (Academic paper) New Jersey Institute of Technology. December 22, 2006.

Zlatunich, Nicole. "Prom Dreams and Prom Reality: Girls Negotiating Perfection at the High School Prom." *Sociological Inquiry*, Vol. 79, No. 3 (August 2009): 351–375.

Journal Articles, Academic Papers, and Research Center Reports

Cornell, Jodi L. "Adolescents Tell Us Why Teens Have Oral Sex." *Journal of Adolescent Health*. (April 29, 2005): 299–301.

Durham, Meenakshi Gigi. "Sex and Spectacle in Seventeen Magazine" A Feminist Myth Analysis." Journalism and Mass Communications Publications. University of Iowa. May 25, 2007.

Finders, Margaret J. "Queens and Teen Zines: Early Adolescent Females Reading Their Way toward Adulthood." *Anthropology and Education Quarterly*, Vol. 27, No. 1 (March 1996), pp. 71–89.

Hegland, Jane Elizabeth. "The High School Prom: A Case Study of Expectations and

Newspapers, Magazines, and Trade Papers

Abel, David. "She Can't Bring Same-Sex Date to Catholic School Prom." *The Boston Globe*, April 27, 2007.

"Adult Spy Goes to High School," *Life*, May 5, 1967, 97.

Barclay, Dorothy, "Prom Begins: Parents Start Nail-Nibbling," *The New York Times*, April 30, 1957, 47.

Barker, Olivia. "Why Freak Dancing Freaks Out Schools." *USA Today*. June 1, 2001.

Barnes, Brook. "Disney Looking Into Cradle for Customers." *The New York Times*, February 6, 2011.

_____. "For Disney, a Younger Princess." *The New York Times*. December 12, 2011, B-9.

Basham, Megan. "Bringing Up Princess: Turning Girls Into Narcissists." *The Wall Street Journal*, June 12, 2009.

Bennett, Jessica. "Tales of a Modern Diva." *Newsweek*. April 6, 2009, 42–43.

Benson, Elisa. "Be His Dream Date." *Seventeen Prom* 2011, 262.

The Billboard, April 3, 1961, 6.

"The Black Teen Explosion." *Ebony*. April 2004, 72–73.

"Boy, 17, Seeks to Take Male Date to the Prom." *The New York Times*, April 11, 1979.

Chambers, Marcia, "High School Dropout Rate at 45%, Macchiarola Reports to City Board." *The New York Times*, October 17, 1979.

"Changing Times," *The Kiplinger Magazine*, June 1950, 33.

Cohen, Bari Nan. "Belle of the Bash." *Young and Modern Prom Special*. Spring, 1998, 64.

"Crime." *Jet*. November 21, 1957, 45.

"The Date of His Choice." *The New York Times*, April 15, 1979.

Deagon, Brian. "Searches Give View of Society; Prom Dress, Engagement Ring Marketing Had Been Too Early." *Investor's Business Daily*. September 5, 2008.

deFever, Dana. "Fenton High School Hosts Prom, Graduation, Senior Picture Expo." *The Flint Journal*, Nov. 3, 2011.

della Cava, Marco R. "No Dancing Around It: Proms Are Getting Strict." *USA Today*. May 21, 2003, A-1.

D'innocenzio, Anne. "Magazines Drop Print for Web to Reach Teens." *USA Today*, August 29, 2006.

Ebony, Aug. 1991, 48.

Eckholm, Erik. "In Isolated Utah City, New Clubs for Gay Students." *The New York Times*, January 1, 2011.

Editors of Time-Life Books, *Our American Century: Time of Transition: The 70s*. Alexandria, VA: Time-Life Books, 1998, 111–21.

Elkin, Toby. "Teens Now Spend More Time Online Than Watching TV." *Advertising Age*. July 28, 2003.

Elliott, Stuart. "MTV Strives to Keep Up With Young Viewers." *The New York Times*. January 31, 2011, B5.

"GAC's Plan Brings Bands to Teens and Vice-Versa," *The Billboard*, May 19, 1958.

Gentil, Gerard. "Prom Dresses." *Seventeen*. March, 1982, 134.

"Georgia High School Students Return to Segregated Prom." *Jet*. May 26, 2003, 18.

Gibbs, Nancy, "How Should We Teach Our Kids about SEX?" *Time*, May 24, 1993.

Gordon, Beverly, "Blue Jeans as Self-Expression." *America's Decades*, 218–20.

"Got a Date for Prom? Enough to Fill a Bus." *The Seattle Times*, May 5, 2010.

Graeber, Laurel. "Long Live the Prom." *Seventeen*, April 1980, 176.

"Fake Bake Debate." *Newsweek*. April 15, 2008.

Fix, Janet L., "Teen Spending Power: Awesome!" *USA Today*, Dec. 10, 1992, B1.

Freas, Ralph, *The Billboard*, 1957.

Hallman, Tom, Jr. "Grinding Rubs Teachers Wrong Way." *The Oregonian*. November 11, 2010, A-4.

Hanes, Stephanie. "Little Girls or Little Women? The Disney Princess Effect." *The Christian Science Monitor*, September 24, 2011.

Hare, Mary Gail. "Prom Invitations Are Elaborate at McDonogh School." *Baltimore Sun*, June 3, 2011.

Harvey, Brett, "Fitting In for Fifties Women," *The 1950s* (Greenhaven Press, 2000), 156.

Haughney, Christine. "Florida to California, Prom Dresses Selling." *The New York Times*. May 3, 2009.

Hays, Matthew. "All Dressed Up, No Place to Go?" *The Advocate*. May 14, 2002.

Henderson, William. "A Prom for All." *The Advocate*, June 20, 2006, 27.

Hernandez, Raymond. "From the Suburbs to the Inner City, Proms Endure As a Rite of Passage." *The New York Times*. June 14, 1993.

"High School Senior in Alabama Shares Prom Night With His Mom." *Jet*. May 29, 2000.

Himchak, Elizabeth Marie. "Prom Expo is Sunday at Rancho Bernardo High." *Pomerado News*, March 3, 2011.

"Homosexual Denied Male Escort Plans to Picket Providence Prom." *The New York Times*, April 22, 1979.

"Homosexual Receives Approval to Take a Male Friend to Prom." *The New York Times*. May 13, 1979.

Hu, Winnie. "Holding Prom on a School Night." *The New York Times*. April 13, 2010.

Ingersoll, E.G., "Spare-Time Jobs for High School Kids," *The Kiplinger Magazine*, April, 1954, 39.

"Integrated High School Prom." *Jet*. April 30, 2007, 46.

Jouvenal, Justin. "Gay Male Student Named Prom Queen." *The Washington Post*. June 1, 2011.

Kane, Eugene. "Proms Take Unfortunate Steps Backward." *Milwaukee Journal Sentinel*. May 14, 2003.

Kaplan, Thomas. "Next on Cuomo's Agenda: Preparing His 16-Year-Olds for Their Driver's Licenses." *The New York Times*. July 26, 2011, A-16.

Kaufman, Burton I., "The War of October 1973 and the Oil Embargo," Mark Ray Schmidt, ed. San Diego, Greenhaven Press, 2000.

Kelly, Katy. "Prom Dress Obsessed: Searching for that Special, Memory-making Gown." *USA Today*, May 14, 1997, 1-D.

The Kiplinger Magazine, June 1950.

Kirn, Walter. "Will Teenagers Disappear?" *Time*. February 21, 2000.

Kizer, Rich and Georgeanne Bender. "Marketing to Millennials." *Craftrends*. June 2005.

Koch, Wendy. "High Schools Join Call to Action Against Student Drinking." *USA Today*. October 17, 2007.

Koepnick, Jenny. "New Rule Requires Prom Bus." *Paly Voice*. October 21, 2002.

Lehoczky, Etelka. "Young, Gay and Okay." *The Advocate*, February 1, 2005, 31.

"Life Goes to a Party," *Life*, May 31, 1937, 82.

Lombardi, Kate Stone. "Planning and Policing Prom Night." *The New York Times*. May 6, 2007.

Jaffe, Rona, "Listening In on New York's Elite Teenagers." *New York Magazine*, May 12, 1972, 56 & 63.

Jayson, Sharon. "Study Challenges Myths of Teen Sex." *USA Today*. May 20, 2008, D-7.

Jepson, Christy. "Mormon Prom Deep in the Heart of Texas." *Mormon Times*. April 11, 2009.

Jet, Sept. 16, 1991, 35.

Klampe, Michelle L. "Elsinore High School Special Education Prom Is a Celebration of Friendship." *The Press-Enterprise*. May 10, 2010.

Kilgannon, Corey. "A Prom for Students Who Don't Want One." *The New York Times*, June 6, 2011.

Klaus, Mary. "Midstate Girl Scouts Get the Gold Through Community Service." *The Patriot-News*. June 25, 2011.

Kranz, Cindy. "Adults Freak Over Teens' Dancing." *The Cincinnati Enquirer*. May 29, 2001.

La Gorce, Tammy. "Confronting Prom Night Drinking." *The New York Times*. June 1, 2008.

Landers, Ann, "Straight Talk on Sex and Growing Up," *Life*, Aug. 18, 1961, 74.

Laucius, Joanne. "Princess Culture Turning Girls Into Overspending Narcissists." *The Ottowa Citizen*, August 18, 2010.

Lowery, Jan A., "Dance Through the Ages." *Ebony Jr.*, Nov. 1978, 27.

"Male Student Wearing Dress Denied Entrance to Prom." *Jet*. June 12, 2006, 10.

Manning, Anita, "Teens and Sex in the Age of AIDS." *USA Today*, Oct. 3, 1988.

Marko, Deborah M. "Senior Guys Primp for VHS Prom." *The Daily Journal*. June 3, 2011.

Martin, Douglas, "Randy Wood, 94, Founder of Dot Records," *The New York Times*, April 15, 2011, A25.

Meltzer, Marisa. "The Prom Dress Moves Into the Designer Leagues." *The New York Times*, June 1, 2011.

Milbank, Dana. "How the Journalist Prom Got Out of Control." *The Washington Post*. April 28, 2011.

Miller, Heather. "Almost 300 at Iberia Parish Special-Needs Prom." *The Daily Iberian*. May 18, 2010.

"Mom's First Prom." *Jet*. August 10, 1998.

"Name Band Failings," *The Billboard*, April 21, 1951, 24.

"Norwalk Denied Permit for Post-Prom Party," *The New York Times*, June 7, 1958.

O'Connor, Brian. "International DJ Expo's Pearls of Wisdom." *DJ Times*, vol. 6, no. 12, December, 2003.

O'Donnell, Jayne. "Economic Downturn May Be Pulling Necklines Up." *USA Today*. March 9, 2009, B-1.

_____. "Marketers Keep Pace With Tweens: Fashion-minded Girls Prove Rich, But Fast-Moving Target." *USA Today*. April 11, 2007, B1.

Olkon, Sara and Steve Schmadeke. "Mormon Prom a Modest Good Time." *Chicago Tribune*, April 30, 2007.

Painter, Kim, "Teenagers Ponder: Is Everyone Doing It?" *USA Today*, March 5, 1991.

Parker, Suzi. *The Christian Science Monitor*. "Constance McMillan Case: Proms as Gay-Rights Battlegrounds." March 23, 2010.

Parle, Richard H., "Party After Prom to Charter Train." *The New York Times*, June 5.

Perna, Michael. Jr., "*Junior Prom—1929.*" *Shrewsbury Chronicle*, Sept. 22, 2009.

Peterson, Karen S. "In High School, Dating is a World Unto Itself." *USA Today*. September 3, 1997, D1.

_____. "Girls Stand Up to Boys; Studies Find, and Teens Agree, That Sexual Boundaries Are Being Set." *USA Today*. April 23, 2002, D8.

_____. "Knowledgeable Teens Still Starve for Attention." *USA Today*. July 18, 1997, D-8.

_____. "Teens Try to Squeeze Flash, Fashion Into School Rules." *USA Today*. August 30, 1999. D-6.

Phelan, Hayley. "Slutty Chic a Popular Prom Dress Trend at Your School?" *Teen Vogue*. March 30, 2010.

Phillips, Susy. "TuxDeluxe." *Arkansas Business*, March 20, 2000, 23.

Poinsett, Alan, "The Dixie Schools Charade." *Ebony*, Aug. 1971, 144.

"Prom Parties, 'tis the Season." *The Rotarian*, June 1958.

"The Prom Went On and On." *Life*, June 9, 1958.

Puente, Maria. "Tech-savvy Teens Primp for the Prom Online." *USA Today*. April 26, 2000, D-10.

"Queen Bee of the School." *Life*, October 11, 1963, 73.

Quenqua, Douglas. "Upload a Prom Dress Photo, and Hope." *The New York Times*. May 12, 2010.

Reddick, DeWitt C., "It Was Only Fifty Years Ago." *The Alcade*, March 1975, 17.

Rotelle, Gabriel. "Shall We Dance?" *The Advocate*. July 3, 2001, 72.

St. George, Donna. "Study of Teen Cellphone Use Reinforces Impression That They're Always Using Them." *Washington Post*. April 20, 2010, B01.

Samuels, Allison. "Bye-Bye Bad Hair Days." *Newsweek*. June 20, 2005.

Scelfo, Julie. "Out at the Prom." *Newsweek*. June 9, 2003.

Schuckel, Kathleen. "School Daze." *Indianapolis Monthly*. September 2002, 173.

Scrivener, Leslie. "A Happily Dateless Prom." *The Toronto Star*. June 29, 2003.

Shapiro, Anna. "Separate But Equal?" *Spin*. May 2003, 96 & 99.

"Sharp Tongue." *The Advocate*. July 5, 2005, 29.

"Should Teenagers Have Steady Dates?" *Jet*, October 1, 1959, 25.

Sisson, Carmen K. "Southern School Holds First Prom for Blacks and Whites." *Christian Science Monitor*. April 25, 2007.

Staples, Gracie Bonds. "Programs Target Alcohol, Drugs During Prom Season." *Atlanta Journal Constitution*. April 1, 2011.

"Style: A Night to Forget." *Newsweek*. May 12, 2003.

"Teenagers Give Out." April 3, 1961. *The Billboard*.

Thomas, Janet. "A Night to Remember." *New Era*. February 2007, 31.

Thompson, Arienne. "16, Pregnant — and Famous." *USA Today*. November 23, 2010. D-1.

Tugend, Aline. "Peeking at the Negative Side of High School Popularity." *The New York Times*. June 18, 2010.

Unger, Craig, "Attitude." *New York Magazine*. July 26, 1982, 26.

Vanderkam, Laura. "Sexually Active Girls Lament: Why Didn't I Wait?" *USA Today*. June 12, 2003, A-15.

Vitello, Paul. "Hold the Limo: The Prom's Canceled as Decadent." *The New York Times*. December 10, 2005.

"Wackiest Proposals." *Seventeen*, Prom issue 2012, 238.

Weldon, Jason. "Program Your Way to More Paydays." *DJ Times*, vol. 18, no. 6, June, 2005.

Welsh, Patrick. "Prom View Skirts Key Message." *USA Today*. June 10, 2003, A-12.

_____. "Proms Equalize High School Life — Briefly." *USA Today*. June 4, 2003, A-11.

Wingert, Pat. "Teens, Tans and Truth." *Newsweek*. May 10, 2008.

"What Goes Around Comes Around." *Newsweek*. October 1, 2009.

Woodyard, Chris. "Generation Y: The Young and Boundless are Taking Over Pop Culture." *USA Today*. October 6, 1998.

Yankelovich, Daniel, "The Search for Self-Fulfillment." *America's Decades: The 1970s*. Mark Ray Schmidt, ed. San Diego, Greenhaven Press, 2000, 231.

"Youth: Crestubilee." *Time*, June 1, 1953.

Web Sites/Articles

"Album-Oriented Rock," last modified June 29, 2011, http://en.wikipedia.org/wiki/Album-oriented_rock#Freeform_and_progressive. Accessed June 29, 2011.

American Prom Blog. "Honor Democracy with an Egyptian Themed Prom." http://american prom.wordpress.com/2011/02/17/honor-democracy-with-an-egyptian-themed-prom/. Posted February 17, 2011. Accessed November 26, 2011.

Amos, Denise Smith. "Students Honor Special Needs Students at Prom." *The Cincinnati Enquirer*. May 15, 2011. http://content.usatoday.net/dist/custom/gci/InsidePage.aspx?cId=cinc innati&sParam=47198902.story. Accessed August 22, 2011.

"Anti-Prom: Super Prom." http://www.nypl.org/events/programs/2011/06/03/anti-prom-super-prom. Accessed August 23, 2011.

Babbs, Dena and Crystal Zobrist, "Gen Xers Lead Piercing and Tattoo Fad," last modified June 1, 1997, http://www.jour.unr.edu/out-post/specials/genx.tattoo1.html. Accessed June 22, 2011.

"Biography: Nancy Reagan," http://www.pbs.org/wgbh/americanexperience/features/biog raphy/reagan-nancy/. Accessed June 7, 2011.

Box Office Mojo. "Twilight." http://www.box officemojo.com/movies/?id=twilight08.htm. Accessed January 23, 2012.

"Brown v. Board of Education." The National Archives. http://www.ourdocuments.gov/doc.php?flash=true&doc=87. Accessed on August 12, 2011.

"The Brownie Camera Page," www.brownie camera.com. Accessed 3/27/11.

Buddenberg, Laura and Kathy McGee. "Prom's Real Purpose." Parenting.org, 2011. http://www.parenting.org/article/proms-real-pur pose. Accessed on September 18, 2011.

"By 2011, Teen Market Shrinks, Spending Clout Soars to $200 Billion." http://www.market ingvox.com/by-2011-teen-market-shrinks-spending-clout-soars-to-200b-031001. Accessed August 12, 2011.

Cairns, John. "High School Musical 3 Rocks the Box Office with $42 Million." *Film School Rejects*, October 26, 2008. http://www.film

schoolrejects.com/news/high-school-musical-3-rocks-the-box-office-with-42-million.php. Accessed January 11, 2011.

Case, Tony. "After 65 Years, Seventeen Still One of the Cool Kids." *MPA Reports*, June 23, 2009. http://www.magazine.org/news/mpa_reports/mpa-reports-2009-seventeen-solutions.aspx. Accessed October 26, 2011.

"Cell Phones Key to Teens' Social Lives, 47% Can Text With Eyes Closed." http://www.marketingcharts.com/interactive/cell-phones-key-to-teens. Aug. 2008. Accessed July 21, 2011.

"Christian School Tells Boy to Skip Prom." Associated Press. Posted on msnbc.msn.com May 8, 2009. Accessed August 15, 2011.

Clippard, Todd. "Should Christian Teens Attend the Prom?" http://faughnfamily.word press.com/2007/03/20/should-christian-teens-attend-the-prom-by-todd-clippard. Posted March 20, 2007. Accessed August 15, 2011.

Crouch, Katie and Grady Hendrix. "Writing Young Adult Fiction." *Slate Magazine*, June 22, 2011. http://www.slate.com/articles/arts/culturebox/2011/06/writing_youngadult_fiction.html. Accessed December 12, 2011.

Donovan, Cathy K. "When a Princess Costume Becomes a Culture." *Rutgers Focus*. February 6, 2008. http://www.news.rutgers.edu/focus/issue.2008-02-05.0513554387/article. Accessed January 28, 2011.

Erickson, Tammy. "Trophies for Everyone? Debunking Another Gen Y Myth." *Harvard Business Review, HBR Blog Network*. http://blogs.hbr.org/Erickson/2008/06/trophies_for_everyone_debunkin.html. Accessed July 19, 2011.

"FAQs: Popular 20th Century American Foods," http://www.foodtimeline.org/fooddecades.html#1960s. Accessed May 13, 2011.

"Flashy You Tube 'Prom-posals' Rival Marriage Proposals." ABC News. http://abcnews.com/Technology/youtube-prom-posals-rival-marriage-proposals. Accessed May 15, 2011.

Gay, Gale Horton. "Confessions of a Prom Limo Driver." *Champion Newspaper.com*. April 4, 2011. http://www.championnewspaper.com/news/890confessions-of-a-prom-limo-driver-890.html. Accessed November 16, 2011.

Gibbons, Sheila. "Teen Magazines Send Girls All the Wrong Messages." *WeNews*. October 29, 2003. http://www.womensnews.org/story/uncovering-gender/031029/teen-magazines-send-girls-all-the-wrong-messages. Accessed October 3, 2011.

Gillie, Brian. "Florida School Selects the Nation's First Transgendered Prom Queen." Examiner.com. http://www.examiner.com/strange-news-in-national/florida-school-awards-the-nations-first-transgendered-prom-queen. June 1, 2011.

Gregory, Brad. "Blockbuster Prom Season." *LCT* (Limousine, Charter & Tour). June 3, 2010. http://blogs.lctmag.com/limorace/archive/2010/06/03/Brad-Update-2-Blockbuster-Prom-Season.aspx. Accessed November 16, 2011.

Hansen, Ric. "Nasty Song Packaged for Teens." http://www.schooldancenetwork.com/about and http://www.schooldancenetwork.com/2011/09/21/nasty-song-packaged-for-teens/ Posted September 21, 2011. Accessed November 21, 2011.

____. "A School Dance Do Not Play!" *Mobile Beat*, November 8, 2011. www.mobilebeat.com/a-school-dance-do-not-play/ Posted November 8, 2011. Accessed November 21, 2011.

Harding, Kate. "How Lesbians Ruined the Prom." Salon.com/mwt/broadsheet/2010/03/11/prom_cancelled. March 11, 2010. Accessed on January 19, 2011.

Heller, Steven. "Hey, Stinky! You're Too Fat, and Your Breath's Bad, Too." *Imprint*, 2010. http://imprint.printmag.com/branding/hey-stinky-you're-too-fat-and-you're-skin's-bad-too/ Accessed October 17, 2011.

"High School Dropout Rates by Race/Ethnicity," last modified 2009, http://www.infoplease.com/us/education/high-school-dropouts-race.html. Accessed May 13, 2011.

Hildebrandt, Peter. "Cancel the Prom, Cancel the Limo." *Limousine Digest*. March 6, 2011. http://limodigest.com/OnlineArticles/mar06/cancelprom.html. Accessed November 23, 2011.

"Homeschool Prom." Successful Homeschooling. http://www.successful-homeschooling.com/homeschool-prom.html. Accessed August 23, 2011.

Huston, John P.. "New Trier Unveils Reality Show-Inspired Fashion Marketing Class." *Trib Local*, October 28, 2010. http://www.triblocal.com/wilmette-kenilworth/2010/10/28/new-trier-fashion-marketing-class. Accessed Nov. 3, 2011.

"Houston Limo Guide: How to Select a Great Limousine." *Limousine Digest*. August 5, 2011. http://www.riveroakslimo.com/blog/tag/prom-night. Accessed November 23, 2011.

Ives, Nat. "The Last Page." Ad Age. December 15, 2009. http://adage.com/article/media works/a-guide-magazines-ceased-publication/132779/ Accessed October 21, 2011.

Jacobs, Pat. "FM Radio." http://www.loti.com/radio/Top%2040%20FM%20Radio.htm. Accessed June 29, 2011.

John, Kayona. "West Hills Prom Dresses." http://www.facebook.com/group.php?gid=112005228820084. Accessed July 30, 2011.

Johnston, Garth. "Carrie the Musical Will Ruin

Prom Off-Broadway This January." *The Gothamist.* June 1, 2011. http://gothamist.com/2011/06/01/carrie_the_musical_to_ruin_prom_off.php. Accessed January 21, 2011.

Jones, Michael A. "Take Your Prom Date to Georgia." http://gayrights.change.org/blog/view/take_your_gay_prom_date_to_georgia. Posted March 23, 2010. Accessed November 12, 2010.

"Judith Martin, Miss Manners Quotations." http://nickelkid.net/quotes/manners.html. Accessed on April 22, 2011.

"Keating-Owen Child Labor Act of 1916." www.ourdocuments.gov (National Archives). Accessed March 11, 2011.

Keeter, Scott and Paul Taylor. "The Millennials." *Pew Research Center Publications.* December 11, 2009. http://pewresearch.org/pubs/1437/millennials-profile. Accessed on June 24, 2011.

Keiles, Jamie. "Senior Prom." *The Seventeen Magazine Project.* June 6, 2010. http://www.theseventeenmagazineproject.com/2010/06/senior-prom-part-2.html. Accessed October 26, 2011.

"Ken Davenport Presents the Awesome 80s Prom." http://www.portlandspirit.com/awesome80sprom.php. Accessed February 1, 2012.

"Key Characteristics of Today's Adolescents: The Millennial Generation (1980/83–Present)." www.catholicyouthministryofdallas.org. Accessed on July 17, 2011.

Koweek, Molly. "Hudson High School Makes History: Elects Two Men as Prom King and Queen." Timesunion.com. http://blog.timesunion.com/highschool/Hudson_high_school_makes_history. June 11, 2010. Accessed December 18, 2010.

Krause, K. "Prom Parties Make Florist Top of Mind with Teens." *Society of American Florists,* April 7, 2011. http://safcms.memberfuse.com/?q=node/913. Accessed November 16, 2011.

Kriss, Miriam. "What's Working in the Young Adult Market?" *Writer's Digest,* November 1, 2011. http://www.writersdigest.com/editor-blogs/guide-to-literary-agents/whats-working-in-the-young-adult-market. Accessed on December 12, 2011.

Lanker, Teresa P. "Dancing for Dollars." *Florists' Review.* February, 2011. http://www.floristsreview.com/main/February2011/Dancing/html. Accessed November 23, 2011.

Lenhart, Amanda. "Teens, Cell Phones and Texting." Pew Research Center Publications. http://pewresearch.org/pubs/1572/teens-cell-phones-text-messages. April 20, 2010. Accessed July 21, 2011.

"Local Florist Recognized For Innovative Prom Marketing Program." PRLog.org. April 10, 2010. http://www.prlog.org/10619908-local-florist-recognized-for-innovative-prom-marketing.html. Accessed November 16, 2011.

"Loretta Young Quotes," http://www.brainyquote.com/quotes/authors/l/loretta_young.html. Accessed March 3, 2011.

Mapes, Diane. "Virginity's Making a Comeback, Report Says." http://www.msnbc.com/ Posted and accessed on March 3, 2011.

McCarthy, Maureen. "Prom Expo to be Held Saturday in Easton." EnterpriseNews.com. Feb. 5, 2010. http://www.enterprisenews.com/news/x785863553/Prom-Expo-to-be-held-Saturday-in-Easton. Accessed Nov. 14, 2011.

McClintock, Pamela. "Friday Box Office." *The Hollywood Reporter,* April 29, 2011. http://www.hollywoodreporter.com/news/friday-box-office-fast-five-183767. Accessed January 11, 2012.

Medina, Jennifer. "A Second Shot to Have the Best Night of Their Lives." *The New York Times.* May 11, 2011. http://www.nytimes.com/2011/05/12/us/12prom.html?pagewanted=all. Accessed February 1, 2012.

"The Millennials: Confident. Connected. Open to Change." *Pew Research Center Publications.* February 24, 2010. http://pewresearch.org/pubs/1501/millennials-new-survey-generations. Accessed January 7, 2011.

Mom Prom. http://www.momprom.org/ Accessed February 10, 2012.

"Monitoring the Future: Teenage Marijuana Use and Trends." last modified 2006, http://www.drugscience.org/Petition/C4C.html. Accessed May 27, 2011.

Moore, Kathleen. "71% of Online Adults Now Use Video-Sharing Sites." *Pew Internet Reports.* http://pewinternet.org/Reports/2011/Video-sharing-sites.aspx. Posted and accessed on July 26, 2011.

"The Muslim, All-Girl High School Prom." *The Education Wonks.* http://www.educationwonk.blogspot.com/2007/06/all-muslim-girl-high-school-prom. Posted June 11, 2007. Accessed November 11, 2010.

"New Jersey's Derrek Lutz Wore a Dress to Prom. And Was Crowned Prom King." *Queerty.* http://www.queerty.com/new-jerseys-derrek-lutz-wore-a-dress-to-prom-and-was-crowned-prom-king-20100503/. May 3, 2010. Accessed August 19, 2011.

"1958 Kodak Commercial," http://www.youtube.com/watch?v=pHc7-37inrs. Accessed March 27, 2011.

"1961 Commercial: Kodak Film Projector," http://www.youtube.com/watch?v=TiIsLVqSauw. Accessed March 27, 2011.

"Our Thirty-Day Checklist to Plan the Perfect Prom!" *Teen Vogue.* http://www.teenvogue.com/style/2009/03/prom-countdown. Accessed October 25, 2011.

Phelan, Hayley. "'Slutty Chic' a Popular Prom Dress Trend at Your School?" *Teen Vogue*, March 30, 2010. http://www.teenvogue.com/style/blogs/fashion/2010/03slutty-chic. Accessed December 15, 2010.

Phillips, Kimberly. "How Seventeen Undermines Young Women." *Media Awareness Network*. Jan/Feb 1993. http://www.mediaawareness.ca/english/resources/articles/gender_portrayal/seventeen.cfm. Accessed October 3, 2011.

"Piercing Gains Popularity." *Body Jewelry and Piercing Blog*. http://blog.piercingmap.com/archives/141. Posted June 26, 2007. Accessed January 7, 2011.

"A Portrait of Generation Next." Jan. 9, 2007. http://people-press.org/report/300/a-portrait-of-generation-next. Accessed 1/26/2011.

"The Prom Exposed: Seeing It for What It Really Is." SoundVision.com. http://www.soundvision.com/Info/prom/exposed.asp. Accessed November 11, 2010.

"Prom 'Rebel': It Was Worth It." *The Early Show*. http://www.cbsnews.com/stories/2009/05/12/earlyshow/main5008061.shtml. Posted on May 12, 2009. Accessed August 21, 2011.

"Prom Season is Here — Are You Ready?" *LCT*. April 6, 2011. http://www.lctmag.com/Operations/news/13529/Prom-Season-is-Here-Are-You-Ready. Accessed November 16, 2011.

Quinton, Brian. "David's Bridal Takes Prom Dreams Mobile." *Chief Marketer*. June 10, 2009. http://bigfatmarketingblog.com/2009/06/10/davids-bridal-takes-prom-dreams-mobile/ Accessed November 3, 2011.

Schwartz, Rachel. "Teens Spending Like Celebrities on Prom Fashion." 7 Live. http://www.7liveonline.com/Teens-spending-like-celebrities-on-prom-fashions/8069523. Accessed October 17, 2011.

Silence, Sherri Drake. "A Night to Treasure: Collierville Hosts Prom for Special Education Students." *The Commercial Appeal*. http://www.thecommercialappeal.com/news/2009/apr/27/a-night-to-treasure. Posted April 27, 2009. Accessed November 11, 2010.

Snow, Jimmy. "Let the Good Times Roll." http://www.youtube.com/watch?v=mT8dBFrVpLA. Accessed on April 22, 2011.

Sperling, Nicole. "The 'Twilight' Saga." *Entertainment Weekly*. June 16, 2008. EW.com. http://www.ew.com/ew/article/0,,20308569_20211840,00.html. Accessed January 23, 2012.

"State Compulsory Attendance Laws," http://www.infoplease.com/ipa/A0112617.html. Accessed March 11, 2011.

Stebleton, Benn. "Painted and Poked: The Tattooing and Piercing of Generations X and Y," *Nashville Feed*, http://www.nashvillefeed.com/culture/painted-and-poked-the-tattoo

ing-and-piercing-of-generations-x-and-y/. Accessed June 22, 2011.

"Teen's Prom Ban Reversed Amid Outcry." http://www.msnbc.com/id/43004197. Posted May 14, 2011. Accessed May 15, 2011.

"Tips on Tattoos." *Prom Dresses*. http://www.promdressesdirectory.com/promdresses/?p=136. Posted October 26, 2009. Accessed January 7, 2011.

"Vince Lombardi Quotes." http://www.brainyquote.com/quotes/authors/v/vince_lombardi.html. Accessed March 3, 2011.

White, Ayssa. "Is Prom Really a One Night Wonder?" The Towne Crier. June 8, 2011. http://my.hsj.org/Schools/Newspaper/tabid/100/view/frontpage/articleid/447232/newspaperid/2667/Is_Prom_Really_A_One_Night_Wonder.aspx. Accessed June 8, 2011.

Wilhelm, Heather. "Surviving Girl Land: Sex, Lies & Proms. realclearbooks.com. January 25, 2012. Accessed January 25, 2012.

Wind, Rebecca. "No Crystal Ball Needed: Teens Are Going in the Wrong Direction." http://guttmacher.org/media/nr/2009/06//18/index.html. June 18, 2009. Accessed February 3, 2011.

"Wyoming Teen's Duck Tape Creations Make Contest's Top Ten." WZZM13. June 17, 2011. http://wyoming.wzzm13.com/news/education/update-wyoming-teens-duct-tape-creations-make-contests-top-10/58506. Accessed Dec. 3, 2011.

Movies

Buffy the Vampire Slayer. Fran Rubel Kuzui, director. Joss Whedon, writer. Twentieth Century–Fox Film Corp., 1992.

Carrie. Brian dePalma, director. MGM, 1976.

Hello Mary Lou: Prom Night II. Bruce Pittman, director. Norstar Releasing, 1987.

High School Musical 3: Senior Year, Kenny Ortega, dir., John Barsocchini, writer, Disney, 2008.

Never Been Kissed. Raja Gosnell, director. Fox 2000 Pictures, 1999.

Peggy Sue Got Married. Francis Ford Coppola, director. Tristar Pictures, 1986.

Pretty in Pink. Howard Deutch, dir. Paramount Pictures, 1986.

Prom. Joe Nussbaum, director. Screenplay by Katie Wech. Disney, 2011.

Prom Night. Paul Lynch, director. AVCO Embassy Pictures, 1980.

Prom Night. Nelson McCormick, director. Sony Pictures, 2008.

Prom Night III: The Last Kiss. Ron Oliver, Peter R. Simpson, directors. Norstar Releasing, 1990.

Prom Night IV: Deliver Us From Evil. Clay Borris, director. Norstar Home Video, 1992.

Prom Night in Kansas City. Hali Lee, Peter von Ziegesar, directors. Golden Pig Productions, Zeitgeist Films (dist.), 2002.

Prom Night in Mississippi. Paul Saltzman, director. Return to Mississippi Productions and HBO Documentary Films, 2009.

The World's Best Prom. Chris Talbot, Ari Vena, directors. Matson Films, 2006.

TV Shows

Buffy the Vampire Slayer, "The Prom." WB. David Solomon, director, Joss Whedon and Marni Noxon, writers. Original air date, May 11, 1999.

Dawson's Creek. Kevin Williamson, creator. WB, 1998–2003. Season 3, episode 22, "The Anti-Prom." Original air date, May 10, 2000.

Glee. "Prom Queen." Eric Stoltz, director, Ian Brennan, writer. Fox Television, original air date, May 10, 2011.

Grey's Anatomy. Shonda Rhimes, creator. ABC, 2008–. "Losing My Religion," Mark Tinker, director, Shonda Rhimes, writer. Original air date, May 15, 2006.

One Tree Hill. Mark Schwahn, creator. CW, 2003–. Season 4, episode 16. Thomas J. Wright, director. Original air date, May 2, 2007.

Saved by the Bell. Sam Bobrick, creator. NBC Productions, 1989–93. Season 4, episode 17, "The Senior Prom." Don Barnhart, director. Original air date, November 7, 1992.

The Suite Life on Deck. Pamela Eells, Jim Geoghan, Danny Kallis, creators. Walt Disney Television. Season 3, episode 21. Disney Channel. Original air date March 18, 2011.

Index

Numbers in ***bold italics*** indicate pages with photographs.

215